What Color Is Your Parachute?

"Job-Hunting in Hard Times" Edition **2010**

SPENCER
Future Care Costs & Vocational Experts

Phyllis Spencer, BA, MA, CDP, RRP
Partner / Vocational Consultant
phyllis@spencerexperts.com

1000-255 Queens Avenue
London, Ontario N6A 5R8

116-1361 Ouellette Avenue
Windsor, Ontario N8X 1J6

Ph: 519-660-3639 • Fax: 888-798-1028 • TF: 866-295-9195
spencerexperts.com

The 2010 "Job-Hunting
in Hard Times" Edition

What Color Is
Your Parachute?

A Practical
Manual for
Job-Hunters and
Career-Changers

by Richard N. Bolles

TEN SPEED PRESS
Berkeley

This is an annual. That is to say, it is revised each year, often substantially, with the new edition appearing in the early fall. Counselors and others wishing to submit additions, corrections, or suggestions for the 2011 edition must submit them prior to February 1, 2010, using the form provided in the back of this book, or by e-mail (RNB25@aol.com). Forms reaching us after that date will, unfortunately, have to wait for the 2012 edition.

PUBLISHER'S NOTE

This publication is designed to provide accurate and authoritative information in regard to the subject matter covered. It is sold with the understanding that the publisher is not engaged in rendering professional career services. If expert assistance is required, the service of the appropriate professional should be sought.

Published in the United States by Ten Speed Press, an imprint of the Crown Publishing Group, a division of Random House, Inc., New York.

www.crownpublishing.com
www.tenspeed.com

Ten Speed Press and the Ten Speed Press colophon are registered trademarks of Random House, Inc.

The drawings on pages vi–vii, 37, 109, 176, 224–25 are by Steven M. Johnson, author of *What the World Needs Now*.

Illustration on page 49 by Beverly Anderson.

ISBN: 978-1-58008-987-6 (paper)
ISBN: 978-1-58008-989-0 (cloth)

ISSN: 8755-4658

Printed in Canada on recycled paper (100% PCW)

Mixed Sources
Product group from well-managed forests, controlled sources and recycled wood or fibre
www.fsc.org   Cert no. SW-COC-000952
© 1996 Forest Stewardship Council
FSC

Design by Betsy Stromberg

10 9 8 7 6 5 4 3 2 1

Revised Edition

The wonderful actress
Anne Bancroft (1931–2005) was once
loosely quoted as saying
about her husband, Mel Brooks,
My heart flutters whenever I hear his key
Turning in the door, and I think to myself,
Oh goody, the party is about to begin.

That is exactly how I feel
about my wife,
Marci Garcia Mendoza Bolles,
God's angel from the Philippines,
whom I fell deeply in love with, and married
on August 22, 2004.

What an enchanted marriage this is!

The 2010
Table of Contents

PART II
Finding a Life . . .

The Green Pages

Preface: The Diary of a Grateful Man

June 17, 2009

People often say to me, "Oh yes, I've read your book." With 10,000,000 copies out there, this happens a lot.

I'm flattered, and pleased, of course. And when I'm in a playful mood, I go on to inquire, *"When?"* Because, if the most recent edition you've read was 2005 or earlier, there's a lot that's changed since then.

Developments have been moving swiftly out there, in the world—as I hardly need tell you. Each new edition of this book represents an attempt to keep up. With the economy in general, the actions of the Fed, the housing crisis, rising foreclosures, the loss of equity in homes, the loss of jobs in particular industries, the credit crunch, the rising costs of gasoline, the rising food prices and shortages, pandemics, health, airlines going belly-up (*MaxJet, Eos, Aloha, ATA, and on and on*), diminishing retirement funds, longer working lives, free trade, outsourcing, BRIC (the emerging economies of Brazil, Russia, India and China, and their ravishing appetites for energy and everything else), new technologies, Web 2.0, Web 3.0(!), Google, YouTube, MySpace, FaceBook, blogs, IM, Twitter, LinkedIn, the explosion of social networks online, omnibus job-search engines like Indeed or SimplyHired, Checkster, Workblast (video resumes), etc., and—of course—changing job-hunting techniques, soft skills, social networks, portfolios, Behavioral Interviews, counselors' associations, individual job-hunters' stories, it all adds up to the fact that the world is spinning faster and faster.

I've worked especially long and hard on the five most recent editions—this one, the 2010, as well as 2009, 2008, 2007, and 2006—and readers

tell me they are more helpful and useful than all the editions before them, stretching back to 1970.

People ask how I keep up, so let me briefly tell you. I come from a newspaper family, and have a voracious appetite for information. I read four newspapers every day (the *New York Times*, the *San Francisco Chronicle*, *USA Today*, plus a local paper), three news or business magazines every week (*Business Week*, *Time*, and *Newsweek*), and I relentlessly search the Internet, daily. Also, four times a year, for five days in a row, I do nothing but interact with job-hunters, gathered in my home. I stay very up-to-date on the current problems men and women are running into, out there in the job-market.

I do not think of this any longer as just *a book*. It's much more *a living organism*, evolving, changing, growing. It takes on a life of its own, each year. I love this work. It's thrilling and exciting, and you never know what's going to happen next.

And what have I learned, when all is said and done? I have learned that when any of us turns into a job-hunter or career-changer, as we inevitably do, we need two things above all else: we need hope—desperately. And we need tools for discovering our truest vision for our own life, plus practical strategies for finding that vision, that work, and that mission.

Hopefully, this book will give you both.

I think a lot about gratitude. I didn't get here, alone. I do not stay here, alone. I am not inspired, alone. I am not able to write, alone.

I thank God that I am still in splendid, vigorous health, that I still have all my marbles and wits about me, that I love to write more than ever, that I love to help people more than ever—and that I am enchanted by every moment of my life with such a wondrous woman as my wife, Marci.

I'm grateful for her two grown children, Adlai and Janice, with husband Marcel, and new son, Logan; and my own dear children, and their families: Stephen, Mark, Gary, and Sharon, plus their most-loving mother, my former wife, Jan; not to mention my former stepdaughter, Dr. Serena Brewer, whom I helped raise for twenty years. I love them all dearly.

Thanks to Marci for playing hostess to the Five-Day Workshops we conduct quarterly, in our home in the San Francisco Bay Area. It is a rare woman who will let twenty-one strangers come be guests in her home for five days at a time, cooking breakfast and lunch for them all, while radiating grace and individual concern for each, throughout. (For details, e-mail fivedayworkshop@aol.com.)

In addition, I want to express my gratitude to my dearest friend (*besides Marci*), Daniel Porot of Geneva, Switzerland—we taught together two weeks every summer, for nineteen years; Jim Kell of Texas, who helped me out for almost as long a time; Dave Swanson, ditto; plus my international friends, Brian McIvor of Ireland; John Webb and Madeleine Leitner, of Germany; Yves Lermusi, of *Checkster* fame, who came from Belgium; Pete Hawkins of Liverpool, England; Debra Angel MacDougall of Scotland; Byung Ju Cho of South Korea; Tom O'Neil of New Zealand; and Howard Figler, beloved friend and co-author of our manual for career counselors; Marty Nemko; Joel Garfinkle; Richard Leider; Richard Knowdell; Rich Feller; Dick Gaither; Warren Farrell; Sue Cullen; and the folks over at Ten Speed Press in Berkeley, California (dear Phil Wood, my friend for forty years, now publisher emeritus, Aaron Wehner, current publisher, George Young, Kara Van de Water, Lisa Westmoreland, Betsy Stromberg), and gracious Jenny Frost, head of the Crown publishing division of Random House—they are the new owners of Ten Speed Press, since February this year; plus all my readers—all ten million of you—for buying my books, trusting my counsel, and following your dream. I have never met so many wonderful souls. I am so thankful for you all.

In closing, I must not fail to record my profound thanks to our Great Creator, Who all my life has been to me the Father of our Lord Jesus Christ, as real to me as breathing, and the Rock of my life through every trial and tragedy, most especially the assassination of my only brother, Don Bolles, with a car bomb, in downtown Phoenix, Arizona, over thirty-four years ago—now memorialized in one of the rooms at the Newseum, in Washington, D.C. I thank God for giving me strength, and carrying me through—*everything*. He is the source of whatever grace, wisdom, or compassion I have ever found, or shared with others. I am grateful beyond measure for such a life, and such a mission as Our Creator has given me: to help people make their lives really count, here on this spaceship Earth.

Dick Bolles
RNB25@aol.com
www.jobhuntersbible.com

GRAMMAR AND LANGUAGE NOTE

I want to explain four points of grammar, in this book of mine: pronouns, commas, italics, and spelling. My unorthodox use of them invariably offends unemployed English teachers so much that instead of finishing the exercises, they immediately write to apply for a job as my editor.

To save us unnecessary correspondence, let me explain. Throughout this book, I often use the apparently plural pronouns "they," "them," and "their" after *singular* antecedents—such as, "You must approach *someone* for a job and tell *them* what you can do." This sounds strange and even wrong to those who know English well. To be sure, we all know there is another pronoun—"you"—that may be either singular or plural, but few of us realize that the pronouns "they," "them," and "their" were also once treated as both plural and singular in the English language. This changed, at a time in English history when agreement in *number* became more important than agreement as to sexual *gender*. Today, however, our priorities have shifted once again. Now, the distinguishing of sexual *gender* is considered by many to be more important than agreement in *number*.

The common artifices used for this new priority, such as "s/he," or "he and she," are—to my mind—tortured and inelegant. Casey Miller and Kate Swift, in their classic, *The Handbook of Nonsexist Writing*, agree, and argue that it is time to bring back the earlier usage of "they," "them," and "their" as both singular and plural—just as "you" is/are. They further argue that this return to the earlier historical usage has already become quite common *out on the street*—witness a typical sign by the ocean that reads, "*Anyone* using this beach after 5 p.m. does so at *their* own risk." I have followed Casey and Kate's wise recommendations in all of this.

As for my commas, they are deliberately used according to my own rules— rather than according to the rules of historic grammar (which I did learn—I hastily add, to reassure my old Harvard professors, who despaired of me weekly, during English class). In spite of those rules, I follow my own, which are: to write conversationally, and put in a comma wherever I would normally stop for a breath, were I *speaking* the same line.

The same conversational rule applies to my use of *italics*. I use *italics* wherever, were I speaking the sentence, I would *emphasize* that word or phrase. I also use italics where there is a digression of thought, and I want to maintain the main flow of the sentence. All in all, I write as I speak. Hence the dashes (—) to indicate a break in my thought.

Finally, some of my spelling (and capitalization) is *weird*. (You say "weird"; I say "playful.") I happen to like writing it "e-mail," for example, instead of "email." Most of the time. Fortunately, since this is my own book, I get to play by my own peculiar interpretations; I'm just grateful that ten million readers have *gone along*. Nothing delights a child (at heart) more, than being allowed to play.

P.S. Speaking of "playful," over the last thirty-five years a few critics (*very* few) have claimed that *Parachute* is not serious enough (they object to the cartoons, here, which poke fun at almost *everything*). On the other hand, a few have complained that the book is *too* serious, and too complicated in its vocabulary and grammar for anyone except a college graduate. Two readers, however, have written me with a different view.

The first one, from England, said there is an index that analyzes a book to tell you what grade in school you must have finished, in order to be able to understand it. My book's index, he said, turned out to be 6.1, which means you need only have finished sixth grade in a U.S. school in order to understand it.

Here in the U.S., a college instructor came up with a similar finding. He phoned me to tell me that my book was rejected by the authorities as a proposed text for the college course he was teaching, because (they said) the book's language/grammar was not up to college level. "What level was it?" I asked. "Well," he replied, "when they analyzed it, it turned out to be written on an eighth grade level."

Sixth or eighth grade—that seems just about right to me. Why make job-hunting complicated, when it can be expressed so simply even a child could understand it?

R.N.B.

PART I

Finding a Job . . .

PART II

Finding a Life . . .

It was the best of times,
It was the worst of times,
It was the age of wisdom,
It was the age of foolishness,
It was the epoch of belief,
It was the epoch of incredulity,
It was the season of light,
It was the season of darkness,
It was the spring of hope,
It was the winter of despair,
We had everything before us,
We had nothing before us,
We were all going direct to heaven,
We were all going direct the other way . . .

CHARLES DICKENS
A Tale of Two Cities

1. Finding a Job . . . Even in Hard Times: Rejection Shock

Charles Dickens had it right. For some of us, this is the worst of times. Our house has been foreclosed, or seen its value drop dramatically. Fuel costs are killing us. Rice is scarce, and getting scarcer. Food prices are soaring. Businesses are folding. Companies are cutting their work force dramatically. Millions are out of work.

But there are others who are barely touched by any of this. They cannot understand what we are going through. At least 138,000,000 people still have jobs, in the U.S. Some of them, well-paying jobs. They are well off, and In some cases, have money to burn. For them, this is the best of times. They cannot understand our pain.

But we, when we are out of work, go looking for another job; but we, when we are finding it difficult to feed our families, go looking for a better-paying job. And that is when we run into the nature of the job-market, and the nature of the job-hunt. It isn't as easy as we thought it was going to be.

Tom Jackson has well characterized the nature of the job-hunt as one long process of rejection. In job-interview after job-interview, what some of us hear the employer say is:

NO NO NO NO NO NO NO NO NO NO NO NO
NO NO NO NO NO NO NO NO NO NO NO NO
NO NO NO NO NO NO NO NO NO NO NO NO
NO NO NO NO NO NO NO NO NO NO NO NO
NO NO NO NO NO NO NO NO NO NO YES.

Before we get to that final YES—or if we are lucky, two YESES, so that we have a choice—before we get there, the job-hunt is nothing but one long process of rejection. And we, so unprepared for this, go into a kind of Rejection Shock.

Naturally, we have questions.

I just lost my job. How many others are in the same predicament?

Well, you've got lots of company. As of June 2009, the number of people out of work totaled at least 14,500,000 individuals. And that's a government figure. In the U.S. there are always many more people out of work than the government will ever admit—regardless of which party is in power.

Will I need a computer and Internet access, to go about my job-hunt in this twenty-first century?

It's not mandatory, and if you don't have a computer, there are non-Internet job-hunting resources, of course. For example, if because you lack a computer you can't access "Job-Postings" by employers on the Internet, you can always look at the "Help Wanted Ads" in your local newspaper, especially the Sunday edition.

There are also regional papers devoted to nothing but job openings, such as *JobDig*, which, at this writing, publishes fourteen local weekly newspapers in twelve states, mostly midwestern (from Minnesota down to Texas). A subscription for thirteen weeks costs job-hunters $65. Call 877-456-2344 to see whether or not there's a local paper covering your part of the country.

According to the latest figures, however, at least 74.7 percent of Americans use the Internet, which adds up to 227 million users. Others, of course, usually have a friend who can go on the Internet for them.

Moreover, if you know how to use a computer but just don't happen to own one at the moment, many public libraries as well as "Internet cafés" can let you use their computer for a fee. (To locate the Internet café nearest you, have a friend use his or her computer, to input your zip code into the comprehensive directory found at www.cybercaptive.com.)

In view of this virtual omnipresence of the computer in our culture now that we are firmly in the twenty-first century, I have freely listed job-hunting resources that are found only on the Internet throughout the rest of this guide.

What are the most helpful job sites on the Web?

For overall free guides to the entire job-hunt process, in addition to my own website, www.jobhuntersbible.com, there are seven sites you will find are the most comprehensive and helpful:

1. www.job-hunt.org, run by Susan Joyce.

2. www.jobstar.org, run by Mary Ellen Mort.

3. www.rileyguide.com, run by Margaret F. Dikel.

4. www.quintcareers.com, run by Dr. Randall Hansen.

5. www.cacareerzone.org, run by the California Career Resource Network. Once you are on the home page, it gives you a choice between running the site under Text, Graphic, or Flash. Choose Graphic.

6. www.asktheheadhunter.com, run by Nick Corcodilos.

7. www.indeed.com, run by a privately held company founded by Paul Forster and Rony Kahan, with the New York Times Company among its shareholders. This is the answer to a job-hunter's prayer. There are lots of "job-boards" out there, thousands in fact; these, if you don't know, are websites that list employers' job-postings, i.e., vacancies. Such postings are also to be found on employers' own company or organization sites. Want to look through every one of them? No, you don't. What you want is something that sweeps through all of them for you, and summarizes what it finds—in just one place. What you need is a site such as **Indeed** (URL above). It is the most comprehensive job search service on the Web, as it "plucks" job listings from thousands of company websites, job boards, newspapers, and associations. It has a UK site, whose URL, not surprisingly, is www.indeed.co.uk.

My picture of the job-hunt during this computer age, is that you call up a search engine, like Indeed, and input the job-title you're looking for, and the geographical area you'd prefer, and by the next morning or within a few days at most, you're told there is a match. A match between your experience and skills, on the one hand, and what some employer is looking for, on the other hand, with a vacancy they're trying to fill.

Ah, you're exactly right. That's how it works, these days. There are thousands of testimonials from job-hunters who have used the Internet successfully, to find a match, and thence a job. But this job-matching doesn't work for every job-hunter. In fact, it doesn't work for the vast majority of job-hunters.

Why not?

Well, job-matching works by using job-titles, and job-titles are, generally speaking, a big problem for the Internet. Well, not a big problem when you're looking for a job that has a simple title, such as "administrative assistant," or "gardener," or "nurse," or "driver," or "waitress," or "mechanic," or "salesperson." Any of these should turn up a lot of matches.

But, you may be looking for a job that various employers call by differing titles, and that's an entirely different ballgame. If you guess wrongly what they call the job you're looking for, then you and those employers will be like two ships passing in the night, on the Internet high seas. Your faithful, hardworking computer will report back to you in the morning: "No matches," when in fact there actually are. You just didn't guess correctly what title those employers are using. Oops!

Another problem: you may be looking for a job-title that essentially has disappeared from the workforce. Over the centuries, our economy has moved from one largely based on agriculture, to one largely based on manufacturing, to one largely based on information and services. As each transition has occurred, certain job-titles have essentially disappeared from the workforce, and in large numbers. Oh, they're still around, but in such small numbers that no one tells the Internet. "Blacksmith" is one example that comes to mind. There are blacksmiths, still; I happen to know of one of them. But I wouldn't count on the Internet turning up many matches, if any, with this title. The same fate generally awaits job-titles with the old words "assembly line" and "manufacturing" in them. As Senator John McCain truthfully told Michigan voters back in 2008, "Those jobs aren't coming back."

Finally, job-titles are a problem for an Internet search because a particular search program on the Internet may depend completely on beginning with a prepared list of job-titles that you are required to choose from, and in the interests of space and speed their menu may only offer you a choice between two dozen or so job-titles, which does not come even close to mentioning all the possibilities; i.e., the 20,000 job-titles that are out there in the workforce—including, of course, the one that you are searching for, in particular.

So sure, Internet job-matching works. Sometimes. Beautifully. You must try it, using Indeed, or a general search engine such as Google, or Metacrawler. Input anything or everything you can think of to describe what you are looking for.

But know ahead of time that you can't count on it necessarily working for You. In the end, it's a big, fat gamble. And not at all the sure thing that so-called experts would have you think it is.

So, how many job-hunters who try to find a match, fail to find a match, on the Internet?

There are various answers to that question. Take your pick: (1) Lots and lots. (2) 90 percent, studies say. (3) ? Big question mark. Studies are notoriously unreliable, so—in the end—we don't really know. We're just left with "lots and lots."

So, if you conclude that Internet job-matching is a big, fat gamble, that's all you really need to know.

Oh, and one more thing. Know this: it doesn't mean there's anything wrong with you, if the Internet can't match you with a job. The problem is the system itself.

Well then, given all this, how long should I expect to be out of work?

This varies, hugely, due to a number of variables: what kind of work you're looking for, what part of the country you live in, the state of the industry, how old you are or how young you are, and—above all else—how you're going about your job-hunt.

But you need to be prepared for the fact that your job-hunt might last nineteen weeks or more. In fact, as of the date I am writing (June 17, 2009), 3,900,000 people in the U.S. had been looking for work for twenty-seven weeks or more. It's possible that you'll find work sooner; but you've got to be prepared for the fact that you may not.

Okay, if there's a chance that my job-hunt may take much longer than I expected, what's the first thing I should do?

Many If Not Most Employers Hunt for Job-Hunters in the Exact Opposite Way from How Most Job-Hunters Hunt for Them

The Way a Typical Employer Prefers to Fill a Vacancy

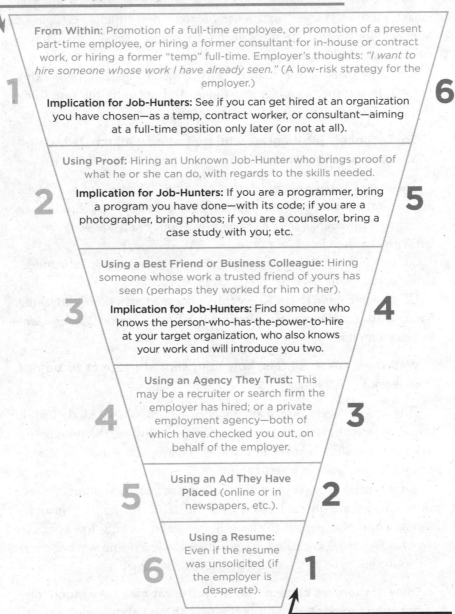

1 **6**

From Within: Promotion of a full-time employee, or promotion of a present part-time employee, or hiring a former consultant for in-house or contract work, or hiring a former "temp" full-time. Employer's thoughts: *"I want to hire someone whose work I have already seen."* (A low-risk strategy for the employer.)

Implication for Job-Hunters: See if you can get hired at an organization you have chosen—as a temp, contract worker, or consultant—aiming at a full-time position only later (or not at all).

2 **5**

Using Proof: Hiring an Unknown Job-Hunter who brings proof of what he or she can do, with regards to the skills needed.

Implication for Job-Hunters: If you are a programmer, bring a program you have done—with its code; if you are a photographer, bring photos; if you are a counselor, bring a case study with you; etc.

3 **4**

Using a Best Friend or Business Colleague: Hiring someone whose work a trusted friend of yours has seen (perhaps they worked for him or her).

Implication for Job-Hunters: Find someone who knows the person-who-has-the-power-to-hire at your target organization, who also knows your work and will introduce you two.

4 **3**

Using an Agency They Trust: This may be a recruiter or search firm the employer has hired; or a private employment agency—both of which have checked you out, on behalf of the employer.

5 **2**

Using an Ad They Have Placed (online or in newspapers, etc.).

6 **1**

Using a Resume: Even if the resume was unsolicited (if the employer is desperate).

The Way a Typical Job-Hunter Prefers to Fill a Vacancy

Chapter One

Sleep. Catch up on your sleep. *You're kidding.* No, I'm not. Overall, you would be wise to think of your job-hunt as an endurance contest, analogous to running a marathon. Especially if it does last nineteen weeks or longer. You need to start training, before you "run" this endurance contest.

Experience teaches us that you should begin by drawing down your "sleep deficit." You've probably got one. Chances are, that up until recently you've been working long hours, trying desperately to survive, so now your body and your brain are at the point of exhaustion, without you even noticing.

The last thing you want to do, is to launch yourself into a long job-hunt when you're this tired. So, let it be your first goal to catch up on your sleep, in order that your body and mind can be working at optimum condition as you set out on your job-hunt. You will think more clearly, and make better decisions, if you're not so tired. For guidance about how much and how long, see www.medicinenet.com/sleep/article.htm.

But I haven't time to catch up on my sleep. Yes, you do. You've probably got nineteen weeks ahead of you. Relax. Start sensibly. Begin by catching up.

Many of us are also helped by a fifteen- to thirty-minute nap during midday, after lunch. It helps keep stress down. I had an aunt who started taking naps at the age of thirty-two, and lived 'til she was ninety-seven. Maybe we humans weren't made to go from wake-up until bedtime, all on one big gulp of sleep. Break the sixteen hours in half. There is wisdom to be learned from countries that have siestas. See http://en.wikipedia.org/wiki/Siesta.

Exercise. The tendency, after you've unexpectedly lost your job, is to curl up in a little ball, assume the fetal position, and turn the electric-blanket up to "9." But job-hunting requires that you get out there. So, begin a regular regimen of daily walking, starting now, even if it's only down to the main road, and back, at first. You can increase the distance, after you've increased your stamina a bit.

Water. And, while you're at it, I know you have enough sense to watch your diet while you're out of work. Eating your way out of feeling low is a real temptation; but putting on, oh, say, one hundred more pounds won't make you look so hot when it comes to the job interview. That's pretty obvious. Not so obvious is your body's need for water. Not "fluids," like coffee, tea, or cola, but actual "water." A lot of things can go wrong with the human body if it gets dehydrated without your even noticing. Believe me, you do not want to be sick while you're job-hunting. If you want to get more guidance about this, see www.watercure.com/faq.html.

"Possibly nineteen weeks or more" is very bad news for me. I'm in a precarious state financially, right now. Where can I go for help with my expenses during my job-hunt?

Unemployment insurance. You probably know all this, but just in case you don't: these are cash benefits that run for a certain number of months while you are unemployed, and are available in the U.S. from your state government, if you regularly report in to them, on how your job-hunt is going. To learn how to apply, go to your computer (or to a computer at your local library, if you don't personally own one) and type the following two pieces of information into your Internet browser (such as Google or Metacrawler): the name of your state, plus the words "unemployment insurance benefits." Once on site, look for the words "unemployment benefits." Or, go to: www.rileyguide.com/claims.html. Free.

(Naturally, greed being what it is, you will find some enterprising souls have put up websites promising that for a fee they will help you file for unemployment benefits. You picture someone sitting down beside you, and helping you fill out the application form, line by line. And maybe showing you the secret of collecting some big bucks. Right? Unfortunately, their "help" is just a booklet, for which they'll charge you around ten bucks, irrevocably ["We do not refund payment for any . . . reason"]—after they first get you to cough up all your personal information. [On the pretext of tailoring their program to your special needs!] All they will then do is send or let you download that booklet [their "program"] telling you how to go file, yourself.

Oh, please!! You can get the same information, and better, costing you absolutely nothing, by just using your Internet browser, as I described above.)

Food stamps. To see if you are eligible for help go to: www.fns .usda.gov/fsp/applicant_recipients/10steps.htm. This is from the U.S. Department of Agriculture, and is titled: "10 Steps to Help You Fill Your Grocery Bag Through the Food Stamp Program: Learn If You or Someone You Know Might Be Eligible for Food Stamps."

How do I find health insurance when I am sort of on my own?

Thanks to the Internet, there are several places you can turn to, for information and help:

1. www.healthinsuranceinfo.net. A site, maintained by the Georgetown Health Policy Institute. Chock full of information. Very comprehensive.

2. www.ehealthinsurance.com. It allows *individuals* to compare policics from different providers, and then purchase the one they like the best. It serves all states, except Maine, Massachusetts, North Dakota, Rhode Island, and Vermont.

3. www.freelancersunion.org. You need to work in one of the occupations served by this union; it is for independent workers or consultants. But browse the site, and see.

Even after all this, I'm still having a really hard time financially. I'm falling behind in paying my bills. I feel like I'm drowning. What can I do?

You have several choices:

a. Get a temporary job: one you hate but it brings in money.

b. Get some financial counseling: to stretch what resources you do have.

c. Move back home temporarily: if your parents invite you to.

Let's start with the last one, first. Moving back home, with our parents, has long been a popular strategy for young adults just out of college, who can't find a job. But, in hard times it becomes more and more common even with people who are already in their thirties, forties, or fifties.

Of course this won't work if you and your parents have never gotten along with each other, and when you were a teenager you couldn't wait to get out of there. Going back, at this later point in your life, would be an exercise in humiliation. Dozens of movies have featured family tensions. Unless you love humiliation, look for any other way you can, to solve your financial problems.

But, assuming you have good relations with your parents, moving back home with them for a temporary period can be a financial lifesaver, as you pay a fair rent and food allowance there, while you save as much as you can 'til you're back on your feet.

However, if you want my advice, don't just appear on your parents' doorstep, without any warning, begging to be taken in. Instead, first write or call and tell them in great detail what's going on in your life, and just ask them if they have any advice.

If they offer you a room in their home for a temporary period, while you get back on your feet, then for heaven's sake, take them up on their kind offer. Pitch in, and help them with everything. Don't just "flop," and lie around all day.

Moving back home can be a redeeming experience if it doesn't last any longer than necessary. Our family offers us a haven when no one else would, they offer us a place of refuge and recovery, when we have nowhere else to turn. Family can turn out to be friends, as defined by Jesus' standard: "I was hungry and you gave me something to eat, I was thirsty and you gave me something to drink, I was a stranger and you invited me in, I needed clothes, and you clothed me, I was sick and you looked after me. . . ."

And it offers you a chance to exercise the good old-fashioned virtue of gratitude. Think it. Say it. Out loud. Daily. Thank you. Thank you.

Next strategy when you're strapped financially: get some financial counseling. You'll have to look around, for this. It's easy to get bad counseling, from someone who thinks they are some big financial expert, but in actuality they don't know what they're talking about. You want good financial counseling. Ask around—at your church, synagogue, or mosque, at your bank, at your local chamber of commerce, at any clubs or associations you belong to, find a helpful soul who knows their business and can show you ways of paying off your bills little by little, but steadily; and can show you how to make what little money you do have to spend, stretch further.

Last strategy, here: a stop-gap job. This is any job, I repeat any job, that will bring in money. It doesn't matter if you hate it, in fact it's better if you hate it. That way you won't linger long, here. But it brings in money, while you're looking for work you enjoy that also pays well. Look in the classified ads in your local newspaper, go inquire about any job that will stop up the gap between when you worked last, and when you work next.

Meanwhile, time to put your thinking cap on.

2. Finding a Job . . .
Even in Hard Times:
Think

---

*He or she who gets hired is not necessarily the one who can
do that job best; but, the one who knows the most about how
to get hired.*

RICHARD LATHROP
in his classic *Who's Hiring Who?*

If there were only three vacancies in the whole country, your job-hunt
would be easy. All you would have to ask yourself is whether or not you
were qualified for any of those three. Period. End of story.

The problem is, there are many more. Many, many more. Vacancies.

How many, exactly?

On March 30, 2004, the brilliant Ben Bernanke gave a speech at
Duke University, in Durham, North Carolina, in the course of which he
revealed that his research showed that "about 30 million jobs are lost
each year in the United States." Fifteen million of them, he said, are
short-term, temporary contracts that run their course, and then end,
as they were supposed to. But the other 15 million become vacancies
that in the job-market game of musical chairs have to be filled. That
works out to at least 1,250,000 vacancies each month. And, his research
revealed, this had been the case for the previous ten years, at least. That
1,250,000 has to be added, each month, to the *net* increase or decrease

the government reports, on the first Friday of each month, in what they call the Monthly Unemployment Report. So if that Report says 20,000 jobs were lost in the previous month, that is a *net* figure; and thus the number of vacancies that had to be filled, totaled 1,250,000 minus 20,000, or 1,230,000 at the very least, during that month. And—don't forget—those 15 million short-term contracts, mentioned above, need to be replaced by 15 million *new* short-term contracts.

This changes the whole ballgame. First, if you are looking for work, you don't have to look at just three vacancies, and ask if you are qualified for any of the three; you have to look at over a million vacancies, with that same question in mind.

Secondly, you have the freedom to approach any places that interest you, using your contacts, whether they are known to have a vacancy or not, because all those vacancies mentioned above were created, and are created, by the constant *churning* of human activity:

People get promoted—thus leaving vacant the job they held.

People retire—thus leaving vacant the job they held.

People quit—thus leaving vacant the job they held.

People decide to move—thus leaving vacant the job they held.

People get injured or get sick—sometimes for a long time, thus leaving vacant for long- or short-term periods, the job they held.

People die—thus leaving vacant the job they held.

And, **people get fired or laid off.**

You don't know whether any or all of these things have happened recently at the places that interest you. Many organizations are notoriously slow to move to fill vacancies. That's why you can approach any organization that interests you—because they're doing work that you would like to do—and ask if they have a vacancy. (This is called "the hidden job-market," as you may have guessed.)

And now, to our questions:

I worked in my industry for a number of years, but now I've been laid off, I've gone job-hunting, and maybe there are a lot of vacancies somewhere in the country. But I just can't find any jobs for someone in my field, with my background and experience, in my geographical area. Now what do I do?

First of all, let me say that I know what a heart-breaking experience this is. It has happened to me. I know what it feels like. You were valued for years and years, and suddenly the job-market is treating you like a disposable Coke can.

It would be nice if the system would fix itself—would find some way to honor all those years of yours, and make you feel valuable again. By "system" I mean the government or industry or education. But it never will. Despite its grandiose promises, the "system" will never evolve programs that exactly recreate the kinds of jobs that have disappeared.

It's sad, but true. No one is going to come and rescue you. Given this fact, there is but one solution: you've got to learn how to rescue yourself.

Okay, where do I start? I was in manufacturing. Those jobs have just disappeared—at least in my geographical area. Now what can I do to rescue myself?

You dust off your brain, and you do some hard thinking. You begin by asking yourself what jobs would be *related to* what you used to do. Think about questions like these:

1. What supplies, equipment, or support services did you use at your last job? Would the suppliers or manufacturers of that equipment or those materials know of other places where their equipment or supplies are used? For example, if you worked at a digital photo place, would suppliers of photo paper or digital equipment tell you where else their customers are? (As I said above, those other places that use their equipment or supplies don't have to have *a known* vacancy. You can approach them anyway. Somebody may have quit just that morning.)

2. What machinery or technologies did you learn, master, or improve upon, at your last job? What other places use such machinery or technology? Would any of them be interested in hiring you?

3. Who supplied training or development to you, at your last job? Would any of them be interested in hiring you?

4. What companies, organizations, or customers did you serve, in your last job? Would any of them be in a position to hire someone with your talents and experience?

5. What communities or service organizations were interested in, or a participant in, your projects at your job? Would any of them be interested in hiring you?

6. Who might be interested in the skills and problem-solving abilities that you learned at your last job?

7. What temp agencies, outsourcing agencies, or sub-contractors were used at your last job? Would any of them be interested in hiring you?

And if I think hard about related jobs, but come up empty, what should I think about, next?

Take a hard look at your spare-time hobbies, over the years. Maybe you've spent quite a bit of time on these, and become something of an informal expert. So, start thinking: is there any kind of work you could look for, related to those hobbies? Put your *hobby words* into a search engine on the Internet—my own personal favorite is Google (www.google.com), which gets about 68 percent of all searches on the Internet, currently.

If you want additional search engines, go to *the* expert, Danny Sullivan, whose lists *at this writing* can be found at http://searchenginewatch .com/links.

Alternative sources of information: go to libraries or stores with large magazine sections. Browse. See if there's a magazine that covers your favorite hobby; buy it, read it from cover to cover for ideas.

Can you give me some idea of what kinds of hobbies might lead to jobs that would value my knowledge and experience?

Oh, almost anything; but just for example: antiques, bicycling, birding, boating, books, camping, cars, collecting, computers, cooking, dance, electronics, exercising, flowers, gardening, genealogy, horses, hunting, martial arts, math, models, motorcycles, oceanography, pets, photography, scrapbooking, sewing, skiing, transportation, volunteer work, and woodworking.

Much more complete lists can be found on the Internet at www.buzzle .com/articles/list-of-hobbies-interests.html and http://en.wikipedia .org/wiki/Category:Hobbies.

If hobbies turn out to be a blind alley, I can guess what to think about, next. I know you advise us to find our passion in life. I've always found it hard to figure out what my passion is. Or if I even have one. What kinds of questions should I be asking myself?

"Your Passion" is a difficult question, and not always easy to find. But here are some clues. Sit down with a note pad, or at your computer, and write down whatever occurs to you about the following questions:

What do I want out of life?

What do I want to give to this life? By the time I die, what do I want my gift to the world, to have been?

What is it about the world that I dislike, am most bothered by, or hate the most; and would most love to correct, fix, or eradicate if I could?

What is the product or service that I think my community, country, or the world, most needs—really, really needs?

What is it that I would love to do, more than anything else in the world?

What is it that most energizes me? What work most exhausts me—and what is the opposite of that work?

What turns me on the most (well, besides *that*)? As the wise David Maister says, "If a thing turns you on, you'll be good at it; if it doesn't, you won't."

In thinking about all this, what do I do if I get no bright ideas? Where do I turn next?

Well, first of all, go back and think harder. And longer. About the questions above. It's amazing how many job-hunters treat *thinking* as a speed-contest. *"Okay, I gave it ten minutes. Now I'm done."* No, no, no. Thinking takes time. Give it more time. Hours. Days. Even weeks, if necessary.

The brain does get rusty. There is much, on the Internet these days, about the plasticity of the brain, and how the brain grows when it is given exercise—both physical and mental.

Helpful sites on the Internet to exercise your brain, that are low cost or free, include:

www.lumosity.com

www.happy-neuron.com

www.sharpbrains.com

There are also systems that are probably beyond the budget of most job-hunters, particularly if you're on the ropes financially; but I mention them here, for the sake of completeness:

www.e-mindfitness.com

www.brainage.com (requires Nintendo DS)

Of course, job-hunting itself is a brain game. That is to say, it pays off rich dividends to those who are willing to take time to take their brain out for a walk.

What kind of brain exercises does job-hunting offer? Besides the ones we've already talked about?

Well, first of all you will profit by thinking out, ahead of time, what employers are looking for. It will vary from individual to individual, of course, but generally speaking, think about these possibilities.

Employers are looking for any or all of the following:

They are looking for talent—*transferable* skills, usually described as verbs.

They are looking for experience—so they don't have to spend a lot of time getting you "up to speed" at the job.

They are looking for self-management skills—do you come in on time, or even ahead of time; do you stay until closing, or even beyond closing, if necessary; do you just try to "get by" or do you go the extra mile?

They are looking for persistence—do you keep at a problem, do you keep at a task, until you've solved it, until it is done?

They are looking for people-skills—do you get along well with co-workers; do you deal with customers caringly and thoroughly?

They are looking for responsibility—every successful worker makes mistakes, but do you try to make mistakes that derive from taking manageable risks—"excellent mistakes" as the author Dan Pink calls them, rather than mistakes resulting from carelessness or stupidity? And do you readily "own up" when the mistake is yours? Responsibility also means knowing when and how to delegate it.

Finally, the employer is trying to avoid mistakes also—in the hiring process. They are looking for retention. They want you to stay, if you're any good. They want to avoid "musical chairs" in the organization. Hiring, and turnover, costs an employer a great deal of money. And time. The best way to reassure them you will stay is to reveal, in the interview, that you've done a good deal of research about this organization before you ever approached it. The reason most employees quit, is they typically do their research of the organization *after* they're hired.

I get it. Let me guess the next brain exercise that job-hunting offers: what is an employer willing to pay for?

Yes. That's a good thing to think about, ahead of time.

One answer is: your skills.

You have three kinds of skills, which employers will pay for; they are characteristically described by different parts of speech.

Nouns describe your special knowledges. Employers will pay for the knowledge that is stored in your brain, which you were taught, or learned through experience. They may be fields, majors, subjects, processes, or "know how." *Samples: how to repair computers, how to do math, how to conduct diplomatic negotiations, how to construct a car from scratch, etc.*

Verbs describe your functional skills. More commonly called *transferable skills.* Things you know how to do, regardless of what field or industry you need to transfer them to. Employers will pay for the different functions you can perform, even if you previously used them in a different field. They are transferable from one field to another, from one industry to another. *Samples: analyzing, lifting, consolidating, running, computing, etc.*

Adjectives or *adverbs* describe the style with which you do things. These are commonly called *traits*, or *personality characteristics. Samples: persistent, thorough, imaginative, loyal, quick, etc.*

What kinds of things will an employer be especially looking for? I need to know because I want to be able to describe how I am different from nineteen other people who can do the same work that I do.

Most often it will be the way you go about doing a task or tasks, something we call your *traits*, or your *style* of doing things—the adjectives or adverbs I mentioned above.

In general, traits describe:

How you deal with time and promptness.

How you deal with people and emotions.

How you deal with authority, and being told *what* to do at your job.

How you deal with supervision, and being told *how* to do your job.

How you deal with impulse vs. self-discipline, within yourself.

How you deal with initiative vs. response, within yourself.

How you deal with crises or problems.

Can you give me some more detailed examples of traits?

Here is a sample list. Check off any of them that you or your colleagues (*using Checkster or similar*) said describes you:

- Accurate
- Achievement-oriented
- Adaptable
- Adept
- Adept at having fun
- Adventuresome
- Alert
- Appreciative
- Assertive
- Astute
- Attentive to details
- Authoritative
- Calm
- Cautious
- Charismatic
- Competent
- Consistent
- Contagious in my enthusiasm
- Cooperative
- Courageous
- Creative
- Decisive
- Deliberate
- Dependable/have dependability
- Diligent
- Diplomatic
- Discreet

- Driving
- Dynamic
- Effective
- Empathetic
- Energetic
- Enthusiastic
- Exceptional
- Exhaustive
- Experienced
- Expert
- Extremely economical
- Firm
- Flexible
- Humanly oriented
- Impulsive
- Independent
- Innovative
- Knowledgeable
- Lots of energy
- Loyal
- Methodical
- Objective
- Open-minded
- Outgoing
- Outstanding
- Patient
- Penetrating
- Perceptive
- Persevering

- Persistent
- Pioneering
- Practical
- Professional
- Protective
- Punctual
- Quick/work quickly
- Rational
- Realistic
- Reliable
- Resourceful
- Responsible
- Responsive
- Safeguarding
- Self-motivated
- Self-reliant
- Sensitive
- Sophisticated/very sophisticated
- Strong
- Supportive
- Sympathetic
- Tactful
- Thorough
- Unique
- Unusual
- Versatile
- Vigorous

Choose your five top favorites, write down a description of a time when you demonstrated that each of them was true of you, and be prepared to share this in the interview, after you have told the employer you can indeed do the work they need done, and you now want to add: what distinguishes you from nineteen other people who can do the same work.

The employer will be paying attention to your traits, as a job-interview begins. Were you punctual? Are you courteous? Do you seem to have a true interest in this position?

Do you seem willing and eager to learn? Sometimes, a person can have all the experience in the world but lack the enthusiasm that leads to doing a great job.

I understand that in a job-interview, the employer may give me a hypothetical situation, and ask me how I would solve it. What kind of answer are they looking for?

Well, not being a mind-reader, I can only speculate. But I would guess they're trying to see how you think:

1. If the situation is one that should be familiar to anyone claiming previous experience with this kind of job, they are testing you to see if you really have the experience you claim. In which case, their expectation is that you will answer it quickly and confidently.
2. If the situation is one you're not likely to have ever encountered before, they are trying to see if you can think on your feet. They deliberately give you a problem they know is new to you, and wait to see how inventive you can be.
3. It is also possible they want to see if you can come up with more than one answer. They want to see if you instinctively search for alternatives, in case your first idea does not work: a plan A, and then a plan B.

I'm about to go on an interview. I know what my transferable skills are. What do I do in an interview—just boast what they are, or what?

No, these days employers want proof. It is no longer sufficient just to say what your skills are. You must give evidence. That has changed the whole way that interviews are conducted in the twenty-first century. Employers call these kinds of interviews "behavioral interviews."

How do I give proof that I have the skills I claim I have?

Before you ever go into an interview you choose the three top skills that you think will be of greatest interest to *this* employer for *this* job, that you are interviewing for. And then, in the case of each of the three you write out a brief description of a situation where you successfully used that skill, each on a separate page.

It may help you to "tighten up" each story, if you answer the following questions to yourself, as you're writing out the story:

a. What was I trying to accomplish?
b. Why did I want to accomplish this?
c. What were the obstacles I faced, or the constraints under which we had to operate?
d. What exactly did I do?
e. What happened as a result?
f. How did I know we were successful?

When done, read the three pages over and over to yourself. You won't be taking these pages into the interview. These are just "crib notes" to help you prepare for the interview. You must be able to offer "proof" that you have each skill, by telling each story as though it were second nature to you—now. Like breathing out and breathing in.

I can see now how job-hunting, in general, and job-interviewing, in particular, are exercises for the brain. But right now I'm still trying to think out how to find a job, and what kind of job to go looking for.

Once your brain is tuned up, if no bright ideas occur to you from all the questions in this chapter, then there is one thing you must do: you need to gather more information about *yourself*.

Of course, being human, our first instinct is to protest that we already know loads of information about ourselves. *After all, we've lived with ourselves all these years. We surely know who we are, by now.* Well, almost four decades of working with job-hunters has taught me this just isn't true. Each of us is blind—not to other people's gifts, but blind to our own uniqueness.

How do I figure out what is unique about me?

One way to do this is to take one piece of paper (just one) and, writing very small, jot down anything and everything that occurs to you about yourself: your history, your hobbies, leisure activities, work, accomplishments—anything. Let's call this sheet something elegant, like: "That One Piece of Paper." When done, read it over and circle the things you think are really unique about you. Copy these on a separate sheet, at that point.

What if I don't trust my own self-perception? After all, I've watched the tryouts of *American Idol*. People sometimes seem prone to wildly exaggerate their own gifts.

Our experience has been that this is rare. But if it worries you, there is a remedy. Go online and use a program invented by a friend of mine, Yves Lermusi, called *Checkster, which is free to individuals* (http:// checkster.com/web/talent.php). You submit the names of six people who know you and your work well—be they colleagues, customers, former supervisors, or friends. Checkster sends them a request, on your behalf, to fill out a short questionnaire about you (five to seven minutes) and submit it back to Checkster within a mandatory seven-day time period. Their names are then separated from their feedback, and an anonymous summary report is given to you summarizing what all these friends and acquaintances together perceive are your strengths and your uniqueness. Only *you* ever get this free report, and you can use it or discard it, as you wish. Use it to see what these people think is unique about you. Discard it if you think they're way off base. Choose six other people, and do it again.

If all else fails, do the paper and pencil exercises, starting on page 157.

3. Things School Never Taught Us about Job-Hunting: **Five Best Ways to Hunt for a Job**

"THE VALUE OF MY HOUSE IS WAY DOWN, THE VALUE OF MY CAR IS PRACTICALLY NOTHING, AND I FOUND OUT THIS SUIT IS ONLY WORTH $23."

We know many, many things about the whole process of job-hunting. Let me give you an example. There are millions of vacancies out there. How many different ways to find them, do you suppose there are? It turns out the answer is: 18.

In a nutshell, they are:

1. Self-Inventory. Before you do anything else, do a thorough self-inventory of the transferable skills and interests that you most

enjoy and do best, so you can define in stunning detail exactly the job(s) you would most like to have, to your family, friends, contacts, network, and employers. And then use this knowledge to focus your search for work.

2. The Internet. Use the Internet, to post your resume and/or to look for employers' "job-postings" (vacancies) on the employer's own website or elsewhere (CareerBuilder, Yahoo/Hot Jobs, Monster, LinkedIn, etc.).

3. Networking. Ask friends, family, or people in the community for job-leads.

4. School. Ask a former professor or teacher for job-leads, or career/alumni services at schools that you attended (high school, trade schools, online schools, community college, college, or university).

5. The Feds. Go to the state/federal unemployment service, or to One-stop career centers (directory at www.careeronestop.org).

6. In Your State. Go to private employment agencies (www.usa.gov/Agencies/State_and_Territories.shtml).

7. Civil Service. Take a civil service exam to compete for a government job (http://federaljobs.net/exams.htm).

8. Newspapers. Answer local "want-ads" (in newspapers, assuming your city or town still has a newspaper, online or otherwise). The Sunday editions usually prove most useful. (See http://tinyurl.com/d58l8z for how to use them; for a directory of their websites, see www.newslink.org.)

9. Journals. Look at professional journals in your profession or field, and answer any ads there that intrigue you (http://tinyurl.com/dlfsdz).

10. Temp Agencies. Go to temp agencies (agencies that get you short-term contracts in places that need your time and skills temporarily) and see if they can place you, in one place after another, until some place says, "Could you stay on, permanently?" At the very least you'll pick up experience that you can later cite on your resume (http://tinyurl.com/dxrdjy).

11. Pickups. Go to places where employers pick up workers: well-known street corners in your town (ask around), or union halls, etc., in order to get short-term work, which may lead to more

permanent work, eventually. For the time being, it may be yard work, or work that requires you to use your hands; but no job is too humble when you're desperate.

12. Job Clubs. Join or form a "job club," where you receive job-leads and weekly emotional support. Check with your local chamber of commerce, and local churches, mosques, or synagogues. Excellent directory at Job-hunt.org (http://tinyurl.com/7a9xbb).

13. Resumes. Mail out resumes blindly to anyone and everyone, blanketing the area.

14. Choose Places That Interest You. Knock on doors of any employer, factory, store, organization, or office that interests you, whether they are known to have a vacancy or not.

15. The Phone Book. Use the index to your phone book's Yellow Pages, to identify five to ten subjects, fields, or interests that intrigue you—that are located in the city or town where you are, or want to be, and then call or visit the organizations listed under these headings.

16. Volunteering. If you're okay financially for a spell, volunteer to work for nothing, short-term, at a place that interests you, whether or not they have a known vacancy, with the hope that down the line they may want to hire you (www.volunteermatch.org or www.networkforgood.org/volunteer).

17. Work for Yourself. Start your own small business, trade, or service, after observing what your community lacks but needs (http://tinyurl.com/yqt7pc).

18. Retraining. Go back to school and get retrained for some other kind of occupation than the one you've been doing.

Researchers discovered, some years ago, that while a typical job-hunt lasted around fifteen to nineteen weeks, depending on the economy, one-third to one-half of all job-hunters simply *give up* by the second month of their job-hunt. They stop job-hunting. *(Of course, they have to resume, somewhere further down the road, when and if things get really desperate.)* But why do they initially *give up?*

It turns out, the answer is related to how many job-hunting methods a job-hunter was using. In a study of 100 job-hunters who were using only one method to hunt for a job, typically 51 abandoned their search by the second month. That's more than one-half of them. On the other hand, of 100 job-hunters who were using several different ways of hunting for a job, typically only 31 of them abandoned their search by the second month. That's less than one-third of them.

You might conclude from this, that the more job-hunting methods you use in looking for a job, the more successful you will be. But, not so fast!

Further research found out that your chances of uncovering a job, does indeed increase with each additional method that you use—but only up to four, in number. If you use more than four methods of job-hunting, your likelihood of success begins to decrease, and continues to decrease with each additional method that you add to your search, beyond four. *Naturally, I have my theories about why these things are so; but for now I just want to give illustrations of my central thesis: that the job-hunt has been researched in exquisite detail, but school never tells us any of this stuff. That's pretty sad, considering that knowing these research findings can go a long way toward taking you out of the ranks of the unemployed!*

Want more examples of things school never taught us?

Okay. It's been discovered that in a job-interview, you are most likely to get hired if you talk half the time, and the interviewer talks half the time. On the other hand, if you talk 90 percent of the time, or the interviewer talks 90 percent of the time, things are not likely to go so well for you there.

Further, it's been discovered that when you are answering questions during a job-interview, you are more likely to get hired if each answer you give is at least twenty seconds in length, but not more than two minutes. *And if your answer just can't fit within the two-minute limit, it's okay if you conclude your two-minute answer with: "I can go into more detail, if you ever want it." Then, if they beg you to go on, go no more than two additional minutes, with the rest of your answer. And then, let it be, let it be!*

Another research finding: it's been discovered that you are much more likely to get hired, if right after the interview you send two thank-you notes, one e-mailed and one hand-written by "snail-mail," as techies now call the U.S. Postal Service. E-mailed for promptness, hand-written for the personal touch. And if your handwriting absolutely sucks, then at least keyboard it, and on nice paper (30 lb. paper, or heavier). U.S. Postal costs for first class mail: 44 cents for the first ounce, but 17 cents for each additional ounce; while e-mail costs nothing, except that it is subject to the dictum: *"Message sent" does not necessarily equal "message received."*

Research Plus

I could go on and on, with examples. But I have made my point: No school has educated us about the job-hunt if all it teaches us is *how to write resumes* and *conduct interviews*. There is so much more we *need* to know, and *can* know, because the job-hunt is one of the most researched of all human activities.

To be sure, the research isn't always *pure*. Many times it is *a mashup*, as it were, of research and hunches, based on long-range observations by those whose business it is, to study and observe these things.

A mashup of research and hunches. This is how we arrive at the following list of the effectiveness of various job-hunting methods, a list of vital importance to every job-hunter or career-changer.

A word about that list.

You will notice that some job-hunting methods are more *ineffective* than others; sometimes much more *ineffective*.

You will further notice that some of our favorite job-hunting strategies since time immemorial, are on the list of *least effective*. Whoops! Guess school should have told us *that*.

Here then are the percentages: they tell us what percentage of job-hunters who use *each method* **succeed** thereby in finding a job.

The Five Worst Ways to Look for a Job

4 to 10%

1. Looking for employers' job-postings on the Internet. The media are filled with stories of job-hunters who have successfully used the Internet to find a job.

One job-seeker, a systems administrator in Taos, New Mexico, who wanted to move to San Francisco posted his resume at 10 p.m. on a Monday night, on a San Francisco online bulletin board (*Craigslist.org*). By Wednesday morning he had over seventy responses from employers.

Again, a marketing professional developed her resume following guidance she found on the Internet, posted it to two advertised positions she found there, and within seventy-two hours of posting her electronic resume, both firms contacted her, and she is now working for one of them.

It is not just the media that are filled with such stories. So is my mail. Here's a letter that I received: "In May I was very unexpectedly laid off from a company I was with for five years. I was given a copy of your book by a ministry in our church that helps people without jobs. I read the book, and it was a great source of encouragement for me. The day I was laid off I committed my job search to the Lord. He blessed us, provided for us, and gave me peace of mind throughout my job-hunt. The Internet was my lifeline in finding the right job. I did 100 percent of my job search and research via the Internet. I found all my leads online, sent all my resumes via e-mail, and had about a 25 percent response rate that actually led to a phone interview or a face-to-face interview. It was a software company that laid me off, and I am [now] going to work for a publishing company, a position I found online."

And another: "Thanks to the Internet, I found what I believe to be the ideal job in [just] eight weeks—a great job with a great company and great opportunities. . . ."

And so we see the Internet can do a marvelous job of making it possible for an employer and a job-hunter to get together, in a way that was rarely possible even a decade or so ago. Internet sites currently devoted to job-hunting—some experts say they number 1,000; some say 5,000; some, 10,000; some 40,000; and some, 100,000 or more—make it possible to get together *faster* than ever before in history.

Of course, it doesn't always work. Aye, and there's the rub! It actually doesn't work for a huge percentage of those who try it. Research has turned up the fact that out of every 100 job-hunters who use the Internet as their search method for finding jobs, 4 of them will get lucky and find a job thereby, while 96 job-hunters out of the 100 will not—if they use only the Internet to search for a job.

Exception: If you are seeking a technical or computer-related job, an IT job, or a job in engineering, finances, or healthcare, the success rate rises, to somewhere around 10 percent. But for the other 20,000 job-titles that are out there in the job-market, the success rate remains at 4 percent only.

Did they teach you this when you were in school? Of course not! So you are left free to suppose that the Internet is working for everyone. And if that is what you think, and you then fail to find a job on the Internet, you can end up with lowered self-esteem, or mammoth depression.

7%

2. Mailing out resumes to employers at random. This job-search method is reported to have a 7 percent success rate. That is, out of every 100 job-hunters who use only this search method, 7 will get lucky, and find a job thereby. Ninety-three job-hunters out of 100 will not—if they use only resumes to search for a job.

I'm being generous here with my percentages for success. One study suggested that outside the Internet only 1 out of 1,470 resumes actually resulted in a job. Another study put the figure even higher: one job offer for every 1,700 resumes floating around out there. We do not know what the odds are if you post your resume on the Internet. We do know that there are reportedly at least 40,000,000 resumes floating around out there in the ether, like lost ships on the Sargasso Sea.[1] No one's bothered to try to count how many of these actually turned up a job for the job-hunter.

7%

3. Answering ads in professional or trade journals, appropriate to your field. This search method, like the one above, has a 7 percent success rate. That is, out of every 100 job-hunters who use only this search method, 7 will get lucky and find a job thereby. Ninety-three job-hunters out of 100 will not—if they use only this method to search for them.

5 to 24%

4. Answering local newspaper ads. This search method has a 5 to 24 percent success rate. That is, out of every 100 job-hunters who use only this search method, between 5 and 24 will get lucky and find a job thereby. Seventy-six to 95 job-hunters out of 100 will not—if they use only this method to search for them.

(The fluctuation between 5 percent and 24 percent is due to the level of salary that is being sought; the higher the salary being sought, the fewer job-hunters who are able to find a job—using only this search method.)

5 to 28%

5. Going to private employment agencies or search firms for help. This method has a 5 to 28 percent success rate—again depending on the

---

1. Some put the estimate way higher.

level of salary that is being sought. Which is to say, out of every 100 job-hunters who use only this method, between 5 and 28 will get lucky and find a job thereby. Seventy-two to 95 job-hunters out of 100 will not—if they use only this method to search for them.

(The range is for the same reason as noted in #4. It is of interest that the success rate of this method has risen slightly in recent years, in the case of women but not of men: in a comparatively recent study, 27.8 percent of female job-hunters found a job within two months, by going to private employment agencies.)

Other Job-Hunting Methods in the Least Effective Category: For the sake of completeness we should note that there are at least four other methods for trying to find jobs, that technically fall into this category of Worst Ways. Those four are:

Going to places where employers pick out workers, such as union halls. This has an 8 percent success rate.

(Only 12.1 percent of U.S. workers are union members, but it is claimed that those who have access to a union hiring hall, have a 22 percent success rate. What is not stated, however, is how long it takes to get a job at the hall, and how temporary and short-lived such a job may be; in the trades it's often just a few days.)

Taking a civil service examination. This has a 12 percent success rate.

Asking a former teacher or professor for job-leads. This also has a 12 percent success rate.

Going to the state or federal employment service office. This has a 14 percent success rate.

The Five Best Ways to Hunt for a Job

Okay, so much for the Worst Ways to hunt for the vacancies that are out there.

But now, let's look at the other side of the coin. What are the job-hunting methods that will pay off better, for the time and energy you have to invest in your job-hunt?

Think about this in terms of *your personal energy*. During your job-hunt, your energies are limited (especially if the job-hunt stretches on for weeks or even months); so, it's important to know which are the best strategies *that you should start with*, in case your energy runs out before you've finished working your way down through all the alternatives. Here goes:

33%

1. **Asking for job-leads from: family members, friends, people in the community, staff at career centers—especially at your local community college or the high school or college where you graduated.** You ask them one simple question: do you know of any jobs at the place where you work—or elsewhere? This search method has a 33 percent success rate. That is, out of every 100 people who use this search method, 33 will get lucky, and find a job thereby. Sixty-seven job-hunters will not—if they use only this method to search for work.

What! This is one of the five best ways to look for a job? Well, yes; but it's all relative. "The fifth best" out of all those job-hunting methods that are out there, isn't necessarily saying much. Sixty-seven job-hunters out of 100 will still not find the jobs that are out there—if they use this so-called "one-of-the-best methods." But to put things in perspective, do note that this method's success rate is almost five times higher than the success rate for resumes. *In other words, by asking for job-leads from your family and friends, you have an almost five times better chance of finding a job, than if you had just sent out your resume.*

47%

2. **Knocking on the door of any employer, factory, or office that interests you, whether they are known to have a vacancy or not.** This search method has anywhere up to a 47 percent success rate. That is, out of every 100 people who use only this search method, 47 will get lucky, and find a job thereby; 53 job-hunters out of 100 will not—if they use only this one method to search for work. But, again for perspective, note that *by going face-to-face* you have an almost seven times better chance of finding a job, than if you had just sent out your resume.

69%

3. **By yourself, using the phone book's Yellow Pages to identify subjects or fields of interest to you in the town or city where you want to work, and then calling up or visiting the employers listed**

in that field, to ask if they are hiring for the type of position you can do, and do well. This method has a 69 percent success rate. That is, out of every 100 job-hunters or career-changers who use only this search method, 69 will get lucky and find a job thereby. Thirty-one job-hunters out of 100 will not—if they use only this one method to search for them. For perspective, however, note that by doing *targeted phone calls by yourself,* you have an almost ten times better chance of finding a job, than if you had just sent out your resume.

84%

4. In a group with other job-hunters, a kind of "job-club," using the phone book's Yellow Pages to identify subjects or fields of interest to you in the town or city where you are, and then calling up or visiting the employers listed in that field, to ask if they are hiring for the type of position you can do, and do well. This method has an 84 percent success rate. That is, out of every 100 people who use only this method, 84 will get lucky and find a job thereby. That's a success rate that is over eleven times higher than if you just sent out resumes.

86%

5. Doing a Life-Changing Job-Hunt. This method, invented by the late John Crystal, depends upon doing extensive homework on *yourself* before you go out there pounding the pavement. This homework revolves around three simple words: What, Where, How.

1. **WHAT.** This has to do with your skills. You need to inventory and identify what skills you have *that you most enjoy using.* I didn't say: *that you are best at.* No, these are the ones you *enjoy* using the most. They are called your transferable skills, because they are transferable to any field/career that you choose, regardless of where you first picked them up.

2. **WHERE.** This has to do with job environments. Think of yourself as a flower. You know that a flower that blooms in the desert will not do well at 10,000 feet up—and vice versa. Every flower has an environment where it does best. So with you. You are like a flower. You need to decide where you want to use your skills, where you would thrive, and where you do your most effective work.

3. **HOW.** You need to decide how to get where you want to go. This has to do with finding out the names of the jobs you would be most interested in, **and** the names of organizations (in your preferred geographical area) that have such jobs to offer, **and** the names of the people or person there who actually has the power to hire you. And, how you can best approach that person to show him or her how your skills can help them with their problems. How, if you were hired there, you would not be part of the problem, but part of the solution.

This method has an 86 percent success rate. That is, out of every 100 job-hunters or career-changers who use only this job-search method, 86 will find a job or new career thereby.

Such an effectiveness rate—86 percent—is astronomically higher than most traditional job-hunting methods. That's why when nothing else is working for you, this is the method that you will thank your lucky stars for.

As usual, it does not work for everyone—specifically, 14 job-hunters out of 100 will still not find the jobs that are out there—if they use only this one method to search for them. But—perspective again—this is twelve times more effective than resumes. In other words, by putting in the hard time that this method requires, you have a 1,200 percent better chance of finding a job than if you just send out resumes!

Well, there's your list. There are 18 alternative ways of looking for those jobs that *are* out there; but these alternatives were not created equal. It would pay you to know which ones are most effective, which ones are less draining of your energy. Even if school never taught you *that*.

Using More Than One of These Alternatives

As we saw earlier, job-hunting success depends on not just using one of these methods, but using up to four of them.

Alternatives keep you from "job-hunting insanity." And what, pray tell, is *that*? It's when something doesn't work, and your response is to just try more of it. It's the type of thinking that says: *500 resumes didn't work? Let's try 1,000.* The only cure for this kind of desperation is alternatives.

The Seven Most Important Truths to Remember So Long as You're Unemployed

1. *Job-hunting is an activity that repeats itself over and over again, in most people's lives.* Lucky you, if that is not the case; but the odds are overwhelming that it will be. According to experts, the average worker, under 35 years of age, will go job-hunting every one to three years. And the average worker over 35 will go job-hunting every five to eight years! And, in this process, so the experts say, we will each of us probably change *careers* three to five times, as we go.

2. *Job-hunting is not a science; it is an art.* Some job-hunters know instinctively how to do it; in some cases, they were born knowing how to do it. Others of us sometimes have a harder time with it, but fortunately for us in the U.S. and elsewhere in the world, there is help, coaching, counseling, and advice—online and off.

3. *Job-hunting is always mysterious.* Sometimes *mind-bogglingly myste-rious.* You may *never* understand why things sometimes do work, and sometimes do not.

4. *There is no always wrong way to hunt for a job or to change careers.* Anything *may* work under certain circumstances, or at certain times, or with certain employers. There are only *degrees of likeli-hood* of certain job-hunting techniques working or not working. But it is crucial to know that likelihood, as we have just seen.

5. *There is no always right way to hunt for a job or to change careers.* Anything *may* fail to work under certain circumstances, or at cer-tain times, or with certain employers. There are only *degrees of likelihood* of certain job-hunting techniques working or not work-ing. But it is crucial to know that likelihood, as we just saw.

6. *Mastering the job-hunt this time, and for the rest of your life, done right, is a lot of hard work and takes some hard thinking.* The more work, the more thinking, you put into pursuing your job-hunt, and doing the homework on yourself, the more successful your job-hunt is likely to be. *Caution: Are you lazy, day by day? Uh, oh! Most people do their job-hunt or career-change the same way they do Life.*

7. *Job-hunting always depends on some amount of luck.* Luck, pure luck. Mastering the job-hunt doesn't mean absolutely, positively,

you will always be able to find a job. It does mean that you can get good at reducing the amount that depends on luck, to as small a proportion as possible.

Wise job-hunters know from the beginning that they are hunting *secondly* for a job but *first* of all for Hope. Alternatives keep Hope alive. And to someone out of work, that is everything.

So, if you answer ads in the newspapers, or if you answer job-postings on the Internet, or send out your resume everywhere, or sign up with agencies, and so far it has turned out to be all in vain, don't just do more of whatever you've been doing. Change your tactics. Try a new strategy.

4. Things School Never Taught Us about Job-Hunting: **How to Deal with Handicaps**

Most of us think that when we go job-hunting, we have some special handicap (hidden or obvious) that is going to keep us from getting a job. We think:

> I have a physical handicap *or*
> I have a mental handicap *or*
> I never graduated from high school *or*
> I never graduated from college *or*

I am just graduating *or*
I just graduated a year ago *or*
I graduated way too long ago *or*
I am too beautiful *or*
I am too handsome *or*
I am too ugly *or*
I am too fat *or*
I am too thin *or*
I am too old *or*
I am too young *or*
I have only had one employer in life *or*
I have hopped from job to job too often *or*
I am too near retirement *or*
I am too wet behind the ears *or*
I have a prison record *or*
I have a psychiatric history *or*
I have not had enough education *or*
I have too much education and am overqualified *or*
I am Hispanic *or*
I am Black *or*
I am Asian *or*
I speak heavily accented English *or*
I am too much of a specialist *or*
I am too much of a generalist *or*
I am ex-clergy *or*
I am ex-military *or*
I am too assertive *or*
I am too shy *or*
I have only worked for volunteer organizations *or*
I have only worked for small organizations *or*
I have only worked for a large organization *or*
I have only worked for the government *or*
I come from a very different culture or background *or*
I come from another industry *or*
I come from another planet.

(In other words, there are approximately three weeks in any of our lives, when we are employable! *Just kidding!*)

If you have a handicap that you think will keep employers from hiring you, take heart! No matter what handicap you have, or think you have, it cannot possibly keep you from getting hired. It will only keep you from getting hired *at some places.*

There is a *mantra* you should keep repeating to yourself again and again, as you go job-hunting:

> **"There is no such thing as 'employers.'**
> **There are at least two different**
> **kinds of employers *out there*:**
>
> **Those who are interested in hiring me**
> for what I *can* do;
> and
> **Those who are not.**
>
> With the latter I should thank them for their time,
> and ask if they know of any other employers
> who might be interested in someone with my skills.
>
> Then, gently take my leave.
> And write and mail them a thank-you note
> **that very night."**

You never know what may occur to them the next day, of some way in which they can help you. A thank-you note jogs their memory.

Now, the biggest handicap any of us can have is our attitude toward our handicap. So, I would like you to think through, with me, what it means to say, "I have a handicap."

First of all, it speaks to the prejudice of some employers. For example, "I'm fat" doesn't necessarily keep you from doing anything. So if an employer won't hire you because of that, it's technically not a handicap that we're talking about; it's a *prejudice.*

A real handicap means there are some things that you can't do. So, let's talk about *that.* Let's begin with however many skills there are, in the world. Nobody knows the number, so let's make one up. Let's say there are 4,341 skills in the world. How many of those 4,341 do you think the average person has? Nobody knows the answer, so let's make one up. Let's say the average person has 1,341 skills. That's a lot. That's 1,341 things the average person *can* do. Now, my question to you: is this average person handicapped?

The answer, of course, is *Yes:* 4,341 minus 1,341 leaves 3,000 things the average person *can't* do. The average person—no, make that: *everybody*—is handicapped. Everybody.

So if, when you go job-hunting, you think you are *handicapped*, then I would agree. But so is everyone. So what? What's so special about your handicap, compared with others'? The answer is *Nothing*. Unless—*unless*—you are obsessed with the fact that you are handicapped, and so disheartened by what you *can't* do, that you have forgotten all the things you *can* do. Unless you're thinking of all the reasons why employers might not hire you, instead of all the reasons why employers would. Unless you're going about your job-hunt feeling like *a job beggar*, rather than as *a resource person.*[1]

Here's a useful exercise for all of us Handicapped Job-Hunters or Career-Changers: take a large piece of paper and divide it into two columns, viz,

Things I Can't Do	Things I CAN Do

Then, look at the (*transferable/functional*) skills list on the next page, and copy as many as you choose onto these lists, putting each skill in the proper column, depending on whether you *can* do this skill, or *cannot*. (*Or not yet, anyway.*) Use additional sheets, as needed.

---

1. This brilliant distinction was coined by Daniel Porot, *the* job expert in Europe.

A LIST OF 246 SKILLS AS VERBS

achieving	acting	adapting	addressing	administering
advising	analyzing	anticipating	arbitrating	arranging
ascertaining	assembling	assessing	attaining	auditing
budgeting	building	calculating	charting	checking
classifying	coaching	collecting	communicating	compiling
completing	composing	computing	conceptualizing	conducting
conserving	consolidating	constructing	controlling	coordinating
coping	counseling	creating	deciding	defining
delivering	designing	detailing	detecting	determining
developing	devising	diagnosing	digging	directing
discovering	dispensing	displaying	disproving	dissecting
distributing	diverting	dramatizing	drawing	driving
editing	eliminating	empathizing	enforcing	establishing
estimating	evaluating	examining	expanding	experimenting
explaining	expressing	extracting	filing	financing
fixing	following	formulating	founding	gathering
generating	getting	giving	guiding	handling
having responsibility	heading	helping	hypothesizing	identifying
illustrating	imagining	implementing	improving	improvising
increasing	influencing	informing	initiating	innovating
inspecting	inspiring	installing	instituting	instructing
integrating	interpreting	interviewing	intuiting	inventing
inventorying	investigating	judging	keeping	leading
learning	lecturing	lifting	listening	logging
maintaining	making	managing	manipulating	mediating
meeting	memorizing	mentoring	modeling	monitoring
motivating	navigating	negotiating	observing	obtaining
offering	operating	ordering	organizing	originating
overseeing	painting	perceiving	performing	persuading
photographing	piloting	planning	playing	predicting
preparing	prescribing	presenting	printing	problem solving
processing	producing	programming	projecting	promoting
proofreading	protecting	providing	publicizing	purchasing
questioning	raising	reading	realizing	reasoning
receiving	recommending	reconciling	recording	recruiting
reducing	referring	rehabilitating	relating	remembering
rendering	repairing	reporting	representing	researching
resolving	responding	restoring	retrieving	reviewing
risking	scheduling	selecting	selling	sensing
separating	serving	setting	setting-up	sewing
shaping	sharing	showing	singing	sketching
solving	sorting	speaking	studying	summarizing
supervising	supplying	symbolizing	synergizing	synthesizing
systematizing	taking instructions	talking	teaching	team-building
telling	tending	testing & proving	training	transcribing
translating	traveling	treating	trouble-shooting	tutoring
typing	umpiring	understanding	understudying	undertaking
unifying	uniting	upgrading	using	utilizing
verbalizing	washing	weighing	winning	working
writing				

When you are done with these two lists, pick out the five top things that you *can* do, and *love* to do; and think of some illustrations and examples of how you demonstrated that, in the past.

What about the things you *can't* do? If your particular handicap or disability has a name, look it up on the Internet. If your issue is mobility, or lack thereof, the ADA may be of help to you. See a companion book to this one: *Job-Hunting for the So-Called Handicapped, or People Who Have Disabilities,* by Dale Susan Brown, and me, which explains all this at length.

Incidentally, there is one handicap that people rarely talk about, and yet it affects, if not job-performance, then the job-hunt itself. And that is, *Shyness.* So, let's close this chapter by taking a look at that handicap, and discussing how to deal with it.

A Word to Those Who Are Shy

The late John Crystal often had to counsel the shy. They were often *frightened* at the whole idea of going to talk to people for information, never mind for hiring. So John developed a system to help the shy. He suggested that before you even begin doing any Informational Interviewing, you first go out and talk to people about *anything* just to get good at *talking to people.* Thousands of job-hunters and career-changers have followed his advice, over the past thirty years, and found it really helps. Indeed, people who have followed John's advice in this regard have had a success rate of 86 percent in finding a job—and not just any job, but *the* job or new career that they were looking for.

Daniel Porot, Europe's premiere job-hunting expert, has taken John's system, and brought some organization to it. He observed that John was really recommending three types of interviews: this interview we are talking about, just for practice. Then Informational Interviewing. And finally, of course, the hiring-interview. Daniel decided to call these three the *"The PIE Method,"* which has now helped thousands of job-hunters and career-changers in both the U.S. and Europe.[2]

Why is it called *"PIE"*?

---

2. Daniel has summarized his system in a book published here in the U.S. in 1996: it is called *The PIE Method for Career Success: A Unique Way to Find Your Ideal Job,* published by JIST Works, Inc. It is a fantastic book, and I give it my highest recommendation. Daniel has a wonderful website of "career games," at www.careergames.com.

SHYNESS VS. ENTHUSIASM

Well, I said it before, but I'm going to say it again. Throughout the job-hunt and career-change, the key to informational "interviewing" is not found in memorizing a dozen questions about what you're supposed to say.

No, the key is just this one thing: now and always, make *sure* you are talking about something you feel *passionate about*.

Enthusiasm is the key—to *enjoying* "interviewing," and conducting *effective* interviews, at any level. What this exercise teaches us is that shyness always loses its power and its painful self-consciousness—*if* and *when* you are talking about something *you love*.

For example, if you love gardens you will forget all about your shyness when you're talking to someone else about gardens and flowers. *"You ever been to Butchart Gardens?"*

If you love movies, you'll forget all about your shyness when you're talking to someone else about movies. *"I just hated that scene where they . . ."*

If you love computers, then you will forget all about your shyness when you're talking to someone else about computers. *"Do you work on a Mac or a PC?"*

That's why it is important that it be your enthusiasms that you are exploring and pursuing in these conversations with others.

P is for the *warm-up* phase. John Crystal named this warm-up "The Practice Field Survey."[3] Daniel Porot calls it **P** for *pleasure*.

I is for "Informational Interviewing."

E is for the employment interview with the-person-who-has-the-power-to-hire-you.

How do you use this **P** for *practice* to get comfortable about going out and talking to people *one-on-one?*

---

3. If you want further instructions about this whole process, I refer you to "The Practice Field Survey," pp. 187–196, in *Where Do I Go from Here with My Life?* by John Crystal and friend, published by Ten Speed Press.

Initial:	Pleasure **P**	Information **I**	Employment **E**
Kind of Interview	Practice Field Survey	Informational Interviewing or Research	Employment Interview or Hiring Interview
Purpose	To Get Used to Talking with People to Enjoy It; To "Penetrate Networks"	To Find Out If You'd Like a Job, Before You Go Trying to Get It	To Get Hired for the Work You Have Decided You Would Most Like to Do
How You Go to the Interview	You Can Take Somebody with You	By Yourself or You Can Take Some-body with You	By Yourself
Who You Talk To	Anyone Who Shares Your Enthusiasm about a (for You) Non-Job-Related Subject	A Worker Who Is Doing the Actual Work You Are Thinking About Doing	An Employer Who Has the Power to Hire You for the Job You Have Decided You Most Would Like to Do
How Long a Time You Ask for	10 Minutes (and DON'T run over— asking to see them at 11:50 a.m. may help keep you hon-est, since most em-ployers have lunch appointments at noon).	Ditto	
What You Ask Them	Any Curiosity You Have about Your Shared Interest or Enthusiasm	Any Questions You Have about This Job or This Kind of Work	You Tell Them What It Is You Like about Their Orga-nization and What Kind of Work You Are Looking For

	Pleasure **P**	**Information** **I**	**Employment** **E**
Initial:			
What You Ask Them (continued)	If Nothing Occurs to You, Ask: **1.** How did you start, with this hobby, interest, etc.? **2.** What excites or interests you the most about it? **3.** What do you find is the thing you like least about it? **4.** Who else do you know who shares this interest, hobby, or enthusiasm, or could tell me more about my curiousity? **a.** Can I go and see them? **b.** May I mention that it was you who suggested I see them? **c.** May I say that you recommended them?	If Nothing Occurs to You, Ask: **1.** How did you get interested in this work and how did you get hired? **2.** What excites or interests you the most about it? **3.** What do you find is the thing you like the least about it? **4.** Who else do you know of who does this kind of work, or similar work but with this difference_____? **5.** What kinds of challenges or problems do you have to deal with in this job? **6.** What skills do you need in order to meet those challenges or problems?	You tell them the kinds of challenges you like to deal with. What skills you have to deal with those challenges. What experience you have had in dealing with those challenges in the past.
	Get their name and address.	Get their name and address.	
Afterward: That Same Night	SEND A THANK- YOU NOTE.	SEND A THANK- YOU NOTE.	SEND A THANK- YOU NOTE.

How to Deal with Handicaps

This is achieved by choosing a topic—*any* topic, however silly or trivial—that is a pleasure for you to talk about with your friends, or family. To avoid anxiety, it should not be connected to any present or future careers that you are considering. Rather, the kinds of topics that work best, for this exercise, are:

- **a hobby** you *love*, such as skiing, bridge playing, exercise, computers, etc.
- **any leisure-time enthusiasm** of yours, such as a movie you just saw, that you liked a lot
- **a long-time curiosity**, such as how do they predict the weather, or what policemen do
- **an aspect of the town or city you live in**, such as a new shopping mall that just opened
- **an issue** you feel strongly about, such as the homeless, AIDS sufferers, ecology, peace, health, etc.

There is only one condition about choosing a topic: it should be something you *love* to talk about with other people; a subject you know nothing about, but you feel a great deal of enthusiasm for, is far preferable to something you know an awful lot about, but it puts you to sleep.

Having identified your enthusiasm, you then need to go talk to someone who is as enthusiastic about this thing, as you are. *For best results with your later job-hunt, this should be someone you don't already know.* Use the Yellow Pages, ask around among your friends and family, *who do you know that* loves *to talk about this?* It's relatively easy to find the kind of person you're looking for.

You love to talk about skiing? *Try a ski-clothes store, or a skiing instructor.* You love to talk about writing? *Try a professor on a nearby college campus, who teaches English.* You love to talk about physical exercise? *Try a trainer, or someone who teaches physical therapy.*

Once you've identified someone you think shares your enthusiasm, you then go talk with them. When you are face-to-face with your *fellow enthusiast*, the first thing you must do is relieve their understandable anxiety. *Everyone* has had someone visit them who has stayed too long, who has worn out their welcome. If your *fellow enthusiast* is worried about you staying too long, they'll be so preoccupied with this that they won't hear a word you are saying.

So, when you first meet them, ask for *ten minutes of their time, only.* Period. Stop. Exclamation point. And watch your wrist-watch *like a hawk,* to be sure you stay no longer. *Never* stay longer, unless they *beg* you to. And I mean, *beg, beg, beg.*[4]

Once they've agreed to give you ten minutes, you tell them why you're there—that you're trying to get comfortable about talking with people, for information—and you understand that you two share a mutual interest, which is . . .

Then what? Well, a topic may have its own unique set of questions. For example, I love movies, so if I met someone who shared this interest, my first question would be, "What movies have you seen lately?" And so on. If it's a topic you love, and often talk about, you'll *know* what kinds of questions you begin with. But, if no such questions come to mind, no matter how hard you try, the following ones have proved to be good conversation starters for thousands of job-hunters and career-changers before you, no matter what their topic or interest.

So, look these over, memorize them *(or copy them on a little card that fits in the palm of your hand),* and give them a try:

Questions Shy People Can Practice With

Addressed to the person you're doing the Practice Interviewing with:

- How did you get involved with/become interested in this? (*"This"* is the hobby, curiosity, aspect, issue, or enthusiasm, that you are so interested in.)
- What do you like the most about it?
- What do you like the least about it?
- Who else would you suggest I go talk to who shares this interest?
- Can I use your name?
- May I tell them it was you who recommended that I talk with them?
- Then, *choosing one person from the list of several names they may have given you, you say,* "Well, I think I will begin by going to talk to this person. Would you be willing to call ahead for me, so they will know who I am, when I go over there?"

---

4. A polite, "Oh, do you have to go?" should be understood for what it is: politeness. Your response should be, "Yes, I promised to only take ten minutes of your time, and I want to keep to my word." This will almost always leave a *very* favorable impression behind you.

Incidentally, during *this* Practice Interviewing, it's perfectly okay for you to take someone with you—preferably someone who is more outgoing than you feel you are. And on the first few interviews, let them take the lead in the conversation, while you watch to see how they do it.

Once it is *your turn* to conduct the interview, it will by that time usually be easy for you to figure out what to talk about.

Alone or with someone, keep at this Practice Interviewing until you feel very much at ease in talking with people and asking them questions about things you are curious about.

In all of this, *fun* is the key. If you're having fun, you're doing it right. If you're not having fun, you need to keep at it, until you are. It may take seeing four people. It may take ten. Or twenty. You'll know.

5. Things School Never Taught Us about Job-Hunting: **Resumes and Contacts**

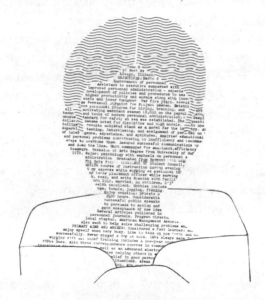

A **resume** is very attractive to an employer, but not for the reasons you think. It offers an easy way to cut down the time employers have to spend on job-hunters. It only takes a skilled human resource person about eight seconds to scan a resume (thirty seconds, if they're really dawdling), so getting rid of fifty job-hunters, I mean fifty *resumes*, takes only half an hour or less. Whereas, interviewing those fifty job-hunters in person would take a minimum of twenty-five hours. Great time savings!

A **resume** is very attractive to a job-hunter. It seems to offer an easy way to do your job-hunt, and to approach an employer. No maddening phone tag, no taking the bus, or driving the car, or sitting in someone's outer office for a blue moon, only to be rejected after all of that. No, with a resume you just take a piece of paper, summarize your qualifications, and mail it to the organization, if you have a particular target in mind. Or post it on the Web if you have no target and you want to cast a wide net—an *Inter*Net. And voilà!—so the myth goes—with your resume "out there," you will automatically find a job. In spite of the statistic that we already saw: *less than 10 percent of all job-hunters or career-changers actually find a job, when they start with their resume.*

Who perpetuates this myth of the magic resume? Well, everyone. For example, some employers—trying to get rid of you, will say, *"Send me your resume"* instead of *"goodbye"* as their way to close out the conversation. Of course, *sometimes* they really do want to see it! And, some coaches who know you will pay them for a concrete product, more than just for handholding and advice. And some resume websites, who know that having *content* on their sites (like, "how to write your resume") will hold visitors longer than just a list of job-postings. And job-hunting authors: some of whom emphatically tell you that a resume is the way to go, because it enables them to show off how good *they* are at writing a resume. And some of them are *very* good!

Of course this is a cynical reading of various parties' perpetuating of resumes; many simply believe, honestly and sincerely, that a resume works, and works superbly, and is the best way to job-hunt. *In spite of that 90 percent failure rate statistic.*

The Most Important Thing
School Should Have Taught Us

Simply this: Resumes and Interviewing are *not* two separate subjects, but one.

The primary purpose of a resume is to get yourself invited in for an interview *(with a prospective employer, of course).*

The primary purpose of that interview is to get yourself invited back for a second interview.

If you keep these two simple truths always in front of you, as you go about your job-hunt or career-change, you will be ahead of 97 percent of all other job-hunters or career-changers.

Important Truths about Resumes

A resume is *one way* to get yourself invited in for an interview. There are other ways, even preferred ways, if your resume fails. Know what they are. *For example: getting introduced there, by a mutual acquaintance or friend (a contact of yours, a business contact, a personal contact or friend, a family contact, or anyone you've ever met and know well enough to have their name and address or phone number).*

A **resume** is more akin to a business card, than to a biography. Evaluate every item you are tempted to include in your resume by this one standard: "Will this item help to get me invited in? Or will this item seem too puzzling, or off-putting, or a red flag?"

I repeat: mention nothing (in your resume) that might keep you from getting invited in. If there is something you feel you would ultimately need to explain, or expand upon, save the explanation for the interview.

A **resume** *on paper* (not by e-mail) first presents itself to the fingers, before it presents itself to the eyes. Picture this scenario: an employer is going through a whole stack of resumes, and on average he or she is giving each resume about eight seconds of their time (true: we checked!). Then that resume goes either into a pile we might call "Forgeddit," or a pile we might call "Bears further investigation."

Yes, the employers' first impression of each resume is how it feels to their fingers, as they first pick it up. By *the message from their fingers* they are either prejudiced in your favor before they even start reading, or prejudiced against you. Before their eyes read even one line. Usually they are not even aware of *why*.

A resume to a particular employer is best not sent solely by e-mail, these days. That route has been overused, and abused; many employers, leery of viruses, will not even open attachments any more, such as your resume. Send it by e-mail if you must, but always send a nicer version of it by the postal service, or UPS, or FedEx, etc.—nicely laid out or formatted, as they say, on good paper; using a decent-sized font, size 12 or even 14 (makes it faster to read), etc.

"**Depending on resumes**" poses three dangers to your job-hunting health:

1. Resumes may create depression in you, and vastly lower your self-esteem. This is the greatest danger, by far, of depending on resumes.

Why depression? Well, if it were just a matter of trying a job-hunting method that didn't work very well, it might be okay. You pick yourself up, and go on, still keeping good self-esteem. But in fact, the danger of resumes is that if you believe in them, and they don't work for you, you start to think something is really, really wrong with *you*. And if some of your friends tell you their resume actually got them a job *(not true: it actually got them an interview)*, you may feel lower than a snake's belly. Many job-hunters never snap out of the depression and feeling of worthlessness that follows. Every resume should carry a warning label: "Using this may be hazardous to your mental health."

2. Resumes make you feel like they're *out there*, working for you. They make you feel as though you're really doing something about your job-hunt. But in fact they may be moribund or comatose. That is, they may not be getting read, at all, even when posted on an employer's own website. As for posting on general sites, well, Pete Weddle, an expert on recruiting, once got some resume sites on the Internet to tell him how many employers actually looked at the resumes on their sites. (Sit down, while I tell you the news.) A site that had 85,000 resumes posted: only 850 employers looked at *any* of those resumes in the previous three months before the survey. Another site with 59,283 resumes posted, only 1,366 employers looked at *any*, in the previous months. Another site with 40,000 resumes, only 400 employers in months. A site with 30,000 resumes, only 15 employers looked in, during the previous three months. So, you send out your resume or post it on the Internet, confident that employers are reading it, when—in a depressing number of cases—nobody is. Some employers, in fact, *hate* resumes (I kid you not). So many lies, on so many resumes. So much exaggeration and distortion of job-hunters' actual experience and knowledge (40 percent of the time, according to studies).

3. Depending on resumes may cause you to give up your job-hunt prematurely. Resumes can be a useful *part* of anybody's job-hunt, but they should never be your entire plan. You can send out tons of resumes, or post them on every resume site on the Internet, and not get a single nibble. Fifty-one percent of all job-hunters who base their job-hunt solely on mailing out or posting their resume,

get discouraged, and abandon their job-hunt by the end of the second month. "Oh well," they say, "obviously there are no jobs out there." Au contraire, there are 30,000,000+ jobs out there, as we saw earlier in this book. Resumes are just the wrong way to find all but a portion of them.

Nonetheless, a resume still has its uses. Experts have been saying, for decades, that a resume is something you should never send ahead of you, but always leave behind you, after the interview. This is, of course, an oversimplification. But, taking its spirit, a resume does have a usefulness to you in helping you organize your own thoughts about yourself, your training, your record, your experience, your usefulness to a prospective employer. And, hand in hand with that, a resume has a usefulness to an employer, which is to jog her or his memory, *after* you've been there, when they are later trying to tell the other decision-makers at that organization, why he or she particularly favors you.

For guidance as to how to write your resume, go on the Internet and type "how to write a resume" into your favorite search engine (e.g., www.google.com or www.metacrawler.com). Alternatively, type in the words "tips on writing a resume" or "keywords on an electronic resume" or "examples of resumes."

This will not only turn up free resources and advice on the Internet, but also the names of books, if you want to get *very* thorough. You should look particularly for books by Yana Parker and Susan Whitcomb.

There are no *rules* about the proper form for a resume, etc. The only question is, *If you send this resume of yours, to a place where you'd like to work, will it persuade the person who has the power to hire, there, to invite you in?* If the answer is, Yes, then it matters not what form it took.

I used to have a hobby of collecting "winning" resumes—that is, resumes that had actually gotten someone a job-interview and, ultimately, a job. I'm kind of playful by nature, so I would show these without comment, to employer friends of mine, over lunch. Many of them didn't like these winning resumes at all. "That resume will never get anyone a job," they would say. Then I would reply, "Sorry, you're wrong. It already has. I think what you mean is that it wouldn't get them a job *with you*."

The resume reproduced on the previous page is a good example of what I mean; you did want an example, didn't you?

E.-J. DYER   Street, City, Zip   Telephone No.

I SPEAK
THE LANGUAGE
OF
MEN
MACHINERY
AND
MANAGEMENT
. . .

OBJECTIVE: Sales of Heavy Equipment

QUALIFICATIONS   * Knowledge of heavy equipment, its use and maintenance.
                  * Ability to communicate with management and with men in the field.
                  * Ability to favorably introduce change in the form of new equipment
                    or new ideas . . . the ability to sell.

EXPERIENCE   * Maintained, shipped, budgeted and set allocation priorities for 85 pieces
                    of heavy equipment as head of a 500-man organization (1975–1977).
Men and
Machinery   * Constructed twelve field operation support complexes, employing a
                    100-man crew and 19 pieces of heavy equipment (1965–1967).
                  * Jack-hammer operator, heavy construction (summers 1956–1957–1958).

Management   * Planned, negotiated and executed large scale equipment purchases on
                    a nation to nation level (1972–1974).

Sales   * Achieved field customer acceptance of two major new computer-
                    based systems:
                    —Equipment inventory control and repair parts expedite system (1968–1971)
                    —Decision makers' training system (1977–1979).
                  * Proven leader . . . repeatedly elected or appointed to senior posts.

EDUCATION   * B.A. Benedictine College, 1959. (Class President; Editor Yearbook;
                    "Who's Who in American Colleges").
                  * Naval War College, 1975. (Class President; Graduated "With Highest
                    Distinction").
                  * University of Maryland, 1973–1974. (Chinese Language).
                  * Middle Level Management Training Course, 1967–1968
                    (Class Standing: 1 of 97).

PERSONAL   * Family: Sharon and our sons Jim (11), Andy (8) and Matt (5) desire to
                    locate in a Mountain State by 1982, however, in the interim will consider
                    a position elsewhere in or outside the United States . . . Health: Excellent . . .
                    Birthdate: December 9, 1937 . . . Completing Military Service with the rank
                    of Lieutenant Colonel, U.S. Marine Corps.

SUMMARY   A seeker of challenge . . . experienced, proven and confident of
                  closing the sales for profit.

Jim Dyer, who had been in the U.S. Marines for twenty years, wanted a job as a salesman for heavy construction and mining equipment, thousands of miles from where he was then living. He devised the resume you see, and had just fifteen copies made. He mailed them out, he said, "to a grand total of seven before I got the job in the place I wanted!"

Like the employer who hired him, I loved this resume. Yet some of the employers I showed it to *(over lunch, as I said)* criticized it for using a picture or for being too long, or for being too short, etc. In other words, had Jim sent that resume to *them*, they wouldn't have even invited him in for an interview.

Trouble is, you don't know which employer likes *what*. That's why many job-hunters, if they use resumes, pray as they mail their resume: *Please, dear God, let them be employers who like resumes in general, and may the form of my resume appeal to those employers I care the most about, in particular.*

Alternatives to a classic resume. Many experts suggest that instead of sending a resume, you send just a "cover letter" instead, summarizing all that a longer resume might have covered. If you don't know what a cover letter is, or how to write it, the Internet can rescue you handily. Just type "cover letters" into your favorite search engine. You'll be surprised at how many tips, examples, etc., you find. Look particularly for Susan Ireland's free Cover Letter Guide (it's at http://susanireland.com/coverletterwork.htm). Incidentally, recent surveys have revealed that many employers prefer a cover letter to a resume.

Another alternative to a classic resume is a Job- or Career-Portfolio. A portfolio may be electronic (posted on the Internet) or on paper/a notebook/or in a large display case (as with artists), of your accomplishments, experience, training, and commendations or awards, from the past. Artists have a portfolio, with samples of their work. You knew that. But portfolios are equally apt in other fields.

Instead of "portfolio" we might just call them "Evidence of What I Can Do and Have Done," or "Proof of Performance." One programmer I know applied for a job, and decided to bring in a kind of portfolio—about twenty to thirty pages of actual programming he had done. None of the other candidates brought in any evidence of what they could do. He got the job.

For guidance on how to prepare a job-portfolio, and what to include, type "job portfolios" into Google; you'll get a wealth of tips and information. I particularly recommend Martin Kimeldorf's site (http://amby .com/kimeldorf/portfolio). Other names to remember (longtime advocates of career portfolios) are Kate Duttro and Carmen Croonquist. (Put their names into Google.) If you want to go deeper, like, to books, I recommend *The Career Portfolio Workbook: Using the Newest Tool in Your Job-Hunting Arsenal to Impress Employers and Land a Great Job!* by Frank Satterthwaite and Gary D'Orsi. There is also: *Proof of Performance: How to Build a Career Portfolio to Land a Great New Job* by Rick Nelles. Try your local bookstore, or online at www.amazon .com or www.barnesandnoble.com.

A Starter Kit, For Writing a Resume (If You Must) Or For Answering Questions In a Behavioral Interview

This is adapted, with the written permission of my friend Tom O'Neil, from an original document of his, which was and is copyright protected under the New Zealand Copyright Act (1994) © cv.co.nz 2001. You may contact Tom at www.cv.co.nz.

A resume is about your past. Here is a framework for recalling your past.

If you cannot think of any achievements under the categories below, don't be concerned, as the Flower Exercise later in this book will help you greatly.

For now, think of your working and personal experiences and skills that you believe you possess innately, or have learned. Which ones are you proud of? What things have you done in your life or work experience that no one else has done? Take some blank sheets of paper and fill in any answers that occur to you, please.

> **It is important to be quantitative when you do this**
> (e.g., mention dates, percents, dollars, brand names, etc.).

Volunteer, Community, and Unpaid Work

1. Have you completed any voluntary or unpaid work for any organization or company? (e.g., church, synagogue, mosque, school, community service, or special needs organization)

Educational

2. Did you work while you were studying? If so, did you receive any promotions or achievements in that role?
3. Did you gain any scholarships?
4. Were you involved in any committees, etc.?
5. Did you win any awards for study?
6. Did you have any high (e.g., A or above) grades? If so, what were the subjects—and grades?

Sales or Account Management

Have you ever been in sales? If so, what were some of your achievements? For example:

7. Have you ever consistently exceeded your set budget in that role? If so, by what percent or dollar value?
8. Have you exceeded your set budget in a particular month(s)/quarter(s) in a role? If so, by what percent or dollar value?
9. What level were you, compared to other sales professionals in your company? (e.g., "Number three out of twenty on the sales team.")
10. Have you ever increased market share for your company? If so, by what percent or dollar value?
11. Have you ever brought in any major clients to your company?
12. What major clients are/were you responsible for managing and selling to?
13. Did you ever manage to generate repeat business or increase current business? If so, by what percent or dollar value?
14. Have you won any internal or external sales awards?

15. Did you develop any new successful promotional or marketing ideas that increased sales?

Administration, Customer Services, and Accounts

Have you ever been in customer service or helped run a business unit? If so:

16. Did you assist in reducing customer complaints, etc.?

17. Did you set up or improve any systems and/or processes?

18. Was there a quantifiable difference in the company or business unit when you first joined the business or project and when you completed the project or left the business?

19. Did you take any old administration- or paperwork-based systems and convert them into an IT-based system?

Responsibility

20. Have you ever been responsible for the purchase of any goods or services in some job? (e.g., air travel or PC acquisition)

21. Have you ever had any budget responsibility? If so, to what level? (e.g., "Responsible for division budget of $200,000 per annum.")

22. Have you ever been responsible for any staff oversight? If so, in what capacity and/or how many staff members were you responsible for?

23. Were you responsible for any official or unofficial training? If so, what type, for whom, and how many people have you trained? (e.g., "Responsible for training twelve new staff in customer service as well as in using the in-house computer system.")

24. Were you responsible for any official or unofficial coaching or mentoring of other staff?

Events or Conference Planning or Logistical Management

25. Have you organized any events or conferences? If so, how large were they (both people attending and total budget if possible) and where and when was the event(s) held?

26. Have you been involved in any major relocation projects?

27. Have you had responsibility with regard to any major suppliers? If so, who?

Computers, PCs, and Macs

28. What systems, software, and hardware experience do you have?

29. What software have you utilized?

30. Have you developed any websites or systems software? If so, what were they, and did it positively affect the business?

31. Were you involved in any special projects that were outside of your job description?

Mechanical

32. Other than computers, have you had experience on any kinds of machines or equipment? Please list them together with the number of years.

33. If you ever worked on transportation devices, what were the airplane, farm equipment, truck, car, machine, or bike brands that you serviced, maintained, or repaired?

Building, Construction, Electrical, and Plumbing

34. If you ever worked in those fields, were there any major projects you have worked on? How much did the project(s) cost? (e.g., "Reception refurbishment—ABC Bank [Auckland Central Head Office] $1.2m.")

General

35. How long have you spent within any industry? (e.g., "Twelve years experience within the fashion industry.")

36. Were you promoted in any of your roles? If so, in what years and to which roles?

37. Was extra authority awarded to you after a period of time within a role? (e.g., "Commenced as receptionist; then, after three months, awarded by being given further clerical responsibilities including data entry and accounts payable.") It is not necessary that these responsibilities awarded to you should have changed your job title and/or salary.

38. Have you been asked to take part in any trainee management courses or management development programs?

39. Were you asked to get involved in any special projects outside your job description? Or, did you ever volunteer for such? What was the result?

Positive Feedback

40. Have you ever received any written or verbal client, customer, or managerial commendations or letters of praise?

41. Can you think of any occasions where you gave excellent customer service? If so, how did you know the customer was satisfied? (Also: What was the outcome? How did it benefit the company?)

42. Did you receive any awards within your company or industry? (e.g., "Acknowledged for support or service of clients or staff, etc.")

Memberships

43. Have you been a representative on any committees (e.g., health and safety committee)? Any special responsibilities there?

44. Do you belong or have you belonged to any professional clubs such as Toastmasters, Lions, or Rotary?

Published or Presented Work

45. Have you had any articles, papers, or features published in any magazines, journals, or books? If so, what publications and when?

46. Have you presented any topics at any conferences or completed any public speaking? If so, what subjects have you talked about and how large was the audience? List in detail.

Looking Ahead

• What value do you think you would add to a potential employer's business? How would you be "a resource" or even "a resource-broker" for them, rather than just "a job beggar"?

• How do you think you would stand out from other applicants who have an equal background?

When Going into a Behavioral Interview

It won't be enough to say, "I'm good at this or that." The interviewer will want to know specifics—when, where, how much—that kind of thing.

To Assist in Drawing Out Your Achievements

If you are having trouble working out your achievements, complete this EASY task below for each role, starting with your current position and working backward.

E   Experiences (What experiences have I had in this role?)
A   Achievements (What achievements have I had in this role?)
S   Skills (What skills have I learned in this role?)
Y   You link to the relevant aspects of the job you are applying for!
(You may wish to start with "skills" to help you in drawing out these achievements.)

How to Get an Interview When Resumes Just Aren't Working

To begin with, most discussions of job-interviewing proceed from a false assumption. They *assume* you are going to be approaching a large organization—you know, the ones where you need a floor-plan of the building, and an alphabetical directory of the staff. There are admittedly *huge* problems in approaching such giants for a hiring-interview, not the least of which is that in troubled times, many do more downsizing than hiring.

But many job-hunters don't want to work for large corporations, anyway. They want to go after the so-called "small organizations"—those with fifty or fewer employees—which, in the U.S., for example, represent 80 percent of all private businesses, and one-fourth of all workers in the private sector.

The Virtues of Small Organizations

Experts have claimed for years that small organizations create up to two-thirds of all new jobs.[1] If that makes you prefer going after a small organization, I have good news: they are *much* easier to get into than large ones, believe me.

---

1. This statistic, first popularized by David Birch of M.I.T., and widely quoted for years, was challenged during the 1990s by economists such as Nobel laureate Milton Friedman and Harvard economist James Medoff. The debate was fueled by a study conducted jointly by Steven J. Davis, a labor economist at the University of Chicago, John Haltiwanger at the University of Maryland, and Scott Schuh at the Federal Reserve. Their study, however, was of U.S. *manufacturing*, not of the economy as a whole. Anyway, what these researchers discovered at that time is that small *manufacturing* companies with fifty or fewer employees created only *one-fifth* of all new manufacturing jobs (*New York Times,* 3/25/94). Other researchers, notably Birch, claim that if you include all small companies, they create as many as two-thirds of all new jobs. Has this changed in the new millennium? Hard to tell. Certainly, the U.S. dot.com meltdown back in 2000 made many people afraid to work for small companies—in the Internet field, at least, and in the so-called "New Economy" for sure.

With a small organization, you don't need to wait until there's a *known* vacancy, because they rarely advertise vacancies even when there is one. You just go there and ask if they need someone.

With a small organization, there is no Personnel or Human Resources Department to screen you out.

With a small organization, there's no problem in identifying the person-who-has-the-power-to-hire-you. It's *the boss*. Everyone there knows who it is. They can point to his or her office door, easily.

With a small organization, you do not need to approach them through the mail; if you use your personal contacts, you can get in to see the boss. And if, by chance, he or she is well protected from intruders, it is relatively easy to figure out how to get around *that*. Contacts again are the answer.

With a small organization, if it is growing, there is a greater likelihood that they will be willing to create a new position for you, *if you quietly convince them that you are too good to let slip out of their grasp.*

For all of these reasons and more, small organizations must be kept in mind, as much as or more than, large organizations, when we begin talking about techniques or strategies for securing a hiring-interview. But let's take each separately, as they involve two different techniques.

Approaching Large Organizations for an Interview

In securing hiring-interviews, it's the large organizations that are the problem—the ones, as I mentioned, where you need a floor-plan of the building, and an alphabetical directory of the staff.

But you can simplify your task, if you keep certain things in mind. To begin with, you don't want to just get into the building. You want to get in to see *a particular person* in that building, and only that person: namely, the person-who-has-the-power-to-hire-you for the job you are interested in.

Most job-hunters *don't* even *try* to find out *who* that person is, before approaching a large organization. Rather, they approach each large organization in what can only be described as a haphazard, scattershot fashion.

There is a far, far more effective way to approach employers—and that, as I was saying, is to identify *who* at that organization has the power to hire you for the position you have in mind, and then to discover what mutual friend the two of you might have in common, who could help you get an appointment. The person-who-has-the-power-to-hire-you will see you because that mutual friend got the appointment for you.

How Do I Find Out Exactly Who Has the Power to Hire Me?

In a small organization with fifty or fewer employees, this is a relatively easy problem. Calling the place and asking for the name of the boss should do it. It's what we call *The One-Minute Research Project*.

But if the place where you are dying to work is a much larger organization, then the answer is: "Through *research and* by asking every *contact* you have."

Let's say that one of the places you are interested in is an organization that we will call *Mythical Corporation*.

You know the kind of job you'd like to get there, but first you know you need to find out the name of the person-who-has-the-power-to-hire-you there. What do you do?

If it's a large organization, you go on the Internet or you go to your local public library, and search the directories there. Hopefully that search will yield the name of the person you want.

But if it doesn't, which will particularly be the case with smaller organizations, *then you turn to your contacts.*

The Virtue of Contacts

So now, to our task. You want to approach *Mythical Corporation* and you know that to get in there, you will need to use your contacts. So, what do you do? Well, you approach as many people from the list below as possible and you ask each of them, "Do you know anyone who works, or used to work, at *Mythical Corporation*?"

You ask that question again and again of *everyone* you know, or meet, until you find someone who says, "*Yes, I do.*"

Then you ask them:

"What is the name of the person you know who works, or used to work, at *Mythical Corporation*? Do you have their phone number and/ or address?"

"Would you be willing to call ahead, to tell them who I am?"

Since this subject of *contacts* is widely misunderstood by job-hunters and career-changers, let's be very specific, here.

Every person you know, is a contact.

Every member of your family.

Every friend of yours.

Every person in your address book.

Every person on your Christmas-card list, or comparable.

Every person you met at any party you attended in the last year or two.

Every co-worker from your last five jobs.

Every person you know at your gym or athletic place.

Every person you know on any athletic team.

Every merchant or salesperson you ever deal with.

Every person who comes to your apartment or house to do any kind of repairs or maintenance work.

Every person you meet in line at the supermarket or bank.

Every checkout clerk you know.

Every gas station attendant you know.

Everyone who does personal work on you: your barber, hairdresser, manicurist, physical trainer, body worker, and the like.

The waiters, waitresses, and manager of your favorite restaurants.

All the people you meet on the Internet. All the people whose e-mail addresses you have.

Every leisure partner you have, as for walking, exercising, swimming, or whatever.

Every doctor, or medical professional you know.

Every professor, teacher, etc., you once knew and maybe still know how to get a hold of.

Every person in your church, synagogue, mosque, or religious assembly.

Everyone you know in Rotary, Kiwanis, Lions, or other service organizations.

Every person you know at any group you belong to.

Every person you are newly introduced to.

Every person you meet, stumble across, or blunder into, during your job-hunt, whose name, address, and phone number you have the grace to ask for. (*Always* have the grace to ask for it.)

Got the picture?

You then phone them yourself and make an appointment to go see them ("*I won't need more than twenty minutes of your time.*"). Once you are talking to them, after the usual polite chit-chat, you ask them the question you are dying to know. Because they are *inside* the organization that interests you, they are usually able to give you the exact answer to the question that has been puzzling you: "Who would have the power to hire me at *Mythical Corporation*, for this kind of position (*which you then describe*)?" If they answer that they do not know, ask if they know *who* might know. If it turns out that they do know, then you ask them not only for that hiring person's name, address, phone, and e-mail address, but also what they can tell you about that person's job, that person's interests, and their style of interviewing.

Then, you ask them if they could help you get an appointment with that person. You repeat this familiar refrain:

"Given my background, would you recommend I go see them?"

"Do you know them, personally? If not, could you give me the name of someone who does?"

"If you know them personally, may I tell them it was you who recommended that I talk with them?"

"If you know them personally, would you be willing to call ahead, to tell them who I am, and to help set up an appointment?"

Also, before leaving, you can ask them about the organization, in general.

Then you thank them, and leave; and you *never never* let the day end, without sitting down to write them a thank-you note. *Always* do it. *Never* forget to.

Getting In

If the contact you talked to doesn't know the person-who-has-the-power-to-hire-you well enough to get you an interview, then you go back to your other contacts—now armed with the name of the person you are trying to get in to see—and pose a new question. Approaching as many of your contacts as possible, you ask each of them, "Do you know Ms. or Mr. See, at *Mythical Corporation,* or do you know someone who does?"

You ask that question again and again of *everyone* you know until you find someone who says, *"Yes, I do."*

Then of course, over the phone or—better—in person, you ask that person these questions, carefully, and in this exact order:

- "What can you tell me about him—or her?"
- "Given the kind of job I am looking for *(which you here describe),* do you think it would be worth my while to go see them?"
- "Do you have their phone number and/or address?"
- "May I tell them it was you who recommended that I talk with them?"
- "Would you be willing to call ahead, to set up an appointment for me, and tell them who I am?"

May-Day, May-Day!

Whenever a job-hunter writes me and tells me they've run into a brick wall, and just can't find out the name of the person-who-has-the-power-to-hire-them, the problem *always* turns out to be: they aren't making *sufficient* use of their contacts. They're making a *pass* at using their contacts, but they aren't putting their whole heart and soul into it.

My favorite (true) story in this regard, concerns a job-hunter I know, in Virginia. He decided he wanted to work for a particular health-care organization in that state, and not knowing any better, he approached them by visiting their Human Resources Department. After dutifully filling out a job application, and talking to someone there in that department, he was told there were no jobs available. Stop. Period. End of story.

Approximately three months later he learned about this technique of approaching your favorite organization by using contacts. He explored his contacts *diligently,* and succeeded in getting an interview with the person-who-had-the-power-to-hire-him for the position he was interested in. The two of them hit it off, immediately. The appointment went swimmingly. "You're hired," said the person-who-had-the-power-to-hire-him. "I'll call Human Resources and tell them you're hired, and that you'll be down to fill out the necessary stuff."

Our job-hunter never once mentioned that he had previously approached that same organization through that same Human Resources Department, and been turned down cold.

Just remember: contacts are the key. It takes about eighty pairs of eyes, and ears, to help find the career, the workplace, the job that you are looking for.

Your contacts *are* those eighty eyes and ears.

They are what will help you get the ideal job you are looking for, and they are key to finding out the name of the person-who-has-the-power-to-hire-you.

The more people you know, the more people you meet, the more people you talk to, the more people you enlist as part of your own personal job-hunting network, the better your job-finding success is likely to be. Therefore, you must try to grow your contacts wherever you go. This, of course, is called "networking." I call it "building your grapevine."

Here's how some people have gone about doing that. If they go to hear a speaker on some subject that interests them, they make it a point to join the crowd that gathers 'round the speaker at the end of the talk, and—with notepad poised—ask such questions as: "Is there anything special that people with my expertise can do?" And here they mention their *generalized* job-title: computer scientist, health professional, chemist, writer, or whatever. Very useful information has thus been turned up. You can also go up to the speaker afterward, and ask if you can contact him or her for further information—"and at what address?"

Conventions, likewise, afford rich opportunities to make contacts. Says one college graduate: "I snuck into the Cable Advertisers Convention at the Waldorf in N.Y.C. That's how I got my job."

Another way people have cultivated contacts, is to leave a message on their telephone answering machine that tells everyone who calls, what information they are looking for. One job-hunter used the following message: "This is the recently laid-off John Smith. I'm not home right now because I'm out looking for a good job as a computer troubleshooter in the telecommunications field; if you have any leads or just want to leave a message, please leave it after the tone."

You may also cultivate contacts by studying the *things* that you like to work with, and then writing to the manufacturer of that *thing* to ask them for a list of organizations in your geographical area that use that *thing.* For example, if you like to work on a particular machine, you would write to the manufacturer of that machine, and ask for names of organizations in your geographical area that use that machine. Or if you like to work in a particular environment, think of the supplies used in that environment. For example, let's say you love darkrooms. You think of what brand of equipment or supplies is usually used in darkrooms, and then you contact the sales manager of the company that makes those supplies, to ask where his (or her) customers are. Some sales managers will not be at all responsive to such an inquiry, but others graciously will, and thus you may gain some very helpful leads.

Because your memory is going to be overloaded during your job-hunt or career-change, it is useful to set up a filing system, where you put the name of each contact of yours on a 3 x 5 card, with addresses, phone numbers, and anything about where they work or who they know that may be of use at a later date. Those of you who are extremely computer literate can, if you prefer, use a database program to do the same thing. Go back over those cards (or their electronic equivalent) frequently.

That does add up to *a lot* of file cards, just because you've got *a lot* of contacts. But that's the whole point.

You may need *every one* of them, *when push comes to shove.*

Rescuing the Employer

As you can see, getting in to see someone, even for a hiring-interview, is not as difficult as people will tell you. It just takes some *know-how,* some *determination,* some *perseverance,* some *going the extra mile.* It works because everyone has friends, including this person-who-has-the-power-to-hire-you. You are simply approaching them through *their* friends. And you are doing this, not *wimpishly,* as one who is coming to ask a favor. You are doing it *helpfully,* as one who is asking to help rescue them.

Rescue? Yes, rescue! I cannot tell you the number of employers I have known over the years, who can't figure out how to find the right employee. It is absolutely mind-boggling, particularly in hard times when job-hunters would seem to be gathered on every street corner.

You're having trouble finding the employer. The employer is having trouble finding you. *What a great country!*

So, if you now present yourself directly to the person-who-has-the-power-to-hire-you, you are not only answering your own prayers. You are hopefully answering the employer's, as well. You will be *just* what the employer is looking for, but didn't know how to find . . . .

if you first figured out what your favorite and best skills are, and

if you then figured out what your favorite Fields of Fascination or *languages* are, and

if you took the trouble to figure out what places *might* need such skills and such *languages*, and

if you researched these places with the intent of finding out what their tasks, challenges, and problems are, and

if you took the trouble to figure out who has the power to hire you there.

Of course, you don't for sure *know* they need you; that remains for the hiring-interview to uncover. But at least by this thorough preparation you have *increased* the chances that you are at the right place—whether they have an announced vacancy or not. And, if you are, you are not imposing on this employer. You are coming not as "job beggar," but as "resource person." You may well be absolutely rescuing him or her, believe me!

And yourself. *"The hiring-interview! I actually got in!"*

Yes, and so, it's time for our next section.

THE TEN GREATEST MISTAKES
MADE IN JOB INTERVIEWS

Whereby Your Chances of Finding a Job Are Greatly Decreased

I. Going after large organizations only (such as the Fortune 500).

II. Hunting all by yourself for places to visit, using ads and resumes.

III. Doing no homework on an organization before going there.

IV. Allowing the Personnel Department (or Human Resources) to interview you—their primary function is to screen you OUT.

V. Setting no time limit when you make the appointment with an organization.

VI. Letting your resume be used as the agenda for the job-interview.

VII. Talking primarily about yourself, and what benefit the job will be for you.

VIII. When answering a question of theirs, talking anywhere from two to fifteen minutes at a time.

IX. Basically approaching them as if you were a job beggar, hoping they will offer you a job, however humble.

X. Not sending a thank-you note right after the interview.

6. Things School Never Taught Us about Job-Hunting: **Interviews**

"I WANT TO EXPERIENCE A WARM CLIMATE, FLY THROUGH THE AIR, SEE SOME COLOR, EAT A PEACH — I WANT TO LIVE!"

An interview resembles *dating*, more than it does buying a used car (*you*). An interview is two people trying to decide if they want "to go steady."

An interview is not to be thought of as *marketing* yourself: i.e., selling yourself to a half-interested employer. Rather, an interview is part of your *research*, i.e., the *data-collecting process* that you have been engaged in, or should have been engaged in, during your whole job-hunt.

While you are sitting there, with the employer, the question you are trying to find an answer to is: "Do I want to work here, or not?" You use the interview to find out. Only when you have concluded, Yes, do you then turn your energy toward *selling* yourself.

An interview is not to be thought of as a test. It's a *data-collecting process* for the employer, too. They are still trying to decide if you *fit*. They are using the interview to find out "Do I want him or her to work here? Do they have skills, knowledge, or experience that I really need? Do they have an attitude toward work, that I am looking for? And, how will they *fit in* with my other employees?"

An interview is best prepared for, *before* you go in, by taking these three steps:

1. Research the organization or company, before going in. Go to their website if they have one, and read everything there that is "About Us." Ask your local librarian for help in finding any news clippings or other information about the place. And, finally, ask all your friends if they know anyone who ever worked there, or works there still, so you can take them to lunch or tea or Starbucks and find out any inside stories. All organizations love to be loved. If you've gone to all this trouble, to find out as much as possible about them, they will be flattered and impressed, believe me, because most job-hunters never go to this amount of trouble. Most just walk in the door, knowing nothing. One time, an IBM recruiter asked a college senior he was interviewing, *What does IBM stand for?* The senior didn't know, and the interview was over. *(Answer: International Business Machines.)*

2. When setting up the interview, specify the time you need. Experts recommend you only ask for twenty minutes, and observe this commitment *religiously*. Once you're into the interview, stay aware of the time, and don't stay one minute longer than the twenty minutes, unless the employer *begs* you to—and I mean, *begs*. Always respond with, "I said I would only take twenty minutes of your time, and I like to honor my agreements." This will always make a big impression on an employer!

3. As you go to the interview, keep in mind that the person-who-has-the-power-to-hire-you is sweating, too. Why? Because, the hiring-interview is not a very reliable way to choose an employee. In a survey conducted many years ago among a dozen top United

Chapter Six

Kingdom employers,[1] it was discovered that the chances of an employer finding a good employee through the hiring-interview was only *3 percent better* than if they had picked a name out of a hat. In a further ironic finding, it was discovered that if the interview was conducted by someone who would be working directly with the candidate, the success rate dropped to *2 percent below* that of picking a name out of a hat. And if the interview was conducted by a so-called human resources expert, the success rate dropped to *10 percent below* that of picking a name out of a hat.

No, I don't know how they came up with these figures, but they sure are a hoot! And, more important, they are totally consistent with what I have learned about the world of hiring during the past forty years. I have watched so-called experts make *wretchedly* bad choices about hiring *in their own office*, and when they would morosely confess this to me some months later, over lunch, I would playfully tease them with, "If *you* don't even know how to hire well for your own office, how do you keep a straight face when you're called in as a hiring consultant by another organization?" And they would ruefully reply, "We act *as though it were* a science." Well, let me tell you, dear reader, the hiring-interview is *not* a science. It is a very, very hazy art, done badly by most of its employer-practitioners, in spite of their own past experience, their very best intentions, and their carloads of goodwill.

The hiring-interview is not what it seems to be. It seems to be one individual (*you*) sitting there, scared to death while the other individual (*the employer*) is sitting there, blasé and confident.

But what it really is, is two individuals (*you* and *the employer*) sitting there scared to death. It's just that the employer has learned to *hide* his or her fears better than you have, because they've had more practice.

But this employer is, after all, a human being just like you. In most cases, they were *not* hired to do *this*. It got thrown in with all their other duties. And they may *know* they're not very good at it. So, they're afraid.

---

1. Reported in the *Financial Times Career Guide* 1989 for the United Kingdom.

The employer's fears include *any* or *all* of the following:

A. That you won't be able to do the job: that you lack the necessary skills or experience, and the hiring-interview didn't uncover this.

B. That if hired, you won't put in a full working day, regularly.

C. That if hired, you'll be frequently "out sick," or otherwise absent whole days.

D. That if hired, you'll only stay around for a few weeks or at most a few months, and then quit without advance warning.

E. That it will take you too long to master the job, and thus it will be too long before you're profitable to that organization.

F. That you won't get along with the other workers there, or that you will develop a personality conflict with the boss himself (or herself).

G. That you will do only the minimum that you can get away with, rather than the maximum that they hired you for.

H. That you will always have to be told what to do next, rather than displaying initiative—always in a responding mode, rather than an initiating mode (and mood).

I. That you will have a work-disrupting character flaw, and turn out to be dishonest, or totally irresponsible, a spreader of dissension at work, lazy, an embezzler, a gossip, a sexual harasser, a drug-user or substance abuser, a drunk, a liar, incompetent, or—in a word— *bad news.*

J. *If this is a large organization, and your would-be boss is not the top person:* that you will bring discredit upon them, and upon their department/section/division, etc., for ever hiring you in the first place—making them lose face, possibly also costing them a raise or a promotion.

K. That you will cost a lot of money, if they make a mistake by hiring you. Currently, in the U.S. the cost to an employer of a bad hire can far exceed $50,000, including relocation costs, lost pay for the period for work not done or aborted, and severance pay—if *they* are the ones who decide to let you go.

No wonder the employer is *sweating.*

And now, to the actual Interview.

An interview is best conducted by You, in the following way:

During the Interview, Determine to Observe the 50-50 Rule

Studies have revealed that, in general, the people who get hired are those who mix speaking and listening fifty-fifty in the interview. That is, half the time they let the employer do the talking, half the time in the interview they do the talking. People who didn't follow that mix, were the ones who didn't get hired, according to the study.[2] My hunch as to the *reason* why this is so, is that if you talk too much about yourself, you come across as one who would ignore the needs of the organization; if you talk too little, you come across as trying to hide something about your background.

In Answering the Employer's Questions, Observe the Twenty-Second to Two-Minute Rule

---

Studies[3] have revealed that when it is your turn to speak or answer a question, you should plan ahead of time not to speak any longer than two minutes at a time, if you want to make the best impression. In fact, a good answer to an employer's question sometimes only takes twenty seconds to give.

Determine to Be Seen as a Part of the Solution, Not as a Part of the Problem

---

Every organization has two main preoccupations for its day-by-day work: the problems or challenges they are facing, and what solutions to

---

2. This one was done by a researcher at Massachusetts Institute of Technology, whose name has been lost in the mists of time.
3. This one was conducted by my friend and colleague, Daniel Porot, of Geneva, Switzerland.

those problems their employees and management are coming up with. Therefore, the main thing the employer is trying to figure out during the hiring-interview with you, is: will you be part of the *solution* there, or just another part of the *problem.*

In trying to answer their concern, you should figure out prior to the interview how a *bad* employee would "screw up," in the position you are asking for—such things as *come in late, take too much time off, follow his or her own agenda instead of the employer's, etc.* Then plan to emphasize to the employer during the interview how much you are the very opposite: your sole goal is to increase the organization's effectiveness, service, and bottom line.

Be aware of the skills all employers are looking for, these days, regardless of the position you are seeking. They are looking for employees: *who are punctual, arriving at work on time or early; who stay until quitting time, or even leave late; who are dependable; who have a good attitude; who have drive, energy, and enthusiasm; who want more than a paycheck; who are self-disciplined, well-organized, highly motivated, and good at managing their time; who can handle people well; who can use language effectively; who can work on a computer; who are committed to teamwork; who are flexible, and can respond to novel situations, or adapt when circumstances at work change; who are trainable, and love to learn; who are project-oriented, and goal-oriented; who have creativity and are good at problem solving; who have integrity; who are loyal to the organization; who are able to identify opportunities, markets, and coming trends.* Above all they want to hire people who can bring in more money than they are paid. *So, plan on claiming all of these that you* legitimately *can, during the hiring-interview, with evidence (short stories).*

Realize That the Employer Thinks the Way You Are Doing Your Job-Hunt Is the Way You Will Do the Job

---

Illustrate by the way you conduct your job-hunt whatever it is you want to claim will be true of you, once hired. For example, if you plan on claiming during the interview that you are very *thorough* in all your work, be sure to be thorough in the way you have researched the company or organization ahead of time. The manner in which you do your

Wild Life, by John Kovalic, © 1989 Shetland Productions. Reprinted with permission.

job-hunt and the manner in which you would do the job you are seeking, are not assumed by most employers to be two unrelated subjects, but one and the same. They can tell when you are doing a slipshod, half-hearted job-hunt (*"Uh, what do you guys do here?"*), and this is taken as a clear warning that you will do a slipshod, half-hearted job, were they foolish enough to hire you. Most people job-hunt the same way they live their lives, and the way they do their work.

Bring Evidence If You Can

Try to think of some way to bring evidence of your skills, to the hiring-interview. For example, if you are an artist, a craftsperson, or anyone who produces a product, try to bring a sample of what you have made or produced—in scrapbook or portfolio form, with photos, or even videos. (Just in case.)

Do Not Bad-Mouth Your Previous Employer(s) During the Interview

Employers often feel as though they are a fraternity or sorority. During the interview you want to come across as one who displays courtesy toward *all* members of that fraternity or sorority. Bad-mouthing a previous employer only makes this employer worry about what you would say about *them*, after they hire you.

I learned this in my own experience. I once spoke graciously about a previous employer during a job-interview. Unbeknownst to me, the interviewer already *knew* that my previous employer had badly mistreated me. He therefore thought very highly of me because I didn't drag it up. In fact, he never forgot this incident; talked about it for years afterward.

Plan on saying something nice about any previous employer, or if you are afraid that the previous employer is going to give you a very bad recommendation, nullify this ahead of time, by saying something simple like, "I usually get along with everybody; but for some reason, my past employer and I just didn't get along. Don't know why. It's never happened to me before. Hope it never happens again."

You Don't Have to Spend a Lot of Time Memorizing 89 "Good Answers" to Potential Questions from the Employer; There Are Only Five Questions That Matter

---

Of course, the employer is going to ask you some questions, as a way of helping them figure out whether or not they want to hire you. Books on *interviewing*, of which there are many, often publish long lists of these questions, with clever answers suggested. They include such questions as:

- What do you know about this company?
- Tell me about yourself.
- Why are you applying for this job?
- How would you describe yourself?
- What are your major strengths?
- What is your greatest weakness?
- What type of work do you like to do best?
- What are your interests outside of work?
- What accomplishment gave you the greatest satisfaction?
- Why did you leave your last job?
- Why were you fired (if you were)?
- Where do you see yourself five years from now?
- What are your goals in life?
- How much did you make at your last job?

The list goes on and on. In some books, eighty-nine questions, or more.

You are then told that you should prepare for the hiring-interview by writing out, practicing, and memorizing some devilishly clever answers to *all* these questions—answers that those books furnish you with.

All of this is well intentioned, and has been *the state of the art* for decades. But, we are in the twenty-first century now, and things have gotten simplified. We now know there are only *five basic questions* that you really need to pay attention to.

Five. Just five. The people-who-have-the-power-to-hire-you want to know the answers to these five, which they may ask directly or try to find out obliquely:

1. "Why are you here?" *They mean by this, "Why are you knocking on my door, rather than someone else's door?"*

2. "What can you do for us?" *They mean by this, "If I were to hire you, would you be part of the problems I already have, or would you be a part of the solution to those problems? What are your skills, and how much do you know about the subject or field that we are in?"*

3. "What kind of person are you?" *They mean by this, "Will you fit in? Do you have the kind of personality that makes it easy for people to work with you, and do you share the values that we have at this place?"*

4. "What distinguishes you from nineteen or nine hundred other people who are applying for this job?" *They mean by this, "Do you have better work habits than the others, do you show up earlier, stay later, work more thoroughly, work faster, maintain higher standards, go the extra mile, or . . . what?"*

5. "Can I afford you?" *They mean by this, "If we decide we want you here, how much will it take to get you, and are we willing and able to pay that amount—governed, as we are, by our budget, and by our inability to pay you as much as the person who would be next above you, on the organizational chart?"*

These are the five principal questions that employers are dying to know the answers to. *This is the case, even if the interview begins and ends with these five questions never once being mentioned overtly by the employer. The questions are still floating beneath the surface of the conversation,* beneath all the things being discussed. Anything you can do, during the interview, to help the employer answer these five questions, will make the interview very satisfying to the employer. Nothing for you to go memorize.

If you just do the Flower Exercise (pages 160–61) in this book, you will know the five answers. Period. End of story.

You Need to Find Out Some Answers Yourself

During the hiring-interview you owe it to yourself to find answers to the same basic questions *as the employer's*, only in a slightly different form. Your questions will come out looking like this:

1. "What does this job involve?" *You want to understand exactly what tasks will be asked of you, so that you can determine if these are the kinds of tasks you would really like to do, and can do.*

2. "What are the skills a top employee in this job would have to have?" *You want to find out if your skills match those that the employer thinks a top employee in this job has to have, in order to do this job well.*

3. "Are these the kinds of people I would like to work with, or not?" *Do not ignore your intuition if it tells you that you would not be comfortable working with these people!! You want to know if they have the kind of personalities that would make it easy for you to accomplish your work, and if they share your most important values.*

4. "If we like each other, and both want to work together, can I persuade them there is something unique about me, that makes me different from nineteen or nine hundred other people who are applying for this job?" *You need to think out, way ahead of time, what does make you different from other people who can do the same job. For example, if you are good at analyzing problems, how do you do that? Painstakingly? Intuitively, in a flash? By consulting with greater authorities in the field? You see the point. You are trying to put your finger on the "style" or "manner" in which you do your work, that is distinctive and hopefully appealing, to this employer.*

5. "Can I persuade them to hire me at the salary I need or want?"
   This requires some knowledge on your part of how to conduct salary negotiation. That's covered in the next chapter.

You will probably want to ask questions one and two out loud. You will *observe* quietly the answer to question three. You will be prepared to make the case for questions four and five, when the *appropriate* time in the interview arises (again, see the next chapter).

How do you introduce these questions? You might begin by reporting to them just exactly how you've been conducting your job-hunt, and what impressed you so much about *their* organization during your research, that you decided to come in and talk to them about a job. Then you can fix your attention, during the remainder of the interview, on finding out the answers to the five questions above—in your own way.[4]

These five questions pop up in a slightly different form (yet again), if you're there to talk *not* about a job that already exists but rather, one that you hope they will *create* for you. In that case, these five questions get changed into five *statements*, that you make to the person-who-has-the-power-to-create-this-job:

1. What you like about this organization.

2. What sorts of needs you find intriguing in this field and in this organization (unless you first hear the word coming out of their mouth, don't use the word "*problems*," as most employers prefer synonyms such as "*challenges*" or "*needs*").

3. What skills seem to you to be needed in order to meet such needs.

4. Evidence from your past experience that demonstrates you have those very skills. Employers are looking for *examples* from your past performance and achievement; not just vague statements like: "I'm good at . . ." They want concrete examples, specifically of your transferable skills, your content skills, and your self-management skills, i.e., traits.

---

4. To help you explore these five, ask:
   What significant changes has this company gone through in the past five years?
   What values are sacred to this company?
   What characterizes the most successful employees this company has?
   What future changes do you see in the work here?
   Who do you see as your allies, colleagues, or competitors in this business?

If you read pages 60–61, you already know this. It's the underlying principle of *Behavioral Interviewing*, or *competency-based interviewing*.

You may be asked, or you can pose the question yourself: "What are the three most important competencies, for this job?" Then, of course, you need to demonstrate during the interview that you *have* those three—for the job that you want them to create.

5. What is unique about the way *you* perform those skills. As I've said before: every prospective employer wants to know *what makes you different* from nineteen or nine hundred other people who can do the same kind of work as you. You *have* to know what that is. And then not merely talk about it, but actually demonstrate it by the way you conduct your part of the hiring-interview.

**Throughout the Interview, Keep in Mind:
Employers Don't Really Care about Your Past;
They Only Ask about It,
in Order to Try to Predict Your Future (Behavior)**

In the U.S. employers may only ask you questions that are related to the requirements and expectations of the job. They cannot ask about such things as your creed, religion, race, age, sexual orientation, or marital status. Any other questions about your past are *fair game*. But don't be fooled by any employer's absorption with your past. You must realize that the only thing any employer can possibly care about is your future . . . with *them*. Since that future is impossible to uncover, they usually try to gauge what it would be by asking about your past (behavior).

Therefore, during the hiring-interview before you answer any question the employer asks you about your past, you should pause to think out what fear about the *future* lies underneath that question—and then address that fear, obliquely or directly.

In most cases, as I have been emphasizing, the person-who-has-the-power-to-hire-you is *anxious*, or *afraid*, or *worried*. And this worry or fear lies beneath all the questions they ask.

Here are some *examples*:

Employer's Question	The Fear Behind the Question	The Point You Try to Get Across	Phrases You Might Use to Get This Across
"Tell me about yourself."	The employer is afraid he/she isn't going to conduct a very good interview, by failing to ask the right questions. Or is afraid there is something wrong with you, and is hoping you will blurt it out.	You are a good employee, as you have proved in the past at your other jobs. (Give the briefest history of who you are, where born and raised, interests, hobbies, and kind of work you have enjoyed the most to date.) *Keep it to two minutes, max.*	In describing your work history, use any *honest* phrases you can about your work history, that are self-complimentary: "Hard worker." "Came in early, left late." "Always did more than was expected of me." Etc.
"What kind of work are you looking for?"	The employer is afraid that you are looking for a different job than that which the employer is trying to fill. E.g., he/she wants an assistant, but you want to be an office supervisor, etc.	You are looking for precisely the kind of work the employer is offering (but don't say that, if it isn't true). Repeat back to the employer, in your own words, what he/she has said about the job, and emphasize the skills you have to do that.	If the employer hasn't described the job at all, say, "I'd be happy to answer that, but first I need to understand exactly what kind of work this job involves." *Then* answer, as at left.
"Have you ever done this kind of work before?"	The employer is afraid you don't possess the necessary skills and experience to do this job.	You have skills that are transferable, from whatever you used to do; and you did it well.	"I pick up stuff very quickly." "I have quickly mastered any job I have ever done."

Employer's Question	The Fear Behind the Question	The Point You Try to Get Across	Phrases You Might Use to Get This Across
"Why did you leave your last job?"—or "How did you get along with your former boss and co-workers?"	The employer is afraid you don't get along well with people, especially bosses, and is just waiting for you to "bad-mouth" your previous boss or co-workers, as proof of that.	Say whatever positive things you possibly can about your former boss and co-workers (without telling lies). Emphasize you usually get along very well with people—and then let your gracious attitude toward your previous boss(es) and co-workers prove it, right before this employer's very eyes (and ears).	If you left voluntarily: "My boss and I both felt I would be happier and more effective in a job where [here describe your strong points, such as] I would have more room to use my initiative and creativity." If you were fired: "Usually, I get along well with everyone, but in this particular case the boss and I just didn't get along with each other. Difficult to say why." You don't need to say anything more than that. If you were laid off and your job wasn't filled after you left: "My job was terminated."
"How is your health?"—or "How much were you absent from work during your last job?"	The employer is afraid you will be absent from work a lot, if they hire you.	You will not be absent. If you have a health problem, you want to emphasize that it is one that will not keep you from being at work, daily. Your productivity, compared with other workers', is excellent.	If you were not absent a lot at your last job: "I believe it's an employee's job to show up every workday. Period." If you were absent a lot, say why, and stress that it was due to a difficulty that is now past.
"Can you explain why you've been out of work so long?"—or "Can you tell me why there are these gaps in your work history?" (Usually said after studying your resume.)	The employer is afraid that you are the kind of person who quits a job the minute he/she doesn't like something at it; in other words, that you have no "stick-to-it-iveness."	You love to work, and you regard times when things aren't going well as challenges, which you enjoy learning how to conquer.	"During the gaps in my work record, I was studying/doing volunteer work/doing some hard thinking about my mission in life/finding redirection." (Choose one.)

Employer's Question	The Fear Behind the Question	The Point You Try to Get Across	Phrases You Might Use to Get This Across
"Wouldn't this job represent a step down for you?"—or "I think this job would be way beneath your talents and experience."—or "Don't you think you would be underemployed if you took this job?"	The employer is afraid you could command a bigger salary, somewhere else, and will therefore leave him/her as soon as something better turns up.	You will stick with this job as long as you and the employer agree this is where you should be.	"This job isn't a step down for me. It's a step up—from welfare." "We have mutual fears; every employer is afraid a good employee will leave too soon, and every employee is afraid the employer might fire him/her, for no good reason." "I like to work, and I give my best to every job I've ever had."
And, last, "Tell me, what is your greatest weakness?"	The employer is afraid you have some character flaw, and hopes you will now rashly blurt it out, or confess it.	You have limitations just like anyone else, but you work constantly to improve yourself and be a more and more effective worker.	Mention a weakness and then stress its positive aspect, e.g., "I don't like to be over-supervised, because I have a great deal of initiative, and I like to anticipate problems before they even arise."

As the Interview Proceeds, You Want to Quietly Notice the Time-Frame of the Questions the Employer Is Asking

---

When the interview is going favorably for you, the time-frame of the employer's questions will often move—*however slowly*—through the following stages.

1. Distant past: *e.g., "Where did you attend high school?"*
2. Immediate past: *e.g., "Tell me about your most recent job."*
3. Present: *e.g., "What kind of a job are you looking for?"*
4. Immediate future: *e.g., "Would you be able to come back for another interview next week?"*
5. Distant future: *e.g., "Where would you like to be five years from now?"*

The more the time-frame of the interviewer's questions moves from the past to the future, the more favorably you may assume the interview is going for you. On the other hand, if the interviewer's questions stay firmly in the past, the outlook is not so good. *Ah well, y' can't win them all!*

When the time-frame of the interviewer's questions moves firmly into the future, *then* is the time for you to get more specific about the job in question. Experts say it is essential for you to ask, at that point, these kinds of questions:

What is the job, specifically, that I am being considered for?

If I were hired, what duties would I be performing?

What responsibilities would I have?

What would you be hiring me to accomplish?

Would I be working with a team, or group? To whom would I report?

Whose responsibility is it to see that I get the training I need, here, to get up to speed?

How would I be evaluated, how often, and by whom?

What were the strengths and weaknesses of previous people in this position?

Why did *you* yourself decide to work here?

What do you wish you had known about this company before you started here? What particular characteristics do you think have made you successful in your job here?

May I meet the persons I would be working with and for (if it isn't you)?

> *Opportunity is missed by most because it is dressed in overalls and looks like work.*
>
> THOMAS ALVA EDISON

Chapter Six

Remember, *the hiring process is more like choosing a mate, than it is like deciding whether or not to buy a new car.* "Choosing a mate" here is a metaphor. To elaborate upon the metaphor a little bit, it means that *the mechanisms* by which human nature decides to hire someone, are *similar* to the mechanisms by which human nature decides whether or not to marry someone. Those mechanisms, of course, are *human:* impulsive, intuitional, nonrational, unfathomable, and often made on the spur of the moment.

Interviews Are Often Lost to Mosquitoes Rather Than to Dragons, and Lost within the First Two Minutes

---

Think about this: you can have all the skills in the world, have researched this organization to death, have practiced *interviewing* until you are a master at giving "right answers," be absolutely the perfect person for this job, and yet lose the hiring-interview because . . . *your breath smells terrible.* Or some other small personal reason. It's akin to your being ready to fight dragons, and then being killed by a mosquito.

It's the reason why interviews are most often lost, when they are lost, *during the first two minutes.*

Let us look at *what* interview-mosquitoes *(as it were)* can fly in, during the first thirty seconds to two minutes of your interview so that *the person-who-has-the-power-to-hire-you* starts muttering to themselves, "*I sure hope we have some other candidates besides this one*":

1. Your appearance and personal habits: interview after interview has revealed that if you are a male, *you are much more likely to get the job if:*

   * you have obviously freshly bathed, have your face freshly shaved or your hair and beard freshly trimmed, have clean fingernails, and are using a deodorant; *and*

   * you have on freshly laundered clothes, pants with a sharp crease, and shoes freshly polished; *and*

   * you do not have bad breath, do not dispense gallons of garlic, on-ion, stale tobacco, or the odor of strong drink, into the enclosed office air, but have brushed and flossed your teeth; *and*

- you are not wafting tons of aftershave cologne fifteen feet ahead of you, as you enter the room.

If you are a female, interview after interview has revealed that *you are much more likely to get the job if:*

- you have obviously freshly bathed; have not got tons of makeup on your face; have had your hair newly cut or styled; have clean or nicely manicured fingernails, that don't stick out ten inches from your fingers; and are using a deodorant; *and*
- you have on freshly cleaned clothes, a suit or sophisticated-looking dress, shoes not sandals, and are not wearing clothes so daring that they call *a lot* of attention to themselves; *and*
- you do not have bad breath; do not dispense gallons of garlic, onion, stale tobacco, or the odor of strong drink, into the enclosed office air, but have brushed and flossed your teeth; *and*
- you are not wafting tons of perfume fifteen feet ahead of you, as you enter the room.

2. Nervous mannerisms: *it is a turnoff for employers if:*
- you continually avoid eye contact with the employer (that's a *big, big* no-no), *or*
- you give a limp handshake, *or*
- you slouch in your chair, or endlessly fidget with your hands, or crack your knuckles, *or* constantly play with your hair during the interview.

3. Lack of self-confidence: *it is a turnoff for employers if:*
- you are speaking so softly you cannot be heard, or so loudly you can be heard two rooms away, *or*
- you are giving answers in an extremely hesitant fashion, *or*
- you are giving one-word answers to all the employer's questions, *or*
- you are constantly interrupting the employer, *or*
- you are downplaying your achievements or abilities, or are continuously being self-critical in comments you make about yourself during the interview.

4. The consideration you show to other people: *it is a turnoff for employers if:*

- you show a lack of courtesy to the receptionist, secretary, and (at lunch) to the waiter or waitress, *or*

- you display extreme criticalness toward your previous employers and places of work, *or*

- you drink strong stuff during the interview process. Ordering a drink if and when the employer takes you to lunch is always an extremely bad idea, as it raises the question in the employer's mind, *Do they normally stop with one, or do they normally keep on going?* Don't . . . ever . . . do . . . it! Even if they do, *or*

- you forget to thank the interviewer as you're leaving, or forget to send a thank-you note afterward. Says one human resources expert: "A prompt, brief, faxed business letter thanking me for my time along with a (brief!) synopsis of his/her unique qualities communicates to me that this person is an assertive, motivated, customer-service-oriented salesperson who utilizes technology and knows the rules of the 'game.' These are qualities I am looking for. . . . At the moment I receive approximately one such letter . . . for every fifteen candidates interviewed."

- Incidentally, *many* an employer watches to see if you smoke, either in the office or at lunch. *In a race between two equally qualified people, the nonsmoker will win out over the smoker 94 percent of the time, according to a study done by a professor of business at Seattle University.*

5. Your values: *it is a complete turnoff for most employers, if they see in you:*

- any sign of arrogance or excessive aggressiveness; any sign of tardiness or failure to keep appointments and commitments on time, including the hiring-interview; *or*

- any sign of laziness or lack of motivation; *or*

- any sign of constant complaining or blaming things on others; *or*

- any signs of dishonesty or lying—especially on your resume or during the interview; *or*

- any signs of irresponsibility or tendency to goof off; *or*
- any sign of not following instructions or obeying rules; *or*
- any sign of a lack of enthusiasm for this organization and what it is trying to do; *or*
- any sign of instability, inappropriate response, and the like; *or*
- the other ways in which you evidence your *values*, such as: what things impress you or don't impress you in the office; *or* what you are willing to sacrifice in order to get this job *and* what you are *not* willing to sacrifice in order to get this job; *or* your enthusiasm for work; *or* the carefulness with which you did or didn't research this company before you came in; and blah, blah, blah.

Well, dear reader, there you have it: the *mosquitoes* that can kill you, when you're on the watch only for dragons, during the hiring-interview.

One favor I ask of you: do not write me, telling me how picayune or asinine some of this is. Believe me, I already *know* that. I'm not reporting the world as it *should* be, and certainly not as I would like it to be. I'm only reporting what study after study has revealed about the hiring world as it *is*.

You may take all this to heart, or just ignore it. However, if you decide to ignore these points, and then—despite interview after interview—you never get hired, you might want to rethink your position on all of this. It may be *mosquitoes*, not dragons, that are killing you.

And, good news: you can *fix* all these mosquitoes. Yes, you control *every one* of these factors.

> *Every great dream begins with a dreamer. Always remember, you have within you the strength, the patience, and the passion to reach for the stars to change the world.*
>
> HARRIET TUBMAN

Read them all over again. There isn't a one of them that you don't have the power to determine, or the power to change. You can decide to bathe before going to the interview, you can decide to shine your shoes, you can decide not to smoke, etc., etc. All the little things that could torpedo your interview are within your control, and *you can fix* them, if they are keeping you from getting hired.

Five Questions You Should Ask
Before You Let the Interview Close

Before you let the interview end, there are five questions you should *always* ask:

#1. *"Can you offer me this job?"* I know this seems stupid, but it is astonishing (at least to me) how many job-hunters have secured a job simply by being bold enough to ask for it, at the end of the interview, in language they feel comfortable with. I don't know *why* this is, I only know *that* it is. Anyway, if after hearing all about this job at this place, you decide you'd really like to have it, you must *ask for it.* The worst thing the employer can say is "No," or "We need some time to think about all the interviews we're conducting."

#2. *"When may I expect to hear from you?"* If the employer says, *"We need some time to think about this,"* or *"We will be calling you for a second interview,"* you don't want to leave this as an undated good intention on the employer's part. You want to nail it down.

#3. *"Might I ask what would be the latest I can expect to hear from you?"* The employer has probably given you their *best* guess, in answer to your previous question. Now you want to know *what is the worst-case* scenario? Incidentally, one interviewer, when I was job-hunting once, and I asked him for the *worst-case* scenario, replied, *"Never!"* I thought he had a great sense of humor. Turned out he was dead serious. I never heard from him, despite repeated attempts at contact.

#4. *"May I contact you after that date, if for any reason you haven't gotten back to me by that time?"* Some employers resent this question. You'll know that is the case if they snap at you. But most employers appreciate your offering them what is in essence a safety-net. They know they can get busy, become overwhelmed with other things, forget their promise to you. It's reassuring, in such a case, for you to offer to rescue them.

(Optional: #5. *"Can you think of anyone else who might be interested in hiring me?"* This question is invoked *only* if they replied *"No,"* to your first question, above.)

Jot down any answers they give you to the questions above, then stand up, thank them sincerely for their time, give a firm handshake, and leave.

Six Reasons for Always Sending a Thank-You Note—
The Same Night, at the Latest

Every expert on interviewing will tell you two things: (1) Thank-you notes *must* be sent after *every* interview, by every job-hunter; and (2) most job-hunters ignore this advice. Indeed, it is safe to say that it is the most overlooked step in the entire job-hunting process.

If you want to stand out from the others applying for the same job, send thank-you notes—to *everyone* you met there, that day. If you need any additional encouragement *(besides the fact that it may get you the job)*, here are six reasons for sending a thank-you note, most particularly to the employer who interviewed you:

First, you were presenting yourself as one who has good skills with people. Your actions with respect to the job-interview must back this claim up. Sending a thank-you note does that. The employer can see you *are* good with people; you remember to thank them.

Second, it helps the employer remember you.

Third, if a committee is involved in the hiring process, the one man or woman who interviewed you has something to show the rest of the committee.

Fourth, if the interview went rather well, and the employer seemed to show an interest in further talks, the thank-you letter can reiterate *your* interest in further talks.

Fifth, the thank-you note gives you an opportunity to correct any wrong impression you left behind. You can add anything you forgot to tell them, that you want them to know. And from among all the things you two discussed, you can underline the main two or three points that you want to stand out in their minds.

Last, if the interview did not go well, and you lost all interest in working there, they may still hear of other openings, elsewhere, that might be of interest to you. In the thank-you note, you can mention this, and ask them to let you know if they hear of anything anywhere. Thus, from kindly interviewers, you may gain additional leads.

In the following days, rigorously keep to all that you said, and don't contact them except with that mandatory thank-you note, until after the *latest* deadline you two agreed upon, in answer to question #4, above. If you do have to contact them after that date, and if they tell you things are still up in the air, you must ask questions #2, #3, and #4, all over again.

Incidentally, it is entirely appropriate for you to insert a thank-you note into the running stream, after *each* interview or telephone contact. Just keep it brief. Very brief.

© ScienceCartoonsPlus.com

"I CAN REMEMBER WHEN ALL WE NEEDED WAS SOMEONE WHO COULD CARVE AND SOMEONE WHO COULD SEW."

When None of This Works, and You Never Get Invited Back

There is no magic in job-hunting. No techniques work all the time. I hear regularly from job-hunters who report that they paid attention to all the matters I have mentioned in this chapter and this book, and are quite successful at securing interviews—but they never get hired. And they want to know what they're doing wrong.

Well, unfortunately, the answer *sometimes* is: "Maybe nothing." I don't know *how often* this happens, but I know it does happen—because more than one employer has confessed it to me, and in fact at one point in my life it actually happened to *moi*: namely, *some* employers play despicable tricks on job-hunters, whereby they invite you in for an interview despite the fact that they have already hired someone for the position in question, and they know from the beginning that they have absolutely no intention of hiring you—not in a million years!

You are cheered, of course, by the ease with which you get these interviews. But unbeknownst to you, the manager who is interviewing you (we'll say it's a *he*) has a personal friend he already agreed to give the job to. Only one small problem remains: the state or the federal government gives funds to this organization, and has mandated that this position be opened to all. So this manager must *pretend* to interview ten candidates, including his favorite, *as though* the job opening were still available. But, he intended, from the beginning, to reject the other nine and give the job to his favorite. You were selected for the honor of being among those nine.

You will of course be baffled as to *why* you got turned down. Trouble is, you will never know.

On the other hand, if you *never* get invited back for a second interview, there is always the chance that no games are being played. You are getting rejected, at place after place, because there is something really wrong with the way you are coming across, during these hiring-interviews.

Employers will rarely ever tell you this. You will never hear them say something like, "You came across as just too cocky and arrogant during the interview." You will almost always be left in the dark as to *what* it is you're doing wrong.

If you've been interviewed by a whole bunch of employers, one way around this deadly silence, is to ask for *generalized* feedback from whoever was the *friendliest* employer that you saw. You can always try phoning, reminding them of who you are, and then asking the following question—deliberately kept generalized, vague, unrelated to just *that* place, and above all, *future-directed*. Something like: *"You know, I've been on several interviews at several different places now, where I've gotten turned down. From what you've seen, is there something about me in an interview, that you think might be causing me not to get hired at those places? If so, I'd really appreciate your giving me some pointers so I can do better in my future hiring-interviews."*

Most of the time they'll *still* duck saying anything hurtful or helpful. First of all, they're afraid of lawsuits. Second, they don't know how you will use what they might have to say. (Said an old veteran to me once, "I used to think it was my duty to tell everyone the truth. Now I only give it to those who can use it.")

But *occasionally* you will run into an employer who is willing to risk giving you the truth, because they think you will know how to use it wisely. If so, thank them from the bottom of your heart, no matter how painful their feedback is. Such advice, seriously heeded, can bring about just the changes in your interviewing strategy that you most need, in order to win the interview.

In the absence of any such help from employers who interviewed you, you might want to get a good business friend of yours to role-play a mock hiring-interview with you, in case they immediately see something glaringly wrong with how you're "coming across."

When all else fails, I would recommend you go to a career coach who charges by the hour, and put yourself in their tender knowledgeable hands. Role-play an interview with them, and take their advice seriously (you've just paid for it, after all).

On Planning for a Raise

I have left out the subject of salary negotiation in this chapter. It requires a chapter of its own (next!).

Hopefully, however, with these tips you will do well in your interviews. And if you do get hired, make one resolution to yourself right there on the spot. Plan to keep track of your accomplishments at this new job, on a weekly basis—jotting them down, every weekend, in your own private diary. Career experts recommend you do this without fail. You can then summarize these accomplishments annually on a one-page sheet, for your boss's eyes, when the question of a raise or promotion comes up.[5]

5. In any good-size organization, you will often be amazed at how little attention your superiors pay to your noteworthy accomplishments, and how little they are aware at the end of the year that you really are entitled to a raise, based on the profits you have brought in. Noteworthy your accomplishments may be, but no one is taking notes . . . unless you do. You may even need to be the one who brings up the subject of a raise or promotion. Waiting for the employer to bring this up may never happen.

THE TEN COMMANDMENTS
FOR JOB-INTERVIEWS

Whereby Your Chances of Finding a Job Are Vastly Increased

I. Go after small organizations with twenty or fewer employees, since they create two-thirds of all new jobs.

II. Hunt for interviews using the aid of, say, eighty friends and acquaintances, because a job-hunt requires eighty pairs of eyes and ears.

III. Do thorough homework on an organization before going there, using Informational Interviews plus the library.

IV. At any organization, identify who has the power to hire you there, for the position you want, and use your mutual friends and acquaintances' contacts, to get an introduction to that person.

V. Ask for just twenty minutes of their time, when asking for the appointment; and keep to your word rigidly.

VI. Go to the interview with your own agenda, your own questions and curiosities about whether or not this job fits you. This always impresses employers.

VII. Talk about yourself only if what you say offers some benefit to that organization, and their "problems."

VIII. When answering a question of theirs, talk only between twenty seconds and two minutes, at any one time.

IX. Basically approach them as if you were a resource person, able to produce better work for that organization than any predecessor; not as a job beggar.

X. Always write a thank-you note the same evening of the interview, and mail it at the latest by the next morning.

Students spend four or more years learning how to dig data out of the library and other sources, but it rarely occurs to them that they should also apply some of the same new-found research skill to their own benefit—to looking up information on companies, types of professions, sections of the country that might interest them.

PROFESSOR ALBERT SHAPERO
The late William H. Davis Professor of
the American Free Enterprise System
at Ohio State University

7. Things School Never Taught Us about Job-Hunting: Salary Negotiation

I remember once talking to a breathless college graduate, who was elated at having just landed her first job. "How much are they going to pay you?" I asked. She looked startled. "I don't know," she said, "I never asked. I just assumed they will pay me a fair wage." *Boy*! did she get a rude awakening when she received her first paycheck. It was so miserably *low*, she couldn't believe her eyes. And thus did she learn, painfully, what you must learn, too: *Before accepting a job, always ask about salary. Indeed, ask and negotiate.*

It's the *negotiate* that throws fear into our hearts. We feel ill-prepared to do this. But, it's not all that difficult. While whole books can be (and have been) written on this subject, there are basically just six secrets to keep in mind.

The First Secret of Salary Negotiation:

Never Discuss Salary Until the End of the Interviewing Process When They Have Definitely Said They Want You

"The end of the interviewing process" is difficult to define. It's the point at which the employer says, or thinks, "We've got to get this person!" That may be at the end of the first (and therefore the last) interview; or it may

be at the end of a whole series of interviews, often with different people within the same company or organization. But assuming things are going favorably for you, whether after the first, or second, or third, or fourth interview, if *you* like them and *they* increasingly like you, a job offer *will* be made. Then, and only then, is it time to deal with the question that is inevitably on any employer's mind: *how much is this person going to cost me?* And the question that is on *your* mind: *how much does this job pay?*

If the employer raises the salary question earlier, in some form like "What kind of salary are you looking for?," you should have three responses ready at your fingertips.

Response #1: If the employer seems like a kindly man or woman, your best and most tactful reply might be: "Until you've decided you definitely want me, and I've decided I definitely could help you with your tasks here, I feel any discussion of salary is premature." That will work, in most cases.

Response #2: There are instances, however, where that doesn't work. You may be face-to-face with an employer who will not be put off so easily, and demands within the first two minutes that you're in the interview room to know what salary you are looking for. At this point, you use your second response: "I'll gladly answer that, but could you first help me understand what this job involves?"

Response #3: That is a good response, *in most cases.* But what if it doesn't work? The employer with rising voice says, "Come, come, don't play games with me. I want to know what salary you're looking for." You have response #3 prepared for *this* very eventuality. It's an answer in terms of a *range.* For example, "I'm looking for a salary in the range of $35,000 to $45,000 a year."

If the employer still won't let it go until later, then consider what this means. Clearly, you are being interviewed by an employer who has no range in mind. Their beginning figure is their ending figure. No negotiation is possible.[1]

This happens, when it happens, because many employers are making salary their major criterion for deciding who to hire, and who not to hire, out of—say—nineteen or even nine hundred possible candidates.

---

1. One job-hunter said his interviews *always* began with the salary question, and no matter what he answered, that ended the interview. Turned out, this job-hunter was doing all the interviewing over the phone. That was the problem. Once he went face to face, salary was no longer the first thing discussed in the interview.

"YOU CHOOSE YOUR OWN SALARY HERE. WOULD YOU CARE TO
WORK AT: 1. NO RISK; 2. SOME RISK; 3. HIGH RISK; OR 4. ARE-
YOU-SURE-YOU-WANT-TO-DO-THIS?"

> It's an old game, played with new determination by many employers during this brutal economy, called "among two equally qualified candidates, the one who is willing to work for the lower salary wins."

If you run into this situation, and you want that job badly enough, you will have no choice but to give in. Ask what salary they have in mind, and make your decision. (Of course you should always say, *"I need a little time, to think about this."*)

However, all the foregoing is merely the *worst-case scenario*. Usually, things won't go this badly. In most interviews, these days, the employer will be willing to save salary negotiation until they've finally decided they want you (and you've decided you want them). And at that point, the salary will be negotiable.

Not until all of the following conditions have been fulfilled—

- *Not until they've gotten to know you, at your best, so they can see how you stand out above the other applicants.*
- *Not until you've gotten to know them, as completely as you can, so you can tell when they're being firm, or when they're flexible.*
- *Not until you've found out exactly what the job entails.*
- *Not until they've had a chance to find out how well you match the job requirements.*
- *Not until you're in the final interview at that place, for that job.*
- *Not until you've decided, "I'd really like to work here."*
- *Not until they've said, "We want you."*
- *Not until they've said, "We've got to have you."*

—should you get into salary discussion with any employer.

If you'd prefer this to be put in the form of a diagram, here it is:[2]

WHEN TO NEGOTIATE SALARY

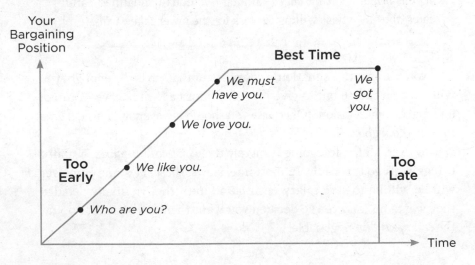

2. Reprinted by permission of Paul Hellman, author of *Ready, Aim, You're Hired!* and president of Express Potential (www.expresspotential.com). All rights reserved.

Why is it to your advantage to delay salary discussion? Because, if you really *shine* during the hiring-interview, they may—at the end—offer you a higher salary than they originally had in mind when the interview started—and this is particularly the case when the interview has gone so well, that they're now *determined* to obtain your services.

The Second Secret of Salary Negotiation:

The Purpose of Salary Negotiation
Is to Uncover the Most That an Employer
Is Willing to Pay to Get You

Salary negotiation would never happen if *every* employer in *every* hiring-interview were to mention, right from the start, the top figure they are willing to pay for that position. *Some* employers do, as I mentioned before. And that's the end of any salary negotiation. But, of course, most employers don't. Hoping they'll be able to get you for less, they start *lower* than they're ultimately willing to go. This creates *a range*. And that range is what salary negotiation is all about.

For example, if the employer wants to hire somebody for no more than $20 an hour, they may start *the bidding* at $12 an hour. In which case, their *range* runs between $12 and $20 an hour.

So, why do you want to negotiate? Because, if a range *is* thus involved, you have every right to try to discover the highest salary that employer is willing to pay you *within that range.*

The employer's goal, is to save money, if possible. Your goal is to bring home to your family, your partner, or your own household, the best salary that you can, for the work you will be doing. Nothing's wrong with the goals of either of you. But it does mean that, where the employer starts lower, salary negotiation is legitimate, and expected.

> *Some men see things as they are and say,*
> *"Why?" I dream of things that never were*
> *and say, "Why not?"*
>
> GEORGE BERNARD SHAW

During Salary Discussion, Never Be the First One to Mention a Salary Figure

Where salary negotiation has been kept *offstage* for much of the interview process, when it finally does come *onstage* you want the employer to be the first one to mention *a figure*, if you possibly can.

Nobody knows why, but it has been observed over the years that where the goals are opposite, as in this case—you are trying to get the employer to pay the most they can, and the employer is trying to pay the least they can—in this back-and-forth negotiation, *whoever mentions a salary figure first, generally loses.* You can speculate from now until the cows come home, as to *why* this is; all we know is *that* it is.

Inexperienced employer/interviewers often don't know this quirky rule. But experienced ones are very aware of it; that's why they will *always* toss the ball to you first, with some innocent-sounding question, such as: "What kind of salary are you looking for?" *Well, how kind of them to ask me what I want*—you may be thinking. No, no, no. Kindness has nothing to do with it. They are hoping *you* will be the first to mention a figure, because they know this strange experiential truth: *whoever mentions a salary figure first, generally loses salary negotiation, at the end.*

Accordingly, if they ask you to name a figure, the *countermove* on your part should be: "Well, you created this position, so you must have some figure in mind, and I'd be interested in knowing what that figure is."

Before You Go to the Interview, Do Some Careful Research on Typical Salaries for Your Field and/or That Organization

As I said, salary negotiation is possible *anytime* the employer does not open discussion of salary by naming the top figure they have in mind, but starts instead with a lower figure.

Okay, so here is our $64,000 question: how do you tell whether the figure the employer first offers you is only their *starting bid*, or is their *final final offer*? The answer is: by doing some research on the field *and* that organization, before you go to the interview.

Oh, come on! I can hear you say. *Isn't this more trouble than it's worth?* No, not if you're determined.

Trust me, salary research pays off *handsomely.* Let's say it takes you from one to three days to run down this sort of information on the three or four organizations that interest you the most. And let us say that because you've done this research, when you finally go in for the hiring-interview you are able to ask for and obtain a salary that is $15,000 a year higher, than you would otherwise have gotten. In just the next three years, you will be earning $45,000 extra, because of your salary research. *Not bad pay, for one to three days' work!* And it can be even more. I know *many* job-hunters and career-changers to whom this has happened. There is a financial penalty exacted from those who are too lazy, or in too much of a hurry, to go gather this information. In plainer language: *if you don't do this research, it'll cost ya!*

Okay then, how do you do this research? There are two ways to go: on the Internet, and off the Internet. Let's look at each, in turn:

SALARY RESEARCH ON THE INTERNET

If you have access to the Internet, and you want to research salaries for particular geographical regions, positions, occupations, or industries, here are some free sites that may give you just what you're looking for:

- The Bureau of Labor Statistics' survey of salaries in individual occupations, *The Occupational Outlook Handbook 2008–2009.*
  www.bls.gov/oco

- The Bureau of Labor Statistics' survey of salaries in individual industries (it's a companion piece to *The Occupational Outlook Handbook 2008–2009*).
  http://stats.bls.gov/oco/cg/cgindex.htm

- "High Earning Workers Who Don't Have a Bachelor's Degree," by Matthew Mariani, appearing first in the Fall 1999 issue of the *Occupational Outlook Quarterly.* For those who want to know how to earn *a lot* without having to go to college first.
  http://stats.bls.gov/opub/ooq/1999/fall/art02.pdf

- The oldest of the salary-specific sites, and one of the largest and most complete lists of salary reviews on the Web; run by a genius (Mary Ellen Mort).

  http://jobstar.org/tools/salary/index.cfm

- The most visited of all the salary-specific job-sites, with fifty online partners that use their "Salary Wizard," such as AOL and Yahoo.

  www.salary.com

- When you need a salary expert, it makes sense to go to the Salary Expert. Lots of stuff on the subject here, including a free "Salary Report" for hundreds of job-titles, varying by area, skill level, and experience. Also has one of the salary calculators mentioned earlier.

  www.salaryexpert.com

Incidentally, if these free sites don't give you what you want, you can always *pay* for the info, and hopefully get more-up-to-date surveys. Salary Source (www.salarysource.com) offers up-to-date salary information services starting at $19.95.

If you "strike out" on all the above sites, then you're going to have to get a little more clever, and work a little harder, and pound the pavement, as I shall describe below.

SALARY RESEARCH OFF THE INTERNET

Off the Internet, how do you go about doing salary research? Well, there's a simple rule: generally speaking, abandon books, and go talk to people. Use books and libraries only as a *second*, or *last*, resort. (Their information is often just way too outdated.)

You can get much more complete and up-to-date information from people who are in the same job *at another company or organization*. Or, people at the nearby university or college who *train* such people, whatever their department may be. Teachers and professors will usually know what their graduates are making.

Now, exactly how do you go about getting this information? Let's look at some concrete examples:

> *First Example:* Working at your first entry-level job, say at a fast-food place.

You may not need to do any salary research. They pay what they pay. You can walk in, ask for a job application, and interview with the manager. He or she will usually tell you the pay, outright. It's usually set in concrete. But at least it's easy to discover what the pay is. (Incidentally, filling out an application, or having an interview there, doesn't force you to take the job—but you probably already know that. You can always decline an offer from *any place*. That's what makes this approach harmless.)

> *Second Example:* Working at a place where you can't discover what the pay is, say *at a construction company*.

If that construction company where you would *hope* to get a job is difficult to research, go visit a *different* construction company in the same town—one that isn't of much interest to you—and ask what they make *there*. Or, if you don't know who to talk to there, fill out one of *their* applications, and talk to the hiring person about what kinds of jobs they have (or might have in the future), at which time prospective wages is a legitimate subject of discussion. Then, having done this research on a place you don't care about, go back to the place that *really* interests you, and apply. You still don't know *exactly* what they pay, but you do know what their competitor pays—which will usually be *close*.

> *Third Example:* Working in a one-person office, say *as an administrative assistant*.

Here you can often find useful salary information by perusing the Help Wanted ads in the local newspaper for a week or two, assuming you still have a local paper! Most of the ads won't mention a salary figure, but a few may. Among those that do, note what the lowest salary offering is, and what the highest is, and see if the ad reveals some reasons for the difference. It's interesting how much you can learn about administrative assistants' salaries, with this approach. I know, because I was an administrative assistant myself, once upon a time.

Another way to do salary research is to find a *Temporary Work Agency* that places secretaries, and let yourself be farmed out to various offices: the more, the merrier. It's relatively easy to do salary research when you're *inside* a place. (Study what that place pays *the agency*, not what the agency pays you after they've taken their "cut.") If you're working temporarily at a place where the other workers *like* you, you'll be able to ask questions about a lot of things, including salary.

The Fifth Secret of Salary Negotiation:

Research the Range That the Employer Likely Has in Mind, and Then Define an Interrelated Range for Yourself

THE EMPLOYER'S RANGE

Before you go into any organization for your final interview, you want more than just *one* salary figure at your fingertips. You want *a range*: what's the *least* the employer may offer you, and what's the *most* the employer may be willing to offer you. In any organization that has more than five employees, that range is relatively easy to figure out. It will be less than what the person *who would be above you* makes, and more than what the person *who would be below you* makes.

If the Person Who Would Be Below You Makes	And the Person Who Would Be Above You Makes	The Range for Your Job Would Be
$45,000	$55,000	$47,000–$53,000
$30,000	$35,500	$31,500–$33,500

One teensy-tiny little problem here: *how* do you find out the salary of those who would be above and below you? Well, first you have to find out their *names* or the names of their *positions*. If it is a small organization you are going after—one with twenty or fewer employees—finding out this information should be *duck soup*. Any employee who works there is likely to know the answer, and you can usually get in touch with one of those employees, or even an ex-employee, through your own personal contacts. Since up to two-thirds of all new jobs are created by companies that size, that's the size organization you are likely to be researching, anyway.

If you are going after a larger organization, then you fall back on our familiar life preserver, namely, every contact you have (family, friend, relative, business, or spiritual acquaintance) who might know the company, and therefore, the information you seek. In other words, you are looking for Someone Who Knows Someone who either is working, or has worked, at the particular place or places that interest you, and who therefore has or can get this information for you.

If, in the end, you absolutely run into a blank wall at a particular organization (everyone who works there is pledged to secrecy, and they have shipped all their ex-employees to Siberia), then seek out information on their nearest *competitor* in the same geographic area. *For example,* let us say you were researching managerial salaries at Bank X, and they were proving to be inscrutable about what they pay their managers. You would then try Bank Y as your research base, to see if the information were easier to come by, there. And if it were, you can then assume the two were similar in their pay scales, and that what you learned about Bank Y was applicable to Bank X.

Experts say that in researching salaries, you should also take note of the fact that most governmental agencies have civil service positions matching those in private industry, and government job descriptions and pay ranges are available to the public. Go to the nearest city, county, regional, state, or federal civil service office, find the job description nearest what you are seeking in private industry, and then ask the starting salary.

Once you've made a guess at what the employer's range might be, for the job you have in mind, you then define your own range *accordingly*. Let me give an example. Suppose you guess that the employer's range is $36,500 to $47,200. Accordingly, you now *invent* an "asking" range for yourself, where your *minimum* "hooks in" just below that employer's *maximum*.

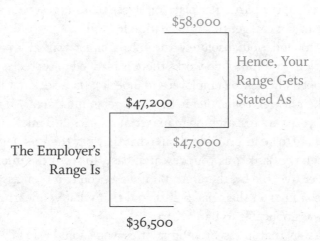

$58,000

Hence, Your Range Gets Stated As

$47,200

The Employer's Range Is

$47,000

$36,500

And so, when the employer has stated a figure (probably around his or her *lowest*—i.e., $36,500), you will be ready to respond with something along these lines: "I understand of course the constraints under which all organizations are operating, considering this brutal economy, but I believe my productivity will be such that it would *justify* a salary"—*and here you mention a range whose bottom figure hooks in just below the top of their range, and goes up from there, accordingly, as shown on the diagram above*—"in the range of $47,000 to $58,000."

It will help a lot during this discussion, if you are prepared to show in what ways you will *make money* or in what ways you will *save money* for that organization, such as would justify the higher salary you are seeking. Hopefully, this will succeed in getting you at least nearer to the salary you want.

Daniel Porot, the job-expert in Europe, suggests that if you and an employer really hit it off, and you're *dying* to work there, but they cannot afford the salary you need, consider offering them part of your time. If you need, and believe you deserve, say $35,000, but they can only afford

$21,000, you might consider offering them three days a week of your time for that $21,000 (21/35 = 3/5). This leaves you free to take work elsewhere during those other two days. You will *of course* produce so much work during those three days per week, that they will be ecstatic about this bargain.

The Sixth Secret of Salary Negotiation:

Know How to Bring the Salary Negotiation to a Close; Don't Leave It "Just Hanging"

Salary negotiation with this employer is not finished until you've also addressed the issue of so-called fringe benefits. "Fringes" such as life insurance, health benefits or health plans, vacation or holiday plans, and retirement programs typically add anywhere from 15 to 28 percent to many workers' salaries. That is to say, if an employee receives $3,000 salary per week, the fringe benefits are worth another $450 to $840 per week.

You should therefore, before you walk into the interview, know what benefits are particularly important to you, so you remember to ask what benefits are offered—and negotiate if necessary for the benefits you particularly care about. Thinking this out ahead of time makes your negotiating easier, by far.

Finally, you want to get *this* summarized, in writing. Always request a letter of agreement—or employment contract.

Many executives unfortunately "forget" what they told you during the hiring-interview, or even deny they ever said such a thing.

Also, many executives leave the company, and their successor or the top boss may disown any *unwritten* promises: *"I don't know what caused them to say that to you, but they clearly exceeded their authority, and of course we can't be held to that."*

Conclusion: The Greatest Secret

All of this, of course, presumes that your interview, and salary negotiation, ends up well. There are times, however, when all seems well; then all of a sudden and without warning it comes totally unraveled. You're hired, told to report next Monday, and then get a phone call on Friday telling you that all hiring has been put, mysteriously, "on hold." You're therefore back out "on the pavement." Having seen this happen so many times, over the years, I remind you of the truth throughout this book: *successful* job-hunters and career-changers *always have alternatives.*

Alternative ideas of what they could do with their life.

Alternative ways of describing what they want to do right now.

Alternative ways of going about the job-hunt (not just the Internet, not just resumes, agencies, and ads).

Alternative job prospects.

Alternative "target" organizations that they go after.

Alternative ways of approaching employers.

And so on, and so forth.

What this means for you, here, is: make sure you are pursuing more than just one employer, until after you start your new job.

TARGET SMALL ORGANIZATIONS

Were I myself looking for a job tomorrow, this is what I would do. After I had figured out, using pages 155–241, what my ideal job looked like, and after I had collected a list of those workplaces that have such jobs, in my chosen geographical area, I would then circle the names and addresses of those that are *small* organizations (personally I would restrict my *first draft* to those with twenty-five or fewer employees)—and then go after them, in the manner I have described in previous chapters. However, as the dot-com bubble back in 2002 taught us, small organizations can sometimes be fraught with danger *(a nova-like birth, a sudden black hole death)*, I would look particularly for small organizations that are *established* or *growing*. And if *"organizations with twenty-five or fewer employees"* eventually didn't turn up enough *leads* for me, then I would broaden my search to *"organizations with fifty or fewer employees,"* and finally—if that turned up nothing—to *"organizations with 100 or fewer employees."* But I would *start* small. Very small.

Remember, job-hunting always involves luck, to some degree. But with a little bit of luck, and a lot of hard work, plus determination, these instructions about how to get hired should work for you, as they have worked for so many hundreds of thousands before you.

Take heart from those who have gone before you, such as this determined job-hunter, who wrote me this heartfelt letter, with which I close:

"Before I read this book, I was depressed and lost in the futile job-hunt using Want Ads Only. I did not receive even one phone call from any ad I answered, over a total of four months. I felt that I was the most useless person on earth. I am female, with a two-and-a-half-year-old daughter, a former professor in China, with no working experience at all in the U.S. We came here seven months ago because my husband had a job offer here.

"Then, on June 11th of last year, I saw your book in a local bookstore. Subsequently, I spent three weeks, ten hours a day except Sunday, reading every single word of your book and doing all of the flower petals in the Flower Exercise. After getting to know myself much better, I felt I was ready to try the job-hunt again. I used Parachute *throughout as my guide, from the very beginning to the very end, namely, salary negotiation.*

"In just two weeks I secured (you guessed it) two job offers, one of which I am taking, as it is an excellent job, with very good pay. It is (you guessed it again) a small company, with twenty or so employees. It is also a career-change: I was a professor of English; now I am to be a controller!

"I am so glad I believed your advice: there are jobs out there, and there are two types of employers out there, and truly there are!

"I hope you will be happy to hear my story."

Two roads diverged in a yellow wood,
And sorry I could not travel both
And be one traveler, long I stood
And looked down one as far as I could
To where it bent in the undergrowth;

Then took the other, as just as fair,
And having perhaps the better claim,
Because it was grassy and wanted wear;
Though as for that the passing there
Had worn them really about the same,

And both that morning equally lay
In leaves no step had trodden black.
Oh, I kept the first for another day!
Yet knowing how way leads on to way,
I doubted if I should ever come back.

I shall be telling this with a sigh
Somewhere ages and ages hence:
Two roads diverged in a wood, and I—
I took the one less traveled by,
And that has made all the difference.

ROBERT FROST (1874–1963)[1]

---

1. The title of this poem is "The Road Not Taken," from *The Poetry of Robert Frost* edited by Edward Connery Lathem, published by Holt, Rinehart & Winston, 1916, 1969. Incidentally, the late M. Scott Peck's classic, *The Road Less Traveled*, took its title from this poem.

8. Things School Never Taught Us about Job-Hunting: **How to Choose a New Career When You Must**

How Much Help Are Vocational Tests?

Okay, so you've got to choose a new career. Or, maybe, if you're just starting out, you've got to choose your very first career.

So, what do you do? Left to our own instincts, most of us will opt for taking a test of one kind or another.

Easy enough to do.

In the U.S. three-quarters of all job-hunters or career-changers have access to the Internet. And tests are everywhere on the Internet.[1]

Except, "tests" are not really "tests." "Instruments" or "assessments" would be a more accurate description. Nonetheless, everyone loves to call them "tests." "Vocational tests." "Psychological tests." Whatever. You can take them all by yourself. That's their virtue.

Or, if you don't want to tackle them all by yourself, you can pay a career coach or career counselor to give them to you *(listings in the back, beginning on page 280)*. Some make *testing* the cornerstone of everything

---

1. A more complete listing of what's on the Internet can be found at: www.jobhuntersbible.com/counseling.

they do with a client. So, they're experienced. One way or another, take a test, and voilà! The test will tell you what you should do, or what you should become.

Or will it?

Six Warnings about Testing

1. You are absolutely unique. There is no person in the world like you. It follows from this that no test can measure YOU; it can only describe the family to which you belong.

Tests tend to divide the population into what we might call groups, tribes, or families—made up of all those people who answered the test the same way. After you've taken any test, don't ever say to yourself, "This must be who I am." (No, no, this must be who your family am.)[2]

I grew up in the Bolles family (surprise!), and they were all very "left-brained." I was a maverick in that family. I was right-brained. Fortunately, my father was an immensely loving man, who found this endearing. When I told him the convoluted way by which I went about figuring out something, he would respond with a hearty affectionate laugh, and a big hug, as he said: "Dick, I will never understand you." Tests are about families, not individuals. The results of any test are descriptors—not of you, but of your family—i.e., all those who answered the test the same way you did. The SAI family. Or the blue family. Or the INTJ family. Or whatever. The results are an accurate description of that family of people, in general; but are they descriptors also of you? Depends on whether or not you are a maverick in that family, the same way I was in mine. These family characteristics may or may not be true in every respect of you. You may be exactly like that group, or you may be different in important ways.

2. Don't predetermine how you want the test to come out. Stay loose and open to new ideas.

It's easy to have an emotional investment that the test should come out a certain way. I remember a job-hunting workshop where I asked everyone to list the factors they liked about any place where they had ever lived; and

---

2. Yes, I know that is bad grammar. But, pressing on: if you want to explore testing in any more depth, there is an excellent course online, from S. Mark Pancer, at Wilfred Laurier University in Waterloo, Ontario, Canada, at www.wlu.ca/page.php?grp_id=265&p=2941. Pay special attention to Lectures 1 and 19.

then prioritize those factors, to get the name of a new place to live. We had this immensely lovable woman from Texas in the workshop, and when we all got back together after a "break" I asked her how she was doing. With a glint in her eye she said, "I'm prioritizing, and I'm gonna keep on prioritizin', until it comes out: Texas!" That was amusing, as she intended it to be; it's not so amusing when you try to make the test results come out a certain way. If you're gonna take tests, you need to be open—to new ideas If you find yourself always trying to outguess the test, so it will confirm you on a path you've already decided upon, then testing is not for you.

3. In taking a test, you should just be looking for clues, hunches, or suggestions, rather than for a definitive picture that tells you exactly what you should do with your life.

And bear in mind that an online test isn't likely to be as insightful as one administered by an insightful psychologist or counselor, who may see things that you don't. But keep saying that mantra to yourself, as you read or hear the test results. Clues. Clues, I'm only looking for clues.

4. Take several tests and not just one. One can easily send you down the wrong path.

People who do a masters or doctorate program in "Testing and Measurement" know that tests are notoriously flawed, unscientific, and inaccurate. Sometimes tests are more like parlor games than anything else. Basing your future on tests' outcomes is like putting your trust in the man behind the curtain in The Wizard of Oz.

5. You're trying, in the first instance with tests, to broaden your horizons, and only later narrow your options down; you are *not* trying to narrow them down from the outset.

Bad career planning looks like this:

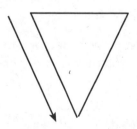

Most computerized tests embody the idea of starting with a wide range of options, and narrowing them down. So, each time you answer a question, you narrow down the number of options. E.g., If you say, "I don't like to work out of doors," immediately all outdoor jobs are eliminated from your consideration, etc., etc.

A model of good career planning looks like this, instead:

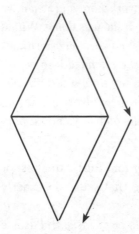

Good career-choice or career planning postpones the "narrowing down," until it has first broadened your horizons, and expanded the number of options you are thinking about. E.g., You're in the newspaper business; but have you ever thought of teaching, or drawing, or doing fashion? You first expand your mental horizons, to see all the possibilities, and only then, do you start to narrow them down to the particular two or three that interest you the most.

So, what's a good test? All together now: a test that shows you more possibilities for your life.

And, what's a bad test? Again, together: a test that narrows the possibilities for your life. Often this is the result of a counselor's interpretation of a test, or rather misinterpretation.

I'll give you an example: I met a man who, many years before, had taken the Strong Inventory.[3] He was told, by his counselor, that this inventory measured that man's native gifts or aptitudes. And, in his particular case, the counselor said, the inventory revealed he had no mechanical aptitude whatsoever. For years thereafter, this man told me, "I was afraid to even pick up a hammer, for fear of maiming myself. But there finally came a time in my life when my house needed aluminum siding, desperately, and I was too poor to hire anyone else to do it for me. So I decided I had to do it myself, regardless of what the test said. I climbed the ladder, and expected to fail. Instead, it was a glorious experience! I had never enjoyed myself so much in my whole life. I later found out that the counselor was wrong. The inventory didn't measure aptitudes; it only measured current interests. Now, today, if I could find that counselor, I would wring his neck with my own bare hands, as I think of how much of my life he ruined with his misinterpretation of that test."

6. Testing will always have "mixed reviews." On the one hand, you can run into successful men and women who will tell you they took this or that test twenty years ago, and it made all the difference in their career direction and ultimate success.

---

3. See www.personalitydesk.com and similar Internet sites.

Other men and women, however, will tell you a horror story about their encounter with testing, like that above.

If you like tests, help yourself. Counselors can give them to you, if you shop around. There are also lots of them on the Internet.

If you want to know where to start, you might try these, which are the tests that I personally like best:

- *The Princeton Review's Career Quiz*
  www.princetonreview.com/cte/quiz/default.asp?menuID=0&careers=6

- *Carolyn Kalil's True Colors Test*
  www.truecolorscareer.com/quiz.asp

- *Dr. John Holland's Self-Directed Search*
  www.self-directed-search.com

- *Supplemented by the University of Missouri's Career Interests Game*
  www.career.missouri.edu/students/explore/thecareer interestsgame.php

- *If you want further suggestions, you can go to my website*
  www.jobhuntersbible.com/counseling

If you don't like tests, what can you do? Well, there's a nice process for determining what to do with your life, later in this book. It's called the Flower Exercise (pages 160–161). It is in a test-free zone.

Seven Rules for Choosing or Changing Careers

When you have to choose or change a career, here are seven rules to keep in mind:

Rule #1 about choosing or changing a career: go for *any* career that seems interesting or even fascinating to you. But *first* talk to people who are already doing that work, to find out if the career or job is as great as it seems at first impression. Ask them: *what do you like best about this work? What do you like least about this work?* And, *how did you get into this work?* This last question, which sounds like mere cheeky curiosity, actually can give you important job-hunting clues about how you could get into this line of work or career.

Rule #2 about choosing or changing a career: make sure that you preserve constancy as well as change, during this transition. In other words, don't change *everything*. Remember the words of Archimedes with his long lever,[4] loosely paraphrased as: *Give me a fulcrum and a place to stand, and with a lever I will move the Earth.* You need a place to stand, when you move your life around, and that place is provided by the things that stay constant about you: your transferable skills, your values, your character, your faith.

We can illustrate this principle about maintaining *some* constancy with a simple diagram of creative career change, below. Let us say you are an accountant, in the television industry, and you want to become a reporter, covering medicine. You can, of course, try to change every-

THREE TYPES OF CAREER-CHANGE, VISUALIZED

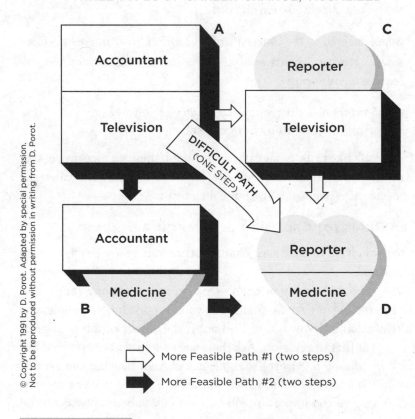

© Copyright 1991 by D. Porot. Adapted by special permission. Not to be reproduced without permission in writing from D. Porot.

⟳ More Feasible Path #1 (two steps)

➡ More Feasible Path #2 (two steps)

---

4. Archimedes (ca. 235 B.C.E.), Greek inventor, mathematician, and physicist.

thing in one big leap (labeled *the difficult path* in this diagram), but that's all change and no constancy. To preserve some constancy, you can first change just your job-title and only later your field. Or you can first change just your field, and only later your job-title (*two steps*). This two-step plan for career-change preserves *some* constancy at every turn, some continuity with the past—and allows you to always claim some past experience and expertise, each time you make a move

Rule #3 about choosing or changing a career: you do better to start with yourself and what *you* want, rather than with the job-market, and what's "hot." The difference is "enthusiasm" or "passion."

Rule #4 about choosing or changing a career: the best *work*, the best career, for you is going to be one that uses: your *favorite* transferable skills, in your *favorite* subjects, fields, or fields of fascination, in a job that offers you your *preferred* people environments, your *preferred* working conditions, with your *preferred* salary or other rewards, working toward your *preferred* goals and values. This requires thorough self-inventory. Detailed instructions are to be found in chapter 11.

Rule #5 about choosing or changing a career: the more time you give to the choosing, the better your choice is going to be. There is a penalty for seeking "quick and dirty" fixes.

Rule #6 about choosing or changing a career: you don't have to get it right, the first time; it's okay to make a mistake, in your choice. You'll have time to correct it, down the road, regardless of your age. Most of us have three to five careers, during our lifetime.

Rule #7 about choosing or changing a career: this should be fun, as much fun as possible. The more fun you're having, the more you can be sure you're doing it right.

Developing a Picture

This builds upon a little-known truth in career-counseling or job-hunting: "*The clearer your vision of what you seek, the closer you are to finding it. For, what you are seeking is also seeking you.*" Sounds kooky, but I've seen it happen too many times, not to believe it. Okay, so how do you make your vision clearer?

Take a large piece of white paper, with some colored pencils or pens, and draw a picture of your ideal life: where you live, who's with you, what you do, what your dwelling looks like, what your ideal vacation looks like, etc.

Don't let *reality* get in the way. Pretend a magic wand has been waved over your life, and it gives you everything you think your ideal life would be.

Now, *of course* you're going to tell me you can't draw. Okay, then make symbols for things, or create little "doodads" or symbols, with labels—anything so that you can *see* all together on one page your vision of your ideal life—however haltingly expressed.

The power of this exercise is sometimes amazing. Reason? By avoiding words and using pictures or symbols as much as possible, it bypasses the left side of the brain ("the safekeeping self," as George Prince calls it) and speaks directly to the right side of your brain ("the experimental self"), whose job it is to engineer change.

Oh, and apropos of Rule #7, this exercise is *fun!*

This done, let's look at the Internet for further clues. In my opinion, the single most useful website with regard to careers, is CNNMoney's (http://money.cnn.com). This site is home to *Money* magazine, *Fortune*, and *Business 2.0*. In the top bar on their home page, choose "Jobs." Then, from the pull-down menu under it, choose "Top 80 Best Jobs." It lists the top twenty jobs for each of several categories, including retirees. Fascinating stuff, and very helpful, as *Money* and *Fortune* always are.

This site also has a fascinating article, about Warren Farrell's research on salaries and careers. The easiest way to find it is to go to any search engine (my favorite is Google), and type in the words *"Where Women's Pay Trumps Men's."* Once you find that article you will find it is chock-full of brilliant ideas about how to make a career choice, when money is the issue. It is based on Warren's blockbuster book (in my opinion) *Why Men Earn More.* Warren is a brilliant, meticulous, highly ethical researcher, but his book is more *news* than it is just another research tome. If I had my way, I would give this book to every female career-chooser or career-changer on the planet.

Try on the Suit First

In your search for a good career, don't believe what lists, tests, experts, or well-meaning friends try to claim is an ideal job *for you.* Just as you would when buying a suit, test it, try it on first, then make up your own mind. *Puh-leeze.*

You do this by going to talk to at least three people who are actually *doing* this career that looks so appealing, and ask them these questions:

How did you get into this field?

What do you like best about it?

What do you like least about it?

How do I get into this career, and how much of a demand is there for people who can do this work?

Is it easy to find a job in this career, or is it hard?

Who else would you recommend or suggest I go talk to, to learn more about this career?

Don't Get a Job by Degrees

Don't go get a college degree in some career field because you think that will guarantee you a job! It will not.

I wish you could see my mail, filled with bitter letters from people who believed this myth, went and got a degree in a field that looked just great, thought it would be a snap to find a job, but are still unemployed two years later. Even in good times. They are bitter (often), angry (always), and disappointed in a society that they feel lied to them.

Now that they have that costly worthless degree, and still can't find a job, they find a certain irony in the phrase, "*Our country believes in getting a job by degrees.*"

If you already made this costly mistake, you know what I mean. It is so sad.

> *The first problem for all of us, men and women, is not to learn, but to unlearn.*
>
> GLORIA STEINEM

9. Things School Never Taught Us about Job-Hunting: **How to Start Your Own Business**

"All I Do the Whole Day Through Is Dream of You . . . "

Sure, you've thought about it, a million times. Hasn't everyone? Every time you're tied up in traffic going to or from work. You've toyed with the idea of not having to go to an office or other place of business, but of running your own business, maybe even out of your own home, making your own product or selling your own services, being your own boss, and keeping all the profits for yourself. It's called *self-employment*, or being *an independent contractor*, or *freelancing*, or *contracting out your services*. Great idea! *But*, nothing's ever come of all this day-dreaming. Until now. Now, you're out of work, and you can't find a job anywhere, and you're thinking to yourself: *Maybe it's now, or never. Maybe I ought to just* do *it.*

The Three Major Problems of Home Businesses

1. The first major problem of home businesses, according to experts, is that on average home-based workers *(in the U.S. at least)* only earn 70 percent of what their full-time office-based equals do. So, you must think carefully whether you could make enough money to survive—never mind *prosper*.

2. The second major problem of home businesses is that it's often difficult to maintain the balance between business and family

time. Sometimes the *family* time gets shortchanged, while in other cases the demands of family (particularly with small children) may become so interruptive, that the *business* gets shortchanged. So, do investigate thoroughly, ahead of time, *how* you would go about doing this *well*.

3. Last, a home business puts you into a perpetual job-hunt.

Some of us when we are unemployed soon learn that we *hate* job-hunting. We are attracted to the idea of a home business because this seems like an ideal way to cut short our job-hunt. The irony is, that a home business makes you in a very real sense a *perpetual* job-hunter—because you have to be *always* seeking new clients or customers—which is to say, new *employers*. (Well, they are *employers*, because they *pay* you for the work you are doing. The only difference between this and a full-time job is that here *the contract is limited*. But if you are running your own business, you will have to *continually* beat the bushes for new clients or customers.)

Of course, the dream of most budding home business people is that you will become so well known, and so in demand, that clients or

"YES, THE BUSINESS HAS BECOME BIGGER, BUT FRED STILL LIKES TO WORK AT HOME."

customers will be literally beating down your doors, and you will be able to stop this endless job-hunt. But that only happens to a relative minority, sorry to report.

The greater likelihood is that you will *always* have to beat the bushes for employers/clients. It may get easier as you get better at it, or it may get harder, if economic conditions continue the present severe downturn. But you must learn to make your peace with it—however grudgingly.

Otherwise, you're probably going to find *a home business* is just a glamorous synonym for *"starving."* I know *many* home business people to whom this has happened, and it happened precisely because they couldn't stomach going out to beat the bushes for clients or customers. If that's true for you, you should plan to start out by *hiring* somebody part-time, who is willing to do this for you—one who, in fact, "eats it up."

When You Don't Know What Kind of Home Business to Start

Okay, let us say the *idea* of being self-employed intrigues the life out of you, but you can't figure out what kind of business to start.

There are fortunately seven steps you can take to nail this down.

First, read. There are oodles of books out there that are filled with ideas for home businesses. Browse in your local independent bookstore or Barnes & Noble.

The best books on home businesses are written by Paul Edwards and Sarah Edwards. Their most recent (2004), and currently most popular, one is called *Best Home Businesses for People 50+*. Earlier works include (2001) *The Best Home Businesses for the Twenty-First Century*, and (1999) *Working from Home*. For other titles, browse the business shelves in your local bookstore.

Second, dream. When looking for ideas, the thing you ought to look at are your dreams. What have you always dreamed about doing? Since childhood? Since last week? Now is the time to dust off those dreams.

You may have been dreaming of earning *more* money. But then again, you may have been dreaming of doing work that you really love, even if it means a lesser salary or income than you have been accustomed to. Don't *judge* your dreams, and don't let anyone else judge them either.

Chapter Nine

Third, look around your own community, and ask yourself what services or products people seem to need the most. Or what service or product already offered in the community could stand a lot of *improving?* There may be something there that *grabs* you.

The underlying theme for 90 percent of the businesses that are *out there* these days is *things that save time or money.* It's what the 140,000,000 who still have jobs in the U.S. most want.

Such ideas as: Daytime or evening office cleaning services and/or home cleaning services. Home repairs, especially in the evening or on weekends, of TVs, computers, smartphones, audio systems, laundries, dishwashers. Lawn care. Care for the elderly in their own homes. Childcare in their own homes. Pickup and delivery of things (even personal stuff, like cleaning) to their office. Automobile care or repair services, with pickup and delivery. Offering short-term business consultancy in various fields.

Fourth, consider mail order. If you find no needs within your own community, you may want to broaden your search, to ask what is needed in this country—or the world. After all, with the Internet at Web 2.0, and even 3.0, businesses can be started *small* at home, and catalogs can can be displayed online, for all the world to see. There is also eBay, as your platform. If this interests you, read up on the subject. Browse the business shelves at your local bookstores.

Fifth, consider telecommuting. Telecommuting is "working at home for others." The people who do this are called *"telecommuters"*—a term coined by Jack Nilles in 1973. To learn more about telecommuting, a good place to start is: http://en.wikipedia.org/wiki/Telecommuting.

One way to go about easing yourself into telecommuting, if you already have a job, is to talk your boss into letting you do at least *some* of your work at home. You can find plans for how you "sell" your employer on the idea, at such sites as: www.workoptions.com.

Your boss, of course, may take the initiative here, before it has even occurred to you, and they may *ask* you to work at home, connected to the office by computer-network telephone lines.

If you are thinking about becoming a telecommuter, I advise you to investigate the idea thoroughly. You can find more telecommuting information, including a database of work-at-home jobs, at: www.careers fromhome.com.

Another similar site with job listings is at www.tjobs.com, and you can find **an association for telecommuters**, TelCoa (The Telework Coalition) with conferences and everything, at: www.telcoa.org.

Sixth, consider a franchise. I'm not sure how good an idea this is, in the present brutal economy. But I list this option for the sake of completeness.

Franchises exist because some people want to have their own business, but don't want to go through the agony of starting it up. They want to *buy in* on an already established business, and they have the money in their savings with which to do that. Fortunately for them, there are a lot of such franchises. You want to keep in mind that some *types* of franchises have a failure rate *far* greater than others. The ten *riskiest* small businesses, according to experts, are local laundries and dry cleaners, used car dealerships (not to mention new car dealerships, since both Chrysler and General Motors slimmed way down), gas stations, local trucking firms, restaurants, infant clothing stores, bakeries, machine shops, grocery or meat stores, and car washes—though I'm sure there will be some new nominees for this list, by the time you read this. *Risky* doesn't mean you can't make them succeed. It only means the odds for failure are greater than you will like.

You want to keep in mind also that some individual franchises are *terrible*—and that includes well-known names. They charge too much for you to *get on board*, and often they don't do the advertising or other commitments that they promised they would.

There isn't a franchising book that doesn't warn you eighteen times to go talk to people who have *already* bought that same franchise, before you ever decide to go with them. And I mean *several* people, not just one. Most experts also warn you to go talk to *other* franchises in the same

Wild Life by John Kovalic, © 1989 Shetland Productions. Reprinted with permission.

Chapter Nine

field, not just the kind you're thinking about signing up with. Maybe there's something better, that such research will uncover.

If you are drawn to the idea of a franchise, because you are in a hurry, and you don't want to do this homework first, 'cause it's just too much trouble, you will deserve what you get, believe me. That way lies madness.

Seventh, if you've invented something, weigh the possibility of doing something with it. If you haven't invented anything yet, but are inclined toward invention or tinkering, you might want to improve something that's already *out there*. Start with something you like, such as bicycles. You might experiment with making—let us say—a folding bicycle. Or, if you like to go to the beach, and your skills run to sewing, you might think about making and selling beach towels with weights sewn in the corners, against windy days.

If you've already invented something, and it's been sitting in your drawer, or the garage, but you've never attempted to duplicate or manufacture it before, now might be a good time to try. Think out very carefully just how you are going to get it manufactured, advertised, and marketed, etc.

There are also promoters out there (on and off the Internet) who claim to specialize in promoting inventions *such as yours*, if *you* will pay *them* a fee. However, there was an old study, done by the Federal Trade Commission, a study of 30,000 people who paid such promoters, and the FTC found that *not a single inventor* ever made a profit after giving their invention to such promoters or firms. Maybe things have changed since, but I'd think this out very carefully, if I were you.

You're much better off if on the Internet you locate other inventors, and ask if they were successful in marketing their own invention. When you find those who were, pick their brains for everything they're worth. (Of course one of the first things they're going to tell you is to go get your invention copyrighted, trademarked, or patented.)

When You Know What Kind of Home Business to Start

The previous seven steps are, of course, in case you don't know what kind of business you'd like to start. But, it may be that you already know exactly *what* business you want to start, because you've been thinking about it for *years*, and may even have been *doing* it for years—only, in the employ of someone else.

But now, you're about to set out on your own. You're thinking about doing this kind of work for yourself, whether it be business services, or consultancy, or repair work, or some kind of craft, or some kind of product, or teaching, or home services, such as childcare or home delivery.

Speaking of home, some jobs are just made for working out of one's home, as when you are some kind of writer, artist, performer, business expert, lawyer, consultant, or the like. On the other hand, your present home may not be big enough for the kind of thing you're dreaming of. For example, your dream may be: *I want a horse ranch, where I can raise and sell horses.* Or *I want to run a bed-and-breakfast place.* Stuff like that.

If it involves a possible move, be sure to go talk to other people who have already done that. Pick their brains for everything they're worth. No need for you to step on the same *land mines* that they did.

A – B = C

As we have seen, the key to successfully starting your own business is: *Find out what's involved, before you hurl yourself into this new world.* Let's talk about this in more detail.

Your **research** has two steps to it:

1. Finding out what skills it takes to make this kind of enterprise work. *This involves figuring out what is "A – B = C."*
2. Then, *going on the Internet, or reading some books.*

Step #1:
Figure Out What Is
"A – B = C"

Over the past forty years I have found it *mind-boggling* how many people start their own business, at home or elsewhere, without *ever* first going to talk to anybody who started that same kind of business before them.

One job-hunter told me she started a home-based soap business, without ever talking to anyone who had started a similar endeavor before her. Not surprisingly, her business went belly-up within a year and a half. She concluded: no one should go into such a business. Ah, but Paula Gibbons for many years ran "Paula's Soap" of Seattle, Washington.[1] *Someone is already doing the work you are dreaming of. The key to your success, is that you go talk to them.*

Here's how to research a potential business you're thinking about:

1. First write out *in as much detail as you can* just exactly what kind of business you are thinking about starting. Do you want to be a freelance writer, or a craftsperson, or a consultant, independent screenwriter, copywriter, digital artist, songwriter, photographer, illustrator, interior designer, video person, film person, counselor, therapist, plumber, electrician, agent, filmmaker, soap maker, bicycle repairer, public speaker, or *what?*

2. Then identify towns or cities that are at least fifty to seventy-five miles away, and by using the Internet or the Yellow Pages or the chamber of commerce, try to identify three businesses in those towns, that are identical or similar to the business you are thinking of starting. Then, journey to that town or city, and talk to the founder or owner of each such business.

3. When you talk to them, you explain that you're exploring the possibility of starting your own business, similar to theirs, but seventy-five miles away. You ask them if they would mind sharing what pitfalls or obstacles they ran into when they started their business. You ask them what skills or knowledge they think are necessary to running that kind of business successfully. Will they give you such information? Yes, most of the time. People love to help others get started in their same business, *if* they love it, although—let's face it—occasionally you may run into owners who are of an ungenerous nature. In such a case, thank them politely for their time, and go on to the next name on your list. When you've found three people willing to help you by relating their own history, you interview each of them in turn, and make a list

---

1. http://paulassoap.com

of the necessary skills and knowledge they all agree were necessary. Give this list a name. Let's call it "A."

4. Back home you sit down and inventory your own skills and knowledge, with the information you will draw from the exercises in chapter 11, in the Flower Exercise. Give this list a name, also. Let's call it "B."

5. Having done this, subtract "B" from "A." This gives you another new list, which you should name. Let's call it "C." "C" is by definition a list of the skills or knowledge that you *don't* have, but must find—either by taking courses yourself, or by hiring someone with those skills, or by getting a friend or family member (who has those skills) to volunteer.

Why fifty to seventy-five miles away? Well, actually, that's a minimum. You want to interview businesses that, *if they were in the same geographical area as you,* would be your rivals. And if they were in the same geographical area as you, they wouldn't likely tell you how to get started. After all, they're not going to train you just so you can then take business away from them.

> How wonderful it is that nobody need wait a single moment before starting to improve the world.
>
> ANNE FRANK

But, when a guy, a gal, or a business is fifty to seventy-five miles away—you're not as likely to be perceived as a rival, unless you plan a rival website, and so they're much more likely to tell you what you want to know about their own experience, and how *they* got started, and where the land mines are hidden.

If your investigation revealed that it takes good accounting practices in order to turn a profit, and you don't know a thing about accounting, go out and hire a part-time accountant *immediately*—or, if you absolutely have no money, talk an accountant friend of yours into giving you some volunteer time, for a while.

It is up to you to do this research thoroughly, weigh the risks, count the cost, get counsel from those intimately involved with you, and then if you decide you want to do it (whatever it is), go ahead and try—no matter what your well-meaning but pessimistic friends or family may say.

You only have one life here on this earth, and that life is *yours* (under God) to say how it will be spent, or not spent. Parents, well-meaning friends, etc., get no vote. Just you, and God.

Doubtless at this point you would like an example of this whole process. Okay. Our job-hunter is a woman who has been making harps for some employer, but now is thinking about going into business for herself, not only *making* harps at home, but also *designing* harps, with the aid of a computer. After interviewing several home-based harp makers and harp designers, and finishing her own self assessment, her chart of A – B = C came out looking like the next page.

If she decides to try her hand at becoming an independent harp maker and harp designer, she now knows what she needs but lacks: *computer programming, knowledge of the principles of electronics, and accounting.* In other words, List **C**. These she must either go to school to acquire for herself, OR enlist from some friends of hers in those fields, on a volunteer basis, OR go out and hire, part-time.

How Can You Do A – B = C, When No One Has Done What You Want to Do?

No matter how inventive you are, you're probably *not* going to invent a job that *no one* has ever heard of before. You're only going to invent a job that *most* people have never heard of before. But the likelihood is *great* that someone, somewhere, in this world of endless creativity, has already put together the kind of job you're dreaming about. Your task: to find them and interview them thoroughly. And then . . . well, A – B = C.

If there isn't someone doing *exactly* what you are dreaming of doing, there is at least someone who is *close.*

For example, let's suppose your dream is—here we take a ridiculous case—to use computers to monitor the growth of plants at the South Pole. And suppose you can't find anybody who's ever done such a thing. The way to tackle this seemingly insurmountable problem, is to break the proposed business down into its parts, which—in this case—are: *computers, plants,* and *the Antarctic.*

Skills and Knowledge Needed to Run This Kind of Business Successfully	Skills and Knowledge That I Have	Skills and Knowledge Needed, Which I have to Learn or Get Someone to Volunteer, or I will Have to Go Out and Hire
Precision-working with tools and instruments	Precision-working with tools and instruments	
Planning and directing an entire project	Planning and directing an entire project	
Programming computers, inventing programs that solve physical problems		Programming computers, inventing programs that solve physical problems
Problem solving: evaluating why a particular design or process isn't working	Problem solving: evaluating why a particular design or process isn't working	
Being self-motivated, resourceful, patient, and persevering, accurate, methodical, and thorough	Being self-motivated, resourceful, patient, and persevering, accurate, methodical, and thorough	
Thorough knowledge of: Principles of electronics	*Thorough knowledge of:*	*Thorough knowledge of:* Principles of electronics
Physics of strings	Physics of strings	
Principles of vibration	Principles of vibration	
Properties of woods	Properties of woods	
Accounting		Accounting

Then you try combining any two parts, together, to identify the kinds of persons you need to go talk to. In this case, that would mean finding someone who's *used computers with plants here in the States*, or someone who's *used computers at the Antarctic*, or someone who has *worked with plants at the Antarctic*, etc. Get names, go talk to them, and along the way you may discover there *is* actually someone who has used computers to monitor the growth of plants at the South Pole. Then again, you may not. In any event, you will learn most of the pitfalls that wait for you, by hearing the experience of those who are in *parallel* businesses or careers.

It is *always* possible—with a little blood, sweat, and imagination—to find out what A – B = C is, for any business you're dreaming of doing.

Step #2:

Going on the Internet

or

Reading Some Books

Websites Dealing with Home-Based Business

I and my Web consultant, my son Mark, have combed through the various home-based business *sites*, testing them for sensible advice, ease of use, and trustworthiness *in our judgment*.

The following list is excerpted from our book, *Job-Hunting Online*.

SELF-EMPLOYMENT AND HOME BUSINESSES

Try these sites for more on self-employment:

Business Owner's Toolkit

www.toolkit.com/small_business_guide/index.aspx

Yikes, there is a lot of information here for the small business owner. Everything about your business: starting, planning, financing, marketing, hiring, managing, getting government contracts, taxes . . . all that stuff.

Small Business Administration

www.sba.gov

The SBA was established to help start, manage, and grow small businesses (bear in mind that it defines "small business" as one with less than five hundred employees; it should be called the "Almost All Businesses Administration"). Lots of useful stuff here; also, check out the Starting a Business resources at www.sba.gov/starting_business/index .html.

The Business Owner's Idea Café

http://businessownersideacafe.com

Great site for the small business owner.

Startup Journal

www.startupjournal.com

The *Wall Street Journal* brings its considerable resources to bear on this site for the entrepreneur. Many articles, how-tos, advice, and resources for the business owner.

Free Agent Nation

www.fastcompany.com/online/12/freeagent.html

The workplace is changing dramatically. Among these changes is the fact that for some, self-employment has become a broader concept than it was in another age. The concept (for some) now includes not only those who own their own business but also free agents: independent contractors who work for several clients; temps and contract employees who work each day through temporary agencies; limited-time-frame workers who work only for a set time, as on a project, then move on to another company; consultants; and so on. This is a fascinating article to help you decide if you want to be part of this trend, on the site of the popular magazine *Fast Company*.

Working Solo

www.workingsolo.com
www.workingsolo.com/resources/resources.html

Working Solo is a good site for the home or small business worker. The best stuff on this site is at the second URL above.

A Home-Based Business Online

www.ahbbo.com
www.ahbbo.com/articles.html

When they say "A Home-Based Business Online," they don't mean "An Online Home-Based Business," or "A Home-Based Online Business"; they mean, "Hey, we've got a lot of information on businesses you can run from your home, and we've put it all on-line for you."

This is a great site, with lots of information for you if you want to get information about a home-based business. There are more than a hundred articles at the second URL.

Nolo Law Center for Small Business

www.nolo.com/lawcenter/index.cfm/catID/
19B45DBF-E85F-4A3D-950E3E07E32851A7

Nolo Press publishes a lot of do-it-yourself law books; this is the part of its website that offers legal resources for the small business person. Really good.

Entrepreneur.com

www.entrepreneurmag.com

Entrepreneur magazine's website. It has lists of home-based businesses, startup ideas, how to raise money, shoestring start-ups, small business myths, a franchise and business opportunity site-seeing guide, and a lot more. As I write, you are allowed access to the magazine's archives, with full text of many articles, stretching back to January of 1999. (This complete, no-fee archive access is unusual for most magazines.) Many resources and articles for the self-employed, home businesses, franchises . . . cool stuff.

World Wide Web Tax

www.wwwebtax.com/miscellaneous/self_employment_tax.htm

Wow. One of the banes of being self-employed is dealing with taxes; this site has more than 1,300 pages to help you handle all of that. Articles, resources, links, downloadable tax forms (going back ten years!) in PDF files . . . of course, the site is selling something (e-filing tax returns), but it has a lot of free information about what self-employed people have to do vis-à-vis taxes, in the United States at least.

AARP

www.aarp.org

In past editions of this book, I have listed AARP's small business center . . . which is no longer there. But I didn't want to just yank this well-known organization's website out of these listings, because there is still *lots* of stuff for the small businessperson—it just isn't in one single place that I can direct you to. Best bet is to do a site search on whatever you want to know ("small business resources" works well; try others), because there are hundreds of articles and useful links on this site; they just aren't particularly well organized at the time I write this.

Jobs and Moms: Work at Home

www.jobsandmoms.com/work_at_home.html

Another article on a popular women's site.

Work at Home Schemes

www.ftc.gov/bcp/edu/pubs/consumer/invest/inv14.shtm

Not everyone using the Internet is as nice as you; there are people in the world who will try to take advantage of your trusting nature. Here is an article to help you protect yourself.

Work at Home Schemes Now Peddled Online

www.scambusters.org/work-at-home.html

A good article from Scambusters.org.

PART-TIME, CONTRACT, AND TEMPORARY WORK

For the most part, I don't advocate people applying for temp jobs through the Internet; you will likely have better luck by going, in person, to a local agency such as Kelly, Manpower, and so on. To find your local agencies, use JobSeek (see below), or go to MapQuest (www.mapquest .com) and type "temp agency" under Business Category.

Here are some sites and articles related to temporary, part-time, and contract work:

The Contract Employee's Handbook

www.cehandbook.com/cehandbook/htmlpages/ceh_main.html

This is an immensely useful handbook, covering every facet of doing temporary or contract work. The site also has a contract employee's newsletter. It's sponsored by the Professional Association of Contract Employees.

JobSeek

www.staffingtoday.net/jobseek/index.html

Best way to find a temp agency. Indicate your area, the kind of work you want, and it kicks back a list—sometimes a very *extensive* list—of temp agencies near you.

SnagAJob

www.snagajob.com

Part-time, restaurant, hourly, summer jobs . . . listings, resources, guidance, advice. Youth oriented, but not exclusively.

Net Temps

www.nettemps.com

"The Hire Power" (groan). I'd be tempted to list this site just for its bad pun, but this is actually a pretty helpful site. Advice on resume writing and such; also a jobs database.

ContractJobHunter

www.cjhunter.com/dcsf/view_some.html?
SearchType=complete

A *huge* listing of firms that hire consultants and contract employees.

Backdoorjobs.com

www.backdoorjobs.com

This site (and the book, by Michael Landes, from which the site takes its title) is mostly aimed at young people who are looking for summer situations, temporary jobs, maybe something outdoors, maybe something overseas for a little while . . . jobs are listed, and there is a sampling of advice from Landes's excellent book, *The Back Door Guide to Short-Term Job Adventures* (published by Ten Speed Press). Basically, this site wants you to buy his book (and it's a good book), but along the way, there's a lot of useful information and news of opportunities online.

Summerjobs.com

www.summerjobs.com/jobSeekers/resources/links.html

This is the links page at SummerJobs.com. There are a number of really useful resources here, including Travel and Adventure, Immigration and Visas, and job sites for overseas and resort employment.

When You're Operating on a Shoestring

Finding clients or customers: With the Internet, came globalization. And this changed everything for the self-employed. You now have a much larger market at your disposal where you can sell your skills, knowledge, services, and products, worldwide.

Finding employees or vendors: In this global age if you're operating on a shoestring, and you need, let us say, to have something printed or produced as inexpensively as possible, you can search for an inexpensive printer, vendor, or manufacturer anywhere in the world, and solicit bids.

At www.virtualecommerce.com, for example, you can list your talent needs or the services required, plus your budget for this task or project, the time by which you need to hire, and some insight into your style or tastes (e.g., your five favorite websites). Vendors from inside the U.S., as well as outside, can bid.

Alternatively, you can type the name of the skill-set you need, plus the word "overseas," and the word "jobs—and see what you can find. For example, if you try "overseas cartoonist jobs" this will turn up a list of sites to try.

Conclusion: New Ways to Work

It takes a lot of guts to try ANYTHING new *(to you)* in today's brutal economy. It's easier, however, if you keep three rules in mind:

1. There is always some risk, in trying something new. Your goal, I hope, is not to avoid risk—there is no way to do that—but to make sure ahead of time that the risks are *manageable*.

2. You find this out before you start, by first talking to others who have already done what you are thinking of doing; then you evaluate whether or not you still want to go ahead and try it.

3. Have a Plan B, laid out, *before you start*, as to what you will do if it doesn't work out; i.e., know where you are going to go, next. Don't wait, *puh-leaze!* Write it out, now. *This is what I'm going to do, if this doesn't work out:* _____

_____   _____

If you're sharing your life with someone, be sure to sit down with that partner or spouse and ask what the implications are *for them* if you try this new thing. Will they have to give up things? If so, what? Are they willing to make those sacrifices? And so on. You have a responsibility to make them full partners in any decision you're facing. Love demands it!

I think there has always been an obsession with youth and beauty. What's missing is the equal obsession with respect for . . . older people . . . and their wisdom and knowledge and courage.

JULIE CHRISTIE, *actress*

10. Things School Never Taught Us about Job-Hunting: **Entering the World of 50+**

The Last Great Change in Our Lives[1]:

The so-called "baby boomers"—the 76 million Americans born between 1945 and 1964—are beginning to enter the time of Life that is traditionally called "retirement."[2] Some people love that word. I'm not one of them. For me, it implies "being put out to pasture"—to borrow an image from a cow. It implies a kind of parole from a thing called *work*, which is assumed to be onerous, and tedious. It implies "disengagement" from both *work* and *Life*, as one patiently—or impatiently—waits to die. It thinks of Life in terms of work; I prefer instead to think of Life in terms of music. My favorite metaphor is that of a symphony. A symphony, traditionally, has four parts to it—four movements, as they're called. So does Life. There is infancy, then the time of learning, then the time of working, and finally, this time that we are talking about, often called "retirement." But if we discourage the use of the word "retirement," then this might better be called the Fourth Movement.

The Fourth Movement, in the symphonic world, is a kind of blank slate. It was and is up to the composer to decide what to write upon it.

---

1. This section is adapted from a book by John E. Nelson and myself, called *What Color Is Your Parachute? for Retirement: Planning Now for the Life You Want* (Berkeley, CA: Ten Speed Press, 2007).
2. The time this disengagement begins, has gotten younger and younger, over the years. Fifty-plus is now the accepted start of some people's *retirement*.

Traditionally, the composer writes of triumph, victory, and joy—as in Beethoven's Symphony #3, the *Eroica*. But it may, alternatively, be a kind of anticlimactic, meandering piece of music—as in Tchaikovsky's Symphony #6, the *Pathetique*. There the Third Movement ends with a bombastic, stirring march. The Fourth Movement, immediately following, is subdued, meditative, meandering, and sounds almost like an afterthought.

Well, there are our choices about our own lives: shall the Fourth Movement, the final movement, of our lives be *pathetique* or *eroica*—pathetic or heroic? Your call!

I like this defining of our lives in terms of *music*, rather than in terms of *work*.

To carry the metaphor onward, in this Fourth Movement of our lives, we have instruments, which we must treat with care. They are: our **body,** our **mind,** our **spirit,** and what we poetically speak of as our **heart,** which Chinese medicine calls "the Emperor."[3] Body, mind, spirit, heart. Some of these instruments are in shiny, splendid condition, in our lives. Others are slightly dented. Or greatly dented. But these are the instruments that play the musical notes and themes of this time of our lives.

The traditional notes are: **sleep, water, eating, faith, love, loneliness, survival** (financial and spiritual), **health care, dreams** (fulfilled or unfulfilled), and **triumph**—over all adversities—and even **death.**

I will share some helpful thoughts, and websites, for each of these notes—at the end of this chapter.

Traditionally, the themes for this period of our lives also include **planning**—as in the phrase "retirement planning." But I believe planning is difficult for the Fourth Movement. It seems to me the outstanding characteristic of the Fourth Movement in our lives is the increased number of things that knock our plans into a cocked hat—the events we call *unexpected*. So I prefer to say that one of the notes we strike during the Fourth Movement in particular, is how to handle **interruptions.** Martin Luther King Jr. perhaps put it best, just before his death:

> "The major problem of life is learning how to handle the costly interruptions—the door that slams shut, the plan that got sidetracked, the marriage that failed, or that lovely poem that didn't get written because someone knocked on the door."

---

3. www.itmonline.org/5organs/heart.htm

Now, in music, interruptions are the pauses between the notes; those pauses that, in fact, keep the notes from just becoming a chaotic jumble. Just listen to the first few bars of Beethoven's Fifth. Thank God for the interruptions, the spaces between the notes.

So, where have we come thus far? Well, I suggested that it is useful to think of Life after 50 as the Fourth Movement in the symphony of our lives—the movement that comes after the first three: Infancy, then The Time of Learning, and then The Time of Working. And it is useful to think that we have instruments, which play certain themes in this movement, as we have seen. That brings us to the $64,000 question: "Toward what end?" "What is the point of all these notes, all these themes, in the Fourth Movement? What are they intended to produce?"

When I think of the overall impression left with me after I hear the Fourth Movement of any great symphony, such as Schubert's Ninth, one impression sticks out, above all others. And that impression is one of *energy*. I am left with an impression of great energy. And the more the better, say I. Energy is lovely to behold, and even lovelier to possess. That energy belongs in the Fourth Movement because it brings the whole symphony to triumphant resolution.

This, it seems to me, is how people evaluate the Fourth Movement of our lives, as well. Not: did we live triumphantly and die victoriously; but: do we manifest energy? Do we manifest enthusiasm? Do we manifest excitement, still?

Ask any employer what they are looking for, when they interview a job candidate who is 50 years or older, and they will tell you: energy. They ask themselves, "Does the candidate (*that's us*) slouch in the chair? Does the candidate look like they're just marking time in Life? Or does the candidate lean slightly forward in the chair as we talk? Does the candidate seem excited about the prospect of working here?"

Energy in people past 50 is exciting to an employer. And to those around us. It suggests the candidate will come in early, and stay late. It suggests that whatever task is given, the task will be done thoroughly and completely, and not just barely or perfunctorily.

All right, then, *energy*. Where shall we find energy, after 50? When we were young, energy resided in the *physical* side of our nature. We were "feeling our oats." We could go all day, and go all night. "My, where do you get all your energy?" our grandmother would ask us. We were a dynamo . . . of *physical* energy.

Can't say the same when we reach 50, and beyond. Oh, some of us still have it. But as we get older the rest of us start to slow down. Physical energy is often harder to come by, despite workouts and exercise and marathons. Increasingly, our energy must more and more come from *within*. It must spring not from our muscles but from our excitement about Life and about what we are doing in this Fourth and final Movement of our lives.

> *This brought back to me a memory I have cherished since childhood. We spent a summer in Balboa in a large cottage on the grand canal and went fishing every day and swimming in the warm southern California water. Next door to us was another cottage with an old couple who always seemed to be sitting on their front porch observing the summer activities. We made friends and the lady wanted to be called Auntie Bess. I think I was twelve and she was probably eighty and her husband the same. Auntie Bess always asked what we were going to do each day and we became friends. Each day we brought home lots of fish and she was really excited when we offered them to her. This continued through the summer and one evening she offered to take us clamming on our beach and explained how we could make a clamming probe with a coat hanger and that we should meet her at low tide around six the next morning.*
>
> *We arrived at the beach in front of the cottage at the same time and I watched her slow progress and unsteady walk and very thick glasses. Her enthusiasm was boundless and she showed us the two holes in the sand that razor clams make and how to pull them out with the coat hanger wire. We probably got ten nice clams and Auntie Bess started to fade and said she would watch us from the porch. I watched her unsteady and slow progress back to her porch. I couldn't forget the energy and enthusiasm that lady had which made her actually quiver with delight in showing two little boys how to bring up clams. Never had I seen anyone burn so bright with so few resources.*
>
> *Oh I hope I can be like that.*
>
> *Phil Wood*

This is why, past 50, we need to spend more time on the questions of our youth—what *are your favorite skills?* where *do you most enjoy using them?* and how *do you find such a place and such a job or endeavor?* These questions are entertaining when we are young, but critical when we are past 50, as they are the doorway to finding our *energy* in the Fourth and final Movement of the symphony of our lives.[4]

Energy is what impresses employers, if you still need (or want) to work, past 50. Employers often worry that older workers have lost their energy and enthusiasm for work. The best way to show that you are not the type to just coast through your remaining work-years, until you give up working, is to display some passion during the interview. Remember, *energy* is what employers are looking for, the most. Figure out what *does* get you excited.

Stay alert, *very* alert, during the whole interview. Lean forward in your chair, ever so slightly. When the employer is speaking, respond with an intelligent question (or curiosity) about what they have just said. When they have asked you a question, don't respond with a long-winded answer. Twenty seconds to two minutes at most, is best.

All in all, your age is irrelevant if you convey energy and enthusiasm— for Life, for work, for helping others. Energy. That's what every employer is looking for, when they interview someone over 50.

The nicest compliment any of us can hear people say about us, as we grow older, is: "What a passion for life she still has! Or, *he* has! It's thrilling to be around them."

Themes and Notes in the
Fourth Movement of Our Lives

THE MIND

By the time we reach the Fourth Movement of our lives, the life of the mind is *everything.*

Sometimes our mind has become puzzling to us in its performance: we experience more short-term memory loss, more inability to concentrate sometimes, more difficulty retrieving words, more difficulty than before, in recognizing faces or remembering names of neighbors, more

---

4. Detailed instructions for getting at these questions can be found in this book in chapter 11.

things becoming "lost," or at least misplaced, at inopportune times, or an increasing inability to follow through on tasks, becoming instead easily distracted or diverted. Or the inability any longer to push ourselves to the limit, as we used to do.

These things can occur when we are young, but they tend to disturb us more when they come in the Fourth Movement of our lives. Oh, *aging*, we think. *Darn!*

Well, not necessarily. The causes are sometimes medicines we are taking—especially for pain or nausea; or abrupt menopause (in women, of course); or anxiety or depression; or medical treatment we have undergone in the past (particularly chemotherapy, in 15 percent of those thus treated—a condition called "chemo brain"); and the largest reason of all for these new behaviors or limits: "I don't know."

Sometimes we obsess. About anything. About everything.

This is a matter of choosing what to think about.

By the Fourth Movement, we've experienced enough injustices, unfairnesses, and psychic injuries, to ourselves or to the vast and vulnerable peoples of the Earth, that we could *brood about* these things, for the rest of our lives. If we so choose.

Again, by then, we've seen enough possible, fearful scenarios for the future of our own lives, and how we shall die, for the future of our people, and for the future of the Earth, that we can live in constant daily fear of a thousand things that will never happen, for the rest of our lives. If we so choose.

Again, by then we've seen the wondrous beauty of the world, in our garden, in the sunset, in music, in a thousand unexpected kindnesses from strangers and loved ones, and in the enchanting spirit of the best people on Earth, that we could think on these things, for the rest of our lives. If we so choose.

Yes, more important than *the life that we choose*, are the thoughts that we choose, day after day after day. They determine the quality of life for us in the Fourth Movement of our lives.

I think that *The Secret*—the phenomenally popular book and DVD— has it right, at its core, even though the melodramatic story and hints of conspiracy in its *presentation* of that core, are more than a little off-putting to some.

The Will

The Will is a metaphor for *the Power of deciding,* which each of us has. We are most familiar with it when we are dieting, or making New Year's resolutions. It often feels like a battlefield, between two opposing impulses: should I eat chocolate? or, should I not eat chocolate?

But in the Fourth Movement of our lives, it is often a larger battlefield, between our diminishing power to decide, and a vast number of crooks, out there, who want to separate us from our money, by false pretense and luring promises that they will make us rich, if only we . . .

So, the Fourth Movement is a great time to relearn, or learn for the first time, *how to decide.*

I mentioned, at the beginning of this book, that this is one of the skills you would *think* school would help us master; but, alas and alack! more often than not, it does not. So, we must pick up clues, wherever we can.

Dr. Jerome Groopman, a *hematologist,*[5] wanted to study *How Doctors Think.* In a brilliant book with that title, published in 2007, he presented his mindings. On average, he discovered, a physician will interrupt a patient describing her symptoms *within eighteen seconds.* By then, often, the doctor has decided what the diagnosis is—often correctly, but sometimes disastrously wrong.

In illuminating how doctors (and we) can make better decisions about our medical treatment, Dr. Groopman illuminates how we can make better decisions about *everything.* Crucial knowledge for those of us over 50.

It is a marvelous book, which I highly recommend. For our purposes, I am summarizing, here, my own learnings about the steps that Dr. Groopman says a doctor (or we, the patient) should take, before making a decision (or diagnosis):

1. Take time. Hurry is the worst enemy of good decisions.
2. Question. *Cogently.* Listen. *Carefully.* Observe. *Keenly.* Think. *Differently.* Questions that will help:

Ask yourself if there is some vital piece of information that is being left out.
Physician to patient: "Tell me the story again, as if I'd never heard it: what you felt, what else you remember about where and when, etc."

---

5. A practitioner in a branch of medicine devoted to the study of blood.

Ask what else we should explore to avoid premature closure. "What else could this possibly be?" Physician: Don't be influenced by how many physicians have previously examined and diagnosed this patient, or what their diagnosis is. This person has come to you because they want to hear something new, not just a reinforcement of what other doctors have said. Bring a fresh mind with the question foremost in your head: "But what if this isn't what others have said it is? What if this is something very different?"

Don't just dismiss the intuitions and feelings of patient or family. Physician to patient: "What are your worst fears, or your family's worst fears, about these symptoms?"

Recheck the initial diagnosis. "In the tests, or in the diagnosis, is there anything that doesn't fit?"

Avoid one-answer solutions to complex problems. Patient to physician: "Is it possible I have more than one problem?"

Work

If you need or want to work past 50, there are some things you need to keep in mind: you have—or should have, if you stop to think about it—lots of contacts, individuals or networks of friends. In a word, *a grapevine.* They can lead you to jobs, they can speak enthusiastically about you. And since, by your age, these contacts are likely to be of all ages, you have a rich pool to pick from. Unlike younger workers.

To find more information, see the article referenced below.[6]

To find jobs that may offer flextime, job-sharing, or telecommuting to either full- or part-time workers, see:

A List of Part-Time Jobs Available in Your Area (Zip Code):
www.snagajob.com

Faith/Spirituality

Past 50, many of us think more strongly about what we believe—about the afterlife, about God, prayer, etc. There is a website that deals with news, etc., about all faiths, which you may want to look at: www.beliefnet.com.

---

6. For the complete article, go to www.jobfinderssupport.com/resources.htm and then, under "Hot Topics" click on "Secrets of Finding a Job When You're Over 50."

Then there is a Jesuit site that leads you in a daily meditation for ten or more minutes (in more than twenty languages with a visual, but otherwise no sound or distraction): http://sacredspace.ie.

There is also a site that gives you a daily podcast of church bells, music, Scripture reading, and meditations or homily, with no visuals, but with sound, and an audio MP3 file that can be sent to your phone, computer, PDA, etc: www.pray-as-you-go.org.

A site dedicated to helping you keep a divine consciousness 24-7: by helping you link up to other people of faith, through prayer circles, sharing of personal stories of faith, etc., aimed especially, but not exclusively, toward young adults. Its ultimate message: you are not alone: www.24-7prayer.com/articles/771.

Lastly, a site dedicated to helping you find a spiritual counselor (or "spiritual director"), as well as retreat centers, in the Christian, Islamic, Buddhist, Jewish, or Interfaith faiths: www.sdiworld.org.

If your spirituality isn't of the traditional kind, at least get out in the outdoors as much as possible. Sit. Walk. Breathe. Observe. Get excited by the simple beauty of just being alive.

PART I
Finding a Job . . .

PART II
Finding a Life . . .

11. Finding a Life . . . The Flower Exercise: The Parachute Workbook (Updated 2010)

What Did You Come into the World to Do?

There is a name for this moment in your life; in fact, there are several names.

We call it "at last going after your dreams."
We call it "finding more purpose and meaning for your life."
We call it "making a career-change."
We call it "deciding to try something new."
We call it "setting out in a different direction in your life."
We call it "getting out of the rat race."
We call it "going after your dream job."
We call it "finding your mission in life, at last."

But what you call it doesn't really matter. It is instantly recognizable as that moment when you decide that *this time* you're not going to do just a traditional job-hunt; you're going to do a life-changing job-hunt or career-change: one that begins with you and what it is that *you* want out of life.

This time it's all about: *Your* agenda. *Your* wishes. *Your* dreams. *Your* mission in life, given you by the Great God, our Creator.

Not a Selfish Activity

You may think that this is a selfish activity—because it deals with You, you, you. But it is not. It is concerned with what *the world* most needs from you. That world currently is *filled* with workers whose week-long question is, *When is the weekend going to be here?* And, then, *Thank God It's Friday!* Their work puts bread on the table *but . . .* they are bored out of their minds. They've never taken the time to think out what they uniquely can do, and what they uniquely have to offer to the world.

What the world most needs *from you* is not to add to their number, but to figure out, and then contribute to the world, what you came into this world to do.

Where Do You Start?

In our search for our dream job, our instinct is to start with some survey of the job-market out there, to find out what's "hot" and what's not. That could take years. No, this is a *journey* you're embarking on, not (yet) a destination.

So, it's useful to recall what travel experts teach about *taking a journey*: before you go, they say, lay out on your bed, two piles. In one pile, put all the clothes, toiletries, and stuff that you think you'll need to take. In the other pile, put all the money you think you'll need to take.

Then, they say, pack only half the clothes, but twice the money.

By coincidence, the same kind of ratio occurs in this journey, This Journey Toward Your Dream Job.

That is: for this journey, you will need only half the information you thought you would need about *the job-market*, but twice the amount of information you thought you would need about *yourself.*

We may paraphrase Alexander Pope, here:

Know then thyself,
Do not the Market scan
Until you've surveyed all You are,
Then you will have your plan.

> Most job-hunters who fail to find their dream job, fail not because they lack information about the job-market, but because they lack information about themselves.

Of course, being human, our first instinct is to protest that we already know loads of information about ourselves. After all, we've lived with ourselves all these years. We *surely* know who we are, by now.

Well, let's test that premise.

1. Take ten sheets of blank paper. Write, at the top of each one, the words: Who Am I?

2. Then write, on each sheet in turn, one answer to that question. And only one.

3. When you're done, go back over all ten sheets and expand now upon what you have written on each sheet. Looking at each answer, write below it, *why* you said that, and *what turns you on* about that answer.

4. When finished with all ten sheets, go back over them and arrange them in order of priority. That is, which identity is the most important to you? That page goes on top. Then, which is next? That goes immediately underneath the top one. Continue arranging the rest of the sheets in order, until the least important identity is at the bottom of the pile.

5. Finally, go back over the ten sheets, in order, and look particularly at your answer, on each sheet, to *What Turns Me On about This?* See if there are any common denominators, or themes, among the ten answers you gave. If so, jot them down on a separate piece of paper. Voilà! You have begun to put your finger on some things that your dream job or career, vocation, mission, or whatever, needs to give you if you are to feel truly excited, fulfilled, useful, effective, and operating at the height of your powers.

Here, incidentally, is an example, of how one man did this exercise:

Who am I?

1. A man
2. An urban dweller (and lover)
3. A loving person
4. A creator
5. A writer
6. A lover of good movies and music
7. A skilled counselor and teacher
8. An independent
9. An executive
10. An enabler

What turns me on about each of these?

1. Taking initiative, having inner strength; being open, growing, playful
2. Excitement, variety of choices available, crowds, faces
3. Feelings, empathizing, playfulness, sex, adoration given, happiness
4. Transforming things, making old things new, familiar, wondrous
5. Beauty of words, variety of images, new perspectives, new relationships of ideas, words, understandings
6. Watching people up close, merging of color, photography, music
7. Using intuition; helping; seeing totalities of people; problem solving; long-term, close, helpful relationships
8. Making own decisions, carrying out own plans
9. Taking responsibility, wise risks, using mind, seeing totalities of problems overall
10. Helping people to become freed-up, to be what they want to be

Any common denominators? Variety, totalities, rearranging of constellations, dealing with a number of different things and showing relationships between them all in a new way, helping others.

What must my career use (and include) for me to be truly happy, useful, and effective? A variety of different things that have to be dealt with, with people, where seeing totalities, rearranging their relationships, and interpreting them to people in a new way are at the heart of the career.

Now, if this exercise was easy, then you do indeed know a lot about yourself. *But* if it was harder than you thought it would be, then you see there is work to be done. It is urgent for you to know more about who you are.

The Three Secrets to Finding Out More about Who You Are

The late Barbara B. Brown, who was the first to bring *biofeedback* to the public's awareness back in 1974, with her then groundbreaking book, *New Mind, New Body*, once gave a public lecture on what *brain scientists* had discovered—on the way to biofeedback—about how best to gather information about yourself, so that you can make better decisions about your life.

Barbara Brown said *brain scientists* had discovered there were three things you can do, that greatly facilitate such decision making.

Their first one was: Put everything you know about yourself, on one piece of paper. Jot down anything and everything that occurs to you about yourself. Write small.

Brain scientists' second finding, according to Barbara, was: Use some kind of graphic on that piece of paper, in order to organize the information *about yourself*. A graphic—any graphic—keeps "That One Piece of Paper" interesting, and not just a mess of words and space.

Their third, and last, finding was: Prioritize all this information, when you have finished gathering it. Put it in its order of importance, to you. Number the top ten things about yourself that you consider most important (to You). That way, when you finally go looking for a dream job or career that matches *you*, if it is not a *perfect* overlap, at least you will know what you should make sure *is* included in the overlap.

I have followed these three prescriptions for the past thirty years, as I have taught millions of job-hunters and career-changers how to find their dream job.

We have called "That One Piece of Paper" by various names over the years: *The Beginning Job-Hunting Map, The Quick Job-Hunting Map, The What Color Is Your Parachute Workbook, The Flower Exercise*, etc.

And, over the years we have tried out various graphics on "That One Piece of Paper": a parachutist and his/her parachute, a Grecian temple, a clown holding a bunch of round balloons, a tree with several branches, etc., etc. The common denominator has been that each graphic has had seven parts, inasmuch as any dream job has seven parts. Ultimately we settled on a diagram of a Flower, with seven petals,[1] because readers preferred it above all other graphics. Something about it being a living entity, beautiful and growing, I guess, and therefore a reflection of them in a sense.

Here's what it came out looking like.

---

1. Seven vs. eight depends on whether you put Goals and Values on one petal, or two.

The Flower

"That One Piece of Paper"

1.

Where Geography-wise? *(in order of priority for me)*

2.

In organizations using THESE **special knowledges:** *(in order of priority for me)*

3.

In organizations having THESE **people-environments:** *(in order of priority for me)*

USING THESE TRANSFERABLE SKILLS: *(in order of priority for me)*

1

2

6.

At THIS level of **responsibility and salary:**

3

4

5

4. Serving THESE
goals/purposes/values:
(in order of priority for me)

5. With THESE
working conditions:
(in order of priority for me)

Readers have asked to see what "That One Piece of Paper" looks like, when it is all filled out, and done. Rich W. Feller, a student of mine back in 1982, now a world-famous professor and expert in this field, filled out his flower as you see, on the facing page. He said "That One Piece of Paper" has been his lifelong companion ever since 1982, and his guiding star, as it has turned out to be more and more a description of where he has gone, and is going, with his life. I hear such testimony, again and again.

Rich Feller, a University Distinguished Teaching Scholar and Professor at Colorado State University, whose own personal "Flower Diagram" is on the facing page, first put his personal "picture" together twenty-five years ago. Here are his comments about its usefulness since, and how "That One Piece of Paper" helped him, how he's used it, and how it's changed.

What the Parachute Flower Has Meant to Me

More than anything I've gained from an academic life, my Flower has given me hope, direction, and a lens to satisfaction. Using it to assess my life direction during crisis, career moves, and stretch assignments, it helps me define and hold to personal commitments. In many ways it's my "guiding light." Data within my Flower became and remain the core of any success and satisfaction I have achieved.

After I first filled out my own Flower diagram in a two-week workshop with Dick Bolles back in 1982, I decided to teach the Flower to others. My academic position has allowed me to do this, abundantly. Having now taught the Flower to thousands of counselors, career development, and human resource specialists, I continually use it with clients, and in my own transitional retirement planning.

I'm overwhelmed with how little has changed within my Flower, over the years. My Flower is the best of what I am. Its petals are my compass, and using my "favorite skills" are the mirror to a joyful day. I trust the wisdom within "That One Piece of Paper." It has guided my work and my life, ever since 1982, and it has helped my wife and I define our hopes for our son.

The process of filling out and acting on "That One Piece of Paper" taught me a lot. Specifically, it taught me **the importance of the following ten things, often running contrary to what my studies and doctoral work had taught me previously.**
I learned from my Flower the importance of:
1. Chasing after passions, honoring strengths, and respecting skill identification
2. Challenging societal definitions of balance and success

(continued)

Chapter Eleven

Example

(Rich Feller's Flower)

Salary and Level of Responsibility

1. Can determine 9/12 month contract **2.** Can determine own projects **3.** Considerable clout in organization's direction without administrative responsibilities **4.** Able to select colleagues **5.** 3 to 5 assistants **6.** $35K to $50K **7.** Serve on various important boards **8.** Can defer clerical and budget decisions and tasks **9.** Speak before large groups **10.** Can run for elected office

Favorite Interests

1. Large conference planning **2.** Regional geography & culture **3.** Traveling on $20/day **4.** Career planning seminars **5.** Counseling techniques / theories **6.** American policies **7.** Fundamentals of sports **8.** Fighting sexism **9.** NASCAR auto racing **10.** Interior design

Geography

1. Close to major city **2.** Mild winters / low humidity **3.** Change in seasons **4.** Clean and green **5.** 100,000 people **6.** Nice shopping malls **7.** Wide range of athletic options **8.** Diverse economic base **9.** Ample local culture **10.** Sense of community (pride)

Favorite Skills

1. Observational / learning skills • continually expose self to new experiences • perceptive in identifying and assessing potential of others **2.** Leadership skills • continually searches for more resonsibility • sees a problem / acts to solve it **3.** Instructing / interpreting / guiding • committed to learning as a lifelong process • create atmosphere of acceptance **4.** Serving / helping / human relations skills • shapes atmosphere of particular place • relates well in dealing with public **5.** Detail / follow-through skills • handle great variety of tasks • resource broker **6.** Influencing / persuading skills • recruiting talent / leadership • inspiring trust **7.** Performing skills • getting up in front of a group (if I'm in control) • addressing small and large groups **8.** Intuitional / innovative skills • continually develop / generate new ideas **9.** Develop / plan / organize / execute • designing rojects • utilizing skills of others **10.** Language / read / write • communicate effectively • can think quickly on my feet

Favorite Working Conditions

1. Receive clinical supervision **2.** Mentor relationship **3.** Excellent secretary **4.** Part of larger, highly respected organization with clear direction **5.** Near gourmet and health food specialty shops **6.** Heterogeneous colleagues (race, sex, age) **7.** Flexible dress code **8.** Merit system **9.** Can bike / bus / walk to work **10.** Private office with window

Favorite People Environment

1. Strong social, perceptual skills **2.** Emotionally and physically healthy **3.** Enthusiastically include others **4.** Heterogeneous in interests and skills **5.** Social changers, innovators **6.** Politically, economically astute **7.** Confident enough to confront / cry and be foolish **8.** Sensitive to nontraditional issues **9.** I and R (see page 204) **10.** Nonmaterialistic

Favorite Values

1. Improve the human condition **2.** Promote interdependence and futuristic principles **3.** Maximize productive use of human / material resources **4.** Teach people to be self-directed / self-responsible **5.** Free people from self-defeating controls (thoughts, rules, barriers) **6.** Promote capitalistic principles **7.** Reduce exploitation **8.** Promote political participation **9.** Acknowledge those who give to the community **10.** Give away ideas

3. Committing to something bigger than oneself
4. Living authentically and with joy
5. Being good at what matters to oneself and its relationship to opportunity
6. Finding pleasure in all that one does
7. Staying focused on well-being and life satisfaction
8. Personal clarity and responsibility for designing "possible selves"
9. Letting the world know, humbly but clearly, what we want and
10. "Coaching" people amidst a world of abundance where individuals yearn for individual meaning and purpose more than they hunger for possessions, abject compliance with society's expectations, or simply fitting in.

This technologically enhanced, global workplace we now face in the twenty-first century certainly challenges all we thought we knew about our life roles. Maintaining clarity, learning agility, and identifying development plans have become elevated to new and critical importance, if we are to maintain choice. As a result I've added the following four emphases to "Rich's Flower": *Have, do, learn,* and *give.* That is to say, I try to keep a running list (constantly updated) of ten things that I want to:

1. Have
2. Do
3. Learn
4. Give

Through the practice of answering the four questions listed above, I can measure change in my growth and development.

I feel so fortunate to have the opportunity to share with others how much I gained from the wisdom and hope embedded within "Rich's Flower."

I humbly offer my resume, home location and design, and family commitments on my website at www.mycahs.colostate.edu/Rich .Feller. I'd be honored to share my journey, and encourage others to nurture and shine light on their garden as well. I believe you'll find about 90 percent of the Flower's items influence our daily experience.

Rich Feller
Professor of Counseling and Career Development
University Distinguished Teaching Scholar
Colorado State University
Fort Collins, CO

STEP 1

What Values Do You Want Your Life to Serve?

You've got talent, no doubt about that. You have special gifts, and skills. The question is: what do you want to accomplish with that talent, those skills, and those gifts? What values do you want your life, ultimately, to serve?

That is the question with which you must begin. Even before you inventory your skills. They can be made to serve any goal or value you choose. To illustrate what I mean, the next time you go to the movies, sit there after the story has come to an end, and watch the credits roll. Their goal was to produce a movie; but just look at the talents and skills it took to do that. You will see such talents listed as: *researcher (especially for movies set in another historical period), travel expert (to scout locations), interior designer (to design sets), carpenter (ditto), painter (ditto), costume designer, hair stylist, make-up artist, lighting technician, sound editor and sound mixer, computer graphics people, singer, conductor, musicians, composer, sound recordist, stunt artists, animal trainer, talent coordinator, camera operator and cinematographer, special effects people, continuity editor, director, art director, casting director, actor, actress, producer, accountant, personal assistants, drivers, first aid people, secretaries, publicists,* and many others, depending on the type of movie it is.

The point is: if what you most want to do is to make movies, It doesn't matter what your skills are, because almost any skills you have can be put to use there.

And so it is, with all goals, fields, and values.

Figure out what cause, what problem, what values, you want your life to serve. Then, almost any talent, skill, or gift you later discover you have, or already know you have, can be put into its service.

The word "values" can refer to almost anything. Do you value chocolate over broccoli? Or do you value broccoli over chocolate? That's a matter of your values.

But "values" in the sense I'm using it here, refers to the broad outcome of your life. What kind of footprint do you want to leave on this earth, after your journey here is done? Figure *that* out, and you're well on your way to finding a life that has purpose and meaning.

I will list nine broad outcomes here; all of them are important, in this life; the question is, which one (or ones) grips you the most?

1. Mind. Is the human mind your major concern? When you are gone, do you want there to be more knowledge, truth, or clarity in the world, because you were here? If so, knowledge, truth, or clarity concerning what, in particular?

2. Body. Is the human body your major concern? When you are gone, do you want there to be more wholeness, fitness, or health in the world, more binding up of the body's wounds and strength, more feeding of the hungry, and clothing of the poor, because you were here? If so, what issue in particular—concerning the human body—do you want to work on?

3. Eyes and Other Senses. Are the human senses your major concern? When you are gone, do you want there to be more beauty in the world, because you were here? If so, what kind of beauty entrances you? Is it art, music, flowers, photography, painting, staging, crafts, clothing, jewelry, or what—that you want your life to contribute toward?

4. Heart. Is the human heart your major concern? When you are gone, do you want there to be more love and compassion in the world, because you were here? If so, love or compassion for whom? Or for what?

5. The Will or Conscience. Is the human will or conscience your major concern? When you are gone, do you want there to be more morality, more justice, more righteousness, more honesty in the world, because you were here? If so, in what areas of human life or history, in particular? And in what geographical area?

6. The Human Spirit. Is the human spirit your major concern? When you are gone, do you want there to be more spirituality in the world, more faith, more compassion, more forgiveness, more love for God, and the human family in all its diversity, because you were here? If so, with what ages, people, or with what parts of human life?

7. Entertainment. When you are gone, do you want there to be more lightening of people's loads, more giving them perspective, more helping them to forget their cares for a spell, do you want there to be more laughter in the world, and joy, because you were here? If so, what particular kind of entertainment do you want to contribute to the world?

8. Possessions. Is the often false love of possessions your major concern? When you are gone, do you want there to be better stewardship of what we possess—as individuals, as a community, as a nation—in the world, because you were here? Do you want to see simplicity, savings, and a broader emphasis on the word *enough*, rather than on the word *more, more*? If so, in what areas of human life in particular?

9. The Earth. Is the planet on which we stand, your major concern? When you are gone, do you want there to be more protection of this fragile planet, more exploration of the world or the universe— *exploration*, not *exploitation*—more dealing with its problems and its energy, because you were here? If so, which problems or challenges in particular, draw your heart and soul?

In sum, remember that all of these are worthwhile values and outcomes, all of these are necessary and needed, in this life. The question is, which one in particular do you most want to bend your energies, your skills and gifts, your life, to serve, while you are here?

The Prioritizing Grid. To help you decide this, you may want to use a little invention of mine, called the Prioritizing Grid, on page 171. You will, in fact, be running into this Grid many times here, so since this is the first time, let me explain in some detail how it works.

Rather than trying to rank a long list, it asks you to compare just two items at a time. You compare them by arbitrarily listing them, as I have done, in Section A—in any order. (Since you are comparing only nine items, here, you cross out all boxes containing the number 10, i.e., the whole bottom row in Section B.)

Then you compare the items, just two at a time, by the shorthand of comparing the numbers, which should recall to you, the items they stand for.

Here, you would begin by comparing just the numbers 1 and 2, in Section A.

Looking at the list in Section A in this sample grid, 1 and 2 would recall MIND, and BODY. You can, of course, flesh these items out further, in your mind, any way you want, so that they are your own definition. So you might phrase "1 vs. 2" to mean:

"Would I like my life to be primarily remembered for
1. MIND. Bringing more knowledge, truth, or clarity to the world?"

OR

"Would I like my life to be primarily remembered for
2. BODY. Bringing more wholeness, fitness, or health to the world, more binding up of the body's wounds and strength, more feeding of the hungry, and clothing of the poor?"

Choose one of these. Even if it's hard, and you only prefer one just an eensy-teensy bit more.

Let's say you choose (2). Then, on the grid in Section B, in the little box where you see just the numbers 1 and 2, you circle the 2, as shown. You only have to decide between two Values at a time, never more than that.

Next, you compare just 2 and 3, or more specifically the Values that those numbers stand for. Choose which one is more important to you, and circle that number in the box that contains only a 2 and a 3.

Etc., etc.

When you're finished choosing just one number (i.e., just one Value) from every box with two numbers in it, in Section B, you then count how many times each number got circled, in the whole grid, and enter that count down in the first empty horizontal row in Section C, right under the number in question. Continue doing this until every number has a count.

Now look at the counts. If you see a tie in the number of times *two* numbers got circled, you break the tie by looking back at the little box where only those two numbers appear, in Section B, and see which number you circled there. Then, give that number an extra half point in the count of how many times it got circled, to break the tie. In our illustration, let us suppose that in the end both #1 and #2 got circled four times. Look back at the box where only #1 and #2 appear, and see which number got circled. We see is was #2. Hence, you assign an extra half point to #2, when you are through with the count. Now no two numbers have the same count.

If you see a tie in the number of times *three* numbers got circled, that's a different problem. It means you gave two inconsistent answers somewhere in Section B, thereby contradicting yourself. How to resolve this? Look at the three numbers, and what they stand for, and by guess and by gosh, decide which is most important to you, which next, and which

PRIORITIZING GRID FOR 10 ITEMS OR LESS

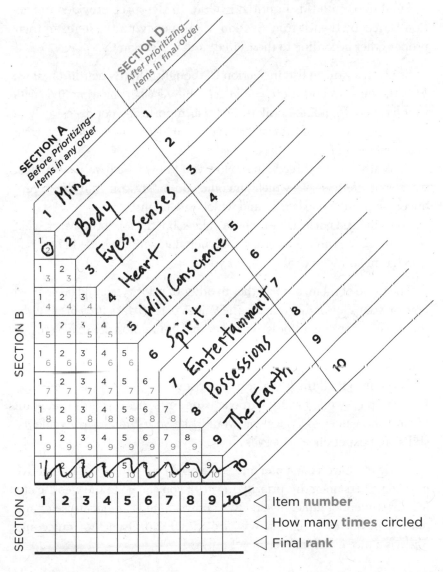

SECTION D
After Prioritizing—
Items in final order

SECTION A
Before Prioritizing—
Items in any order

1 Mind
2 Body
3 Eyes, Senses
4 Heart
5 Will, Conscience
6 Spirit
7 Entertainment
8 Possessions
9 The Earth

SECTION B

SECTION C

◁ Item **number**
◁ How many **times** circled
◁ Final **rank**

next. Give the first one an extra three-quarters point, give the second one an extra half point, and the third one no extra point, in the count of how many times they got circled, thus dissolving the three-way tie.

Next step: look to see which number got circled the most, and give it a Final rank of #1 in that bottom row of Section C, right under the number in question and its count. Then, count which number got circled next most, and give it a Final rank of #2 in the bottom row. Continue until a ranking (#1 to #9, here) has been assigned to every number.

Final step, with this Prioritizing Grid. In the space provided in Section D, recopy the list from Section A, but now with the items in their proper order according to their Final rank in Section C.

Study this ranked list, in Section D, thoughtfully. By definition, now, #1 is the most important to you *in determining what you want to do with your life*, and #9 in Final rank is the least important—not necessarily in the overall scheme of things, *but certainly in determining what you want to do with your life.*

Look at your top three Values. Now you know which Value you most want your life to serve, which outcome you most want your life to produce; plus which one is next and which one is third.

You will need not just one of those Values, but the top three. Mark what they are. Those three top Values, together, determine what will be a Life that has meaning and purpose, for you.

The three of them, put together in order of priority, should be entered now on your Flower diagram, on the Values petal (pages 160–61). Put the top three in your own words, whatever makes the most sense to you.

And if you want to burrow under the headings of your top Three, if you have a computer, go to the Internet, choose a browser (like Google), and type into it all the key words that occur to you—on the same line. For example, "work, beauty, gardens"—or any series of words that point toward the values or issues you would like your life and your talents, skills, and experience, to serve.

P.S. If you have a computer and you would prefer to use an interactive electronic version of this prioritizing grid, you can go to the website of a former student of mine, Beverly Ryle, now a noted career counselor and author, in her own right (www.GroundOfYourOwnChoosing.com). She has a nice electronic version of my grid.

PRIORITIZING GRID FOR 10 ITEMS OR LESS

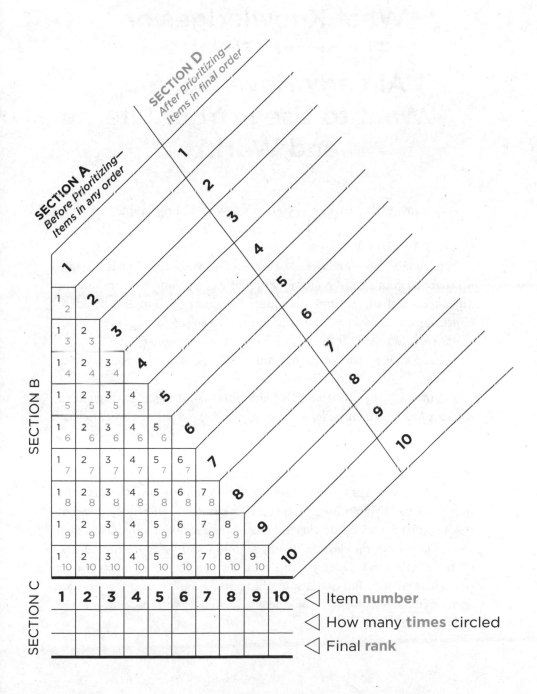

◁ Item **number**

◁ How many **times** circled

◁ Final **rank**

STEP 2

What Knowledges or Expertise That You Already Have Do You Want to Use in Your Life and Work?

As we saw earlier (page 19), you have a whole filing cabinet up there in your head. The number of things that you know *something* about, by this time in your life, is awesome.

You, in fact, have doubtless lost track of all you know. What files are up there in your head? What do you know something, or a lot, about, anyway? Football? Skiing? Antiques? Gardening? Computers? Cars? Knitting? Scrapbooking? Information technology? Management practices? How to raise children? Design? Career counseling?

Let's do an inventory of all that you know, and then pick your favorite subjects.

In order for you to do this, it is helpful to fill out the following chart; *you may first copy it onto a larger piece of paper, if you wish, in order to have more room to write.*

Please note that this chart is asking you what subjects you know *anything* about, not whether you *like* the subject or not. (*Later*, you will ask yourself which of these you like or even *love*.) For now, the task facing you is merely *inventory*. That is a task similar to inventorying what clothes you've got in your closet, before you decide which ones to give away. Only, here, *the closet is your head*, and you're inventorying all the stuff that's in *there*. Don't try to evaluate your degree of mastery of a particular subject. Put down something you've only read a few articles about (*if it interests you*) side by side with a subject you studied for three semesters in school.

Throwaway comes later *(though, obviously, if there's a subject you hate so much you can barely stand to write it down, then . . . don't . . . write . . . it . . . down).*

When filling this chart out, do not forget to list those things you've learned—no matter how—about *Organizations (including volunteer organizations)*, and what it takes to make them work.

It is not necessary that you should have ever taken a course in management or business. Examples of things you may know something about (and should list here) are: *accounting or bookkeeping; administration; applications; credit collection of overdue bills; customer relations and service; data analysis, distribution; fiscal analysis, controls, reductions; government contracts; group dynamics or work with groups in general; hiring, human resources, or manpower; international business; management; marketing, sales; merchandising; packaging; performance specifications; planning; policy development; problem solving or other types of troubleshooting with operations or management systems; production; public speaking/ addressing people; R & D program management; recruiting; show or conference planning, organization, and management; systems analysis; travel or travel planning, especially international travel; etc.*

THE SUBJECTS CHART

Subjects I Know Something About

Which column you decide to put a subject in, below, doesn't matter at all. The columns are only a series of pegs, to hang your memories on. Which peg is of no concern. Jot down a subject anywhere you like.

Column 1	Column 2	Column 3	Column 4	Column 5
Studied in High School or College or Graduate School	Learned on the Job	Learned from Conferences, Workshops, Training, Seminars	Learned at Home: Reading, TV, Tape Programs, Study Courses	Learned in My Leisure Time: Volunteer Work, Hobbies, etc.
Examples: Spanish, Typing, Accounting, Computer Literacy, Psychology, Geography	*Examples: Publishing, Computer Graphics, How an Organization Works, How to Operate Various Machines*	*Examples: Welfare Rules, Job-Hunting, Painting, How to Use the Internet*	*Examples: Art Appreciation, History, Speed Reading, a Language*	*Examples: Landscaping, How to Sew, Antiques, Camping, Stamps*

Chapter Eleven

When you're done, you may want to let this Chart just sit around for a few days, to see if any other items occur to you. But when you're sure you've listed all you want to, then draw the matrix below on a large sheet of paper, and sort the knowledges on the Chart into these four boxes:

YOUR FAVORITE SUBJECTS MATRIX

	HIGH	
E X P E R T I S E	**3.** Subjects for Which You Have Little Enthusiasm but in Which You Have Lots of Expertise	**1.** Subjects for Which You Have Lots of Enthusiasm and in Which You Have Lots of Expertise BINGO!
	Subjects for Which You Have Little Enthusiasm and in Which you Have Little Expertise	**2.** Subjects for Which You Have Lots of Enthusiasm but in Which You Have Little Expertise
	LOW ENTHUSIASM HIGH	

Then, choose your three favorite knowledges, from any of these boxes. You want to pay particular attention to the knowledges you put in box 1 above. And next, those you put in box 2. Last of all, those in box 3.

Let us say it turns out your three favorite knowledges are gardening and carpentry in box 1, and your knowledge of psychiatry in box 2.

What you want to be able to do is to use all three expertises, not just one of them—if you possibly can.

So, put your three favorite knowledges on a series of overlapping circles, as follows:

Now, to figure out how to combine these three, imagine that each circle is a person; that is, in this case, Psychiatrist, Carpenter, and Gardener.

You ask yourself which person took the longest to get trained in their specialty. The answer, here, is the psychiatrist. The reason you ask yourself this question, is that the person with the longest training is most likely to have the largest overview of things. So, you go to see a psychiatrist, either at a private clinic or at a university or hospital. You ask for fifteen minutes of his or her time, and pay them if necessary.

Then you ask the psychiatrist if he or she knows how to combine psychiatry with *one*—just one, initially—of your other two favorite knowledges. Let's say you choose gardening, here. "Doctor, do you know anyone who combines a knowledge of psychiatry with a knowledge of gardening or plants?"

Since I'm talking about a true story here, I can tell you what the psychiatrist said: "Yes, in working with catatonic patients, we often give them a plant to take care of, so they know there is something that is depending on them for its future, and its survival."

"And how would I also employ a knowledge of carpentry?"

"Well, in building the planters, wouldn't you?"

(Parenthetically, healers also use pets as they do plants. See www .sniksnak.com/therapy.html.)

This is the way you explore how to combine your three favorite knowledges, all at once, no matter what those three may be. The Internet can also be useful in this regard.

Put these three on your Knowledges petal of the Flower, on pages 160–61.

STEP 3

What Transferable Skills Do You Most Enjoy Using?

You are looking here for what you may think of as the basic building-blocks of your work. So, if you're going to identify your dream job, and/or attempt a thorough career-change, you should begin by first of all identifying your functional, transferable skills. And while you may think you know what your best and favorite skills are, in most cases your self-knowledge could probably use a little work.

A weekend should do it! In a weekend, you can inventory your *past* sufficiently so that you have a good picture of the *kind* of work you would love to be doing *in the future. (You can, of course, stretch the inventory over a number of weeks, maybe doing an hour or two one night a week, if you prefer. It's up to you as to how fast you do it.)*

A Crash Course on "Transferable Skills"

Many people just "freeze" when they hear the word "skills."

It begins with high school job-hunters: "I haven't really got any skills," they say.

It continues with college students: "I've spent four years in college. I haven't had time to pick up any skills."

And it lasts through the middle years, especially when a person is thinking of changing his or her career: "I'll have to go back to college, and get retrained, because otherwise I won't have any skills in my new field." Or: "Well, if I claim any skills, I'll start at a very entry kind of level."

All of this fright about the word "skills" is very common, and stems from a total misunderstanding of what the word means. A misunderstanding that is shared, we might add, by altogether too many employers, or human resources departments, and other so-called "vocational experts."

By understanding the word, you will automatically put yourself way ahead of most job-hunters. And, especially if you are weighing a change of career, you can save yourself much waste of time on the adult folly called "I must go back to school." I've said it before, and I'll say it again: *maybe* you need some further schooling, but very often it is possible to make a dramatic career-change without any retraining. It all depends. And you won't really *know* whether or not you need further schooling, until you have finished all the exercises in this section of the book.

All right, then, if transferable skills are the heart of your vision and your destiny, let's see just exactly what transferable skills *are*.

Here are the most important truths you need to keep in mind about transferable, functional skills:

1 Your transferable *(functional)* skills are the most basic unit—the atoms—of whatever career you may choose.

You can see this from this diagram:

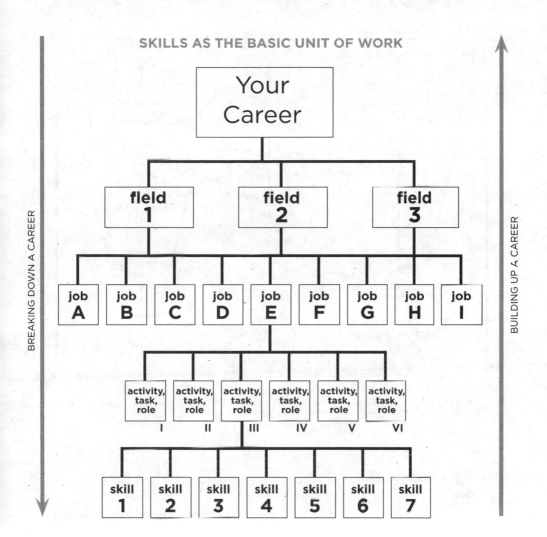

SKILLS AS THE BASIC UNIT OF WORK

Now, let's look at the very bottom level of the above diagram. It says "skill." That means "transferable skills." Here is a famous diagram of them, invented by the late Sidney A. Fine (reprinted by his permission).

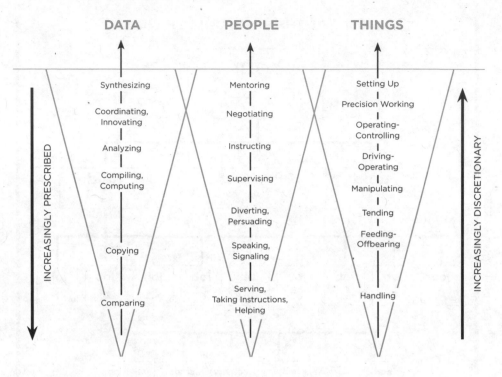

	DATA	PEOPLE	THINGS

DATA

Synthesizing

Coordinating, Innovating

Analyzing

Compiling, Computing

Copying

Comparing

PEOPLE

Mentoring

Negotiating

Instructing

Supervising

Diverting, Persuading

Speaking, Signaling

Serving, Taking Instructions, Helping

THINGS

Setting Up

Precision Working

Operating-Controlling

Driving-Operating

Manipulating

Tending

Feeding-Offbearing

Handling

INCREASINGLY PRESCRIBED

INCREASINGLY DISCRETIONARY

Chart based on information from the *Dictionary of Occupational Titles, Appendix B: Explanation of Data, People, and Things*, 1971, www.occupationalinfo.org/appendxb_1.html.

2 You should always claim the *highest* skills you legitimately can, on the basis of your past performance.

As we see in the functional/transferable skills diagram above, your transferable skills break down into three *families,* according to whether you use them with **Data/Information, People,** or **Things.** And again, as this diagram makes clear, within each family there are *simple* skills, and there are higher, or *more complex* skills, so that these all can be diagrammed as inverted pyramids, with the simpler skills at the bottom, and the more complex ones in order above it, as shown above.

Incidentally, as a general rule—to which there are exceptions—each *higher* skill requires you to be able also to do all those skills listed below it. So of course you can claim *those,* as well. But you want to especially claim the highest skill you legitimately can, on each pyramid, based on what you have already proven you can do, in the past.

3 The *higher* your transferable skills, the more freedom you will have on the job.

Simpler skills can be, and usually are, heavily *prescribed* (by the employer), so if you claim *only* the simpler skills, you will have to *"fit in"*—following the instructions of your supervisor, and doing exactly what you are told to do. The *higher* the skills you can legitimately claim, the more you will be given discretion to carve out the job the way you want to—so that it truly fits *you*.

4 The higher your transferable skills, the less competition you will face for whatever job you are seeking, because jobs that use such skills will rarely be advertised through normal channels.

Not for you the way of classified ads, resumes, and agencies, that we spoke of in earlier chapters. No, if you can legitimately claim higher skills, then to find such jobs you *must* follow the step-by-step process I am describing here.

The essence of this approach to job-hunting or career-change is that once you have identified your favorite transferable skills, and your favorite Fields of Fascination, you may then approach *any organization that interests you, whether they have a known vacancy or not.* Naturally, whatever places you visit—and particularly those that have not advertised any vacancy—you will find far fewer job-hunters that you have to compete with.

In fact, if the employers you visit happen to like you well enough, they may be willing to create for you a job that does not presently exist. *In which case, you will be competing with no one, since you will be the sole applicant for that newly created job.* While this doesn't happen all the time, it is astounding to me how many times it *does* happen. *The reason* it does is that the employers often have been *thinking* about creating a new job within their organization, for quite some time—but with this and that, they just have never gotten around to *doing* it. Until you walked in.

Then they decided they didn't want to let you get away, since *good employees are as hard to find as are good employers.* And they suddenly remember that job they have been thinking about creating for many weeks or months, now. So they dust off their *intention*, create the job on the spot, and offer it to you! And if that new job is not only what *they* need, but is exactly what *you* were looking for, then you have a dream job. Match-match. Win-win.

From our country's perspective, it is also interesting to note this: by this job-hunting initiative of yours, you have helped accelerate the creation of more jobs in your country, which is so much on everybody's mind here in the new millennium. How nice to help your country, as well as yourself!

5 Don't confuse transferable skills with traits.

Functional/transferable skills are often confused with **traits, temperaments,** or **type.**[2] People think transferable skills are such things as: *has lots of energy, gives attention to details, gets along well with people, shows determination, works well under pressure, is sympathetic, intuitive, persistent, dynamic, dependable,* etc. Despite popular misconceptions, these are **not** functional/transferable skills, but traits, or the *style* with which you do your transferable skills. For example, take *"gives attention to details."* If one of your *transferable skills* is *"conducting research"* then *"gives attention to details"* describes the manner or style with which you do the transferable skill called *conducting research.* If you want to know what your traits are, popular tests such as the *Myers-Briggs Type Indicator* measure that sort of thing.

If you have access to the Internet, there are clues, at least, about your traits or "type":

> **Working Out Your Myers-Briggs Type**
>
> www.teamtechnology.co.uk/mb-intro/mb-intro.htm
>
> An informative article about the Myers-Briggs

---

2. The Myers-Briggs Type Indicator, or "MBTI®," measures what is called *psychological type.* For further reading about this, see:

Paul D. Tieger and Barbara Barron-Tieger, *Do What You Are: Discover the Perfect Career for You Through the Secrets of Personality Type* (Revised and Updated). Fourth Edition. 2007. Little, Brown & Company, Inc. For those who cannot obtain the MBTI®, this book includes a method for readers to identify their personality types. This is one of the most popular career books in the world. It's easy to see why. Many have found great help from the concept of personality type, and the Tiegers are masters in explaining this approach to career-choice. Highly recommended.

Donna Dunning, *What's Your Type of Career? Unlock the Secrets of Your Personality to Find Your Perfect Career Path.* 2001. Davies-Black Publishing. This is a dynamite book on personality type. Donna Dunning's knowledge of "Type" is encyclopedic!

David Keirsey and Marilyn Bates, *Please Understand Me: Character & Temperament Types.* 1978. Includes the Keirsey Temperament Sorter—again, for those who cannot obtain the MBTI® (Myers-Briggs Type Indicator)—registered trademark of Consulting Psychologists Press.

The 16 Personality Types

www.16types.com/Request.jsp?hView=DynamicPage&Content
=The16Types

A helpful site about Myers types

What Is Your Myers-Briggs Personality Type?

www.personalitypathways.com/type_inventory.html

www.personalitypathways.com

Another article about personality types; also, there's a Myers-Briggs
Applications page, with links to test resources

Myers-Briggs Foundation home page

www.myersbriggs.org

The official website of the Foundation; lots of testing resources

Human Mètrics Test (Jung Typology)

www.humanmetrics.com/cgi-win/JTypes2.asp

Free test, loosely based on the Myers-Briggs

Myers-Briggs Type Indicator Online

www.discoveryourpersonality.com/testlist.html

On this site you can find the official Myers-Briggs test, $60

The Keirsey Temperament Sorter

www.keirsey.com

Free test, similar to the Myers-Briggs

"I Wouldn't Recognize My Skills If They Came Up and Shook Hands with Me"

Now that you know what transferable skills technically *are*, the problem that awaits you now, is figuring out your own. If you are one of the few lucky people who already know what your transferable skills are, blessed are you. Write them down, and put them in the order of preference, for you, on "That One Piece of Paper" (see page 159).

If, however, you don't know what your skills are (and 95 percent of all workers *don't*), then you will need some help. Fortunately there is an exercise to help.

It involves the following steps:

1. Write a Story (The First of Seven)

Yes, I know, I know. You can't do this exercise because you don't like to write. *Writers are a very rare breed.* That's what thousands of job-hunters have told me, over the years. And for years I kind of believed them—until "blogging" came along. ("Blog" is shorthand, of course, for "web log.") Let's face it: we human beings are "a writing people," and we only need a topic we have a real passion for, or interest in, for the writing genie to spring forth from within each of us, pen or keyboard in hand.

So, call the *Seven Stories* you're about to write your personal *offline blog*, if you prefer. But start writing. Please.

Here is a specific example:

> *"A number of years ago, I wanted to be able to take a summer trip with my wife and four children. I had a very limited budget, and could not afford to put my family up in motels. I decided to rig our station wagon as a camper.*
>
> *"First I went to the library to get some books on campers. I read those books. Next I designed a plan of what I had to build, so that I could outfit the inside of the station wagon, as well as topside. Then I went and purchased the necessary wood. On weekends, over a period of six weeks, I first constructed, in my driveway, the shell for the 'second story' on my station wagon. Then I cut doors, windows, and placed a six-drawer bureau within that shell. I mounted it on top of the wagon, and pinioned it in place by driving two-by-fours under the station wagon's rack on top. I then outfitted the inside of the station wagon, back in the wheel-well, with a table and a bench on either side, that I made.*
>
> *"The result was a complete homemade camper, which I put together when we were about to start our trip, and then disassembled after we got back home. When we went on our summer*

trip, we were able to be on the road for four weeks, yet stayed within our budget, since we didn't have to stay at motels.

"*I estimate I saved $1,900 on motel bills, during that summer's vacation.*"

Ideally, each story you write should have the following parts, as illustrated above:

I.

Your goal: what you wanted to accomplish: "*I wanted to be able to take a summer trip with my wife and four children.*"

II.

Some kind of hurdle, obstacle, or constraint that you faced (self-imposed or otherwise): "*I had a very limited budget, and could not afford to put my family up in motels.*"

III.

A description of what you did, step by step (how you set about to ultimately achieve your goal, above, in spite of this hurdle or constraint): *"I decided to rig our station wagon as a camper. First I went to the library to get some books on campers. I read those books. Next I designed a plan of what I had to build, so that I could outfit the inside of the station wagon, as well as topside. Then I went and purchased the necessary wood. On weekends, over a period of six weeks, I . . ." etc., etc.*

IV.

A description of the outcome or result: *"When we went on our summer trip, we were able to be on the road for four weeks, yet stayed within our budget, since we didn't have to stay at motels."*

V.

Any measurable/quantifiable statement of that outcome, that you can think of: *"I estimate I saved $1,900 on motel bills, during that summer's vacation."*

Now write *your* story, using the next page as a guide.

Don't pick a story where you achieved something *big*. At least to begin with, write a story about a time when you had fun!

Do not try to be too brief. This isn't Twitter.

If you absolutely can't think of any experiences you've had where you enjoyed yourself, and accomplished something, then try this: describe the seven most enjoyable jobs that you've had; or seven roles you've had so far in your life, such as: wife, mother, cook, homemaker, volunteer in the community, citizen, dressmaker, student, etc. Tell us something you did or accomplished, in each role.

MY LIFE STORIES

Column 1	Column 2	Column 3	Column 4	Column 5
Your Goal: What You Wanted to Accomplish	Some Kind of Obstacle (or limit, hurdle, or restraint you had to overcome before it could be accomplished)	What You Did Step by Step (It may help if you pretend you are telling this story to a whining 4-year-old child, who keeps asking, after each of your sentences, "An' then whadja do? An' then whadja do?")	Description of the Result (what you accomplished)	Description of the Result (what you accomplished)

SAMPLE	
"The Halloween Experience. I won a prize on Halloween for dressing up as a horse."	← **THIS WON'T DO**

THIS WILL DO →

SAMPLE

"My Halloween Experience When I Was Seven Years Old. Details: When I was seven, I decided I wanted to go out on Halloween dressed as a horse. I wanted to be the front end of the horse, and I talked a friend of mine into being the back end of the horse. But, at the last moment he backed out, and I was faced with the prospect of not being able to go out on Halloween. At this point, I decided to figure out some way of getting dressed up as the whole horse, myself. I took a fruit basket, and tied some string to both sides of the basket's rim, so that I could tie the basket around my rear end. This filled me out enough so that the costume fit me, by myself. I then fixed some strong thread to the tail so that I could make it wag by moving my hands. When Halloween came I not only went out and had a ball, but I won a prize as well."

2. Analyze your story, to see what transferable skills you used.

On the facing page, write the title of your first story *above* the number 1. Then work your way down the column *below* that number 1, asking yourself in each case: "Did I use this skill in *this story?*"

If the answer is "Yes," color the little square in, with a red pen or whatever you choose.

Example: "Did I use my hands, assembling something, in *this* story?" If so, color in the square under Column 1, and opposite A, 1. If not, leave it blank.

Next: "Did I use my hands constructing something, in *this* story?" If so, color in the square under Column 1, and opposite A, 2. If not, leave it blank.

Work your way through the entire Transferable Skills Inventory that way, with your first story.

Sample: The Halloween Experience

TRANSFERABLE
SKILLS
INVENTORY

1	2	3	4	5	6	7	Name of Skill	Example of a situation where that skill is used
							A. Using My Hands	
							1. assembling	as with kits, etc.
▨							2. constructing	as with carpentry, etc.
							3. or building	
							4. operating tools	as with drills, mixers, etc.
							5. or machinery	as with sewing machines, etc.
							6. or equipment	as with trucks, station wagons, etc.
▨							7. showing manual or finger dexterity	as with throwing, sewing, etc.
							8. handling with precision and/or speed	as with an assembly line, etc.
							9. fixing or repairing	as with autos or mending, etc.
							10. other	
							B. Using My Body	
							11. muscular coordination	as in skiing, gymnastics, etc.
▨							12. being physically active	as in exercising, hiking, etc.
							13. doing outdoor activities	as in camping, etc.
							14. other	
							C. Using Words	
							15. reading	as with books; with understanding
							16. copying	as with manuscripts; skillfully
							17. writing or communicating	as with letters; interestingly
							18. talking or speaking	as on the telephone; interestingly
							19. teaching, training	as in front of groups; with animation
							20. editing	as in improving a child's sentences in an essay, etc.
							21. memory for words	as in remembering people's names, book titles, etc.
							22. other	

continued

The Parachute Workbook (Updated 2010)   189

This side is blank so that when you have completed the grid, you may cut out these four pages and place them side by side to see the total pattern.

Sample Halloween	1	2	3	4	5	6	7	Name of Skill	Example of a situation where that skill is used
								D. Using My Senses (Eyes, Ears, Nose, Taste, or Touch)	
▓								23. observing, surveying	as in watching something with the eyes, etc.
								24. examining or inspecting	as in looking at a child's bumps, etc.
▨								25. diagnosing, determining	as in deciding if food is cooked yet
								26. showing attention to detail	as in shop, in sewing, etc.
								27. other	
								E. Using Numbers	
								28. taking inventory	as in the pantry, shop, etc.
								29. counting	as in a classroom, bureau drawers
								30. calculating, computing	as in a checkbook, arithmetic
								31. keeping financial records, bookkeeping	as with a budget, etc.
								32. managing money	as in a checking account, bank, store, etc.
								33. developing a budget	as for a family, etc.
								34. number memory	as with telephone numbers, etc.
								35. rapid manipulation of numbers	as with doing arithmetic in the head
								36. other	
								F. Using Intuition	
▨								37. showing foresight	as in planning ahead, predicting consequences, etc.
▨								38. quickly sizing up a person or situation accurately	as in everything, rather than just one or two details about them, etc.
								39. having insight	as to why people act the way they do, etc.
								40. acting on gut reactions	as in making decisions, deciding to trust someone, etc.
▓								41. ability to visualize third-dimension	as in drawings, models, blueprints, memory for faces, etc.
								42. other	
								G. Using Analytical Thinking or Logic	
▨								43. researching, information gathering	as in finding out where a particular street is in a strange city
								44. analyzing, dissecting	as with the ingredients in a recipe, material, etc.
					.			45. organizing, classifying	as with laundry, etc.
▓								46. problem solving	as with figuring out how to get to a place, etc.
								47. separating important from unimportant	as with complaints, or cleaning the attic, etc.
								48. diagnosing	as in cause-and-effect relations, tracing problems to their sources
								49. systematizing, putting things in order	as in laying out tools or utensils in the order you will be using them

This side is blank so that when you have completed the grid, you may cut out these four pages and place them side by side to see the total pattern.

Sample Halloween	1	2	3	4	5	6	7	Name of Skill	Example of a situation where that skill is used
								50. comparing, perceiving similarities	as with different brands in the supermarket, etc.
								51. testing, screening	as with cooking, deciding what to wear, etc.
▨								52. reviewing, evaluating	as in looking at something you made, to see how you could have made it better, faster, etc.
								53. other	
								H. Using Originality or Creativity	
▨								54. imaginative, imagining	as in figuring out new ways to do things, or making up stories, etc.
▨								55. inventing, creating	as with processes, products, figures, words, etc.
▨								56. designing, developing	as with new recipes, new gadgets
▨								57. improvising, experiments	as in camping, when you've left some of the equipment home, etc.
								58. adapting, improving	as with something that doesn't work quite right, etc.
								59. other	
								I. Using Helpfulness	
								60. helping, being of service	as when someone is in need, etc.
								61. showing sensitivity to others' feelings	as in a heated discussion, argument
								62. listening	
								63. developing rapport	as with someone who is initially a stranger, etc.
								64. conveying warmth, caring	as with someone who is upset, ill
								65. understanding	as when someone tells how they feel, etc.
								66. drawing out people	as when someone is reluctant to talk, share
								67. offering support	as when someone is facing a difficulty alone, etc.
								68. demonstrating empathy	as in weeping with those who weep
								69. representing others' wishes accurately	as when one parent tells the other what a child of theirs wants, etc.
								70. motivating	as in getting people past hangups, and into action, etc.
								71. sharing credit, appreciation	as when working in teams, etc.
								72. raising others' self-esteem	as when you make someone feel better, less guilty, etc.
								73. healing, curing	as with physical, emotional, and spiritual ailments, etc.
								74. counseling, guiding	as when someone doesn't know what to do, etc.
								75. other	

continued

This side is blank so that when you have completed the grid, you may cut out these four pages and place them side by side to see the total pattern.

Sample Halloween	1	2	3	4	5	6	7	Name of Skill	Example of a situation where that skill is used
								J. Using Artistic Abilities	
								76. composing music	
								77. playing (a) musical instrument(s), singing	
								78. fashioning or shaping things, materials	as in handicrafts, sculpturing, etc.
								79. dealing creatively with symbols or images	as in stained glass, jewelry, etc.
▨								80. dealing creatively with spaces, shapes, or faces	as in photography, art, architectural design, etc.
								81. dealing creatively with colors	as in painting, decorating, making clothes, etc.
								82. conveying feelings and thoughts through body, face, and/or voice tone	as in acting, public speaking, teaching, dancing, etc.
								83. conveying feelings and thoughts through drawing, paintings, etc.	as in art, etc.
								84. using words on a very high level	as in poetry, playwriting, novels
								85. other	
								K. Using Leadership, Being Up-front	
▨								86. beginning new tasks, ideas, projects	as in starting a group, initiating a clothing drive, etc.
								87. taking first move in relationships	as with stranger on bus, plane, train, etc.
								88. organizing a game at a picnic, etc.	as with a Scout troop, a team,
								89. leading, directing others	as with a field trip, cheerleading
								90. promoting change	as in a family, community, organization, etc.
▨								91. making decisions	as in places where decisions affect others, etc.
▨								92. taking risks	as in sticking up for someone in a fight, etc.
▨								93. getting up before a group, performing	as in demonstrating a product, lecturing, making people laugh, entertaining, public speaking
▨								94. selling, promoting, negotiating, persuading	as with a product, idea, materials, in a garage sale, argument, recruiting, changing someone's mind
								95. other	
								L. Using Follow-Through	
▨								96. using what others have developed	as in working with a kit, etc.
								97. following through on plans, instructions	as in picking up children on schedule
								98. attending to details	as with embroidering a design on a shirt, etc.
								99. classifying, recording, filing, retrieving	as with data, materials, letters, ideas, information, etc.
								100. other	

This side is blank so that when you have completed the grid, you may cut out these four pages and place them side by side to see the total pattern.

Chapter Eleven

3. Write Six Other Stories, and Analyze Them for Transferable Skills

Voilà! You are done with Story #1. However, "one swallow doth not a summer make," so the fact that you used certain skills in this first story doesn't tell you much. What you are looking for is **patterns**—transferable skills that keep reappearing in story after story. They keep reappearing because they are your favorites (assuming you chose stories where you were *really* enjoying yourself).

So, now, write Story #2, from any period in your life, analyze it using the keys, etc., etc. And keep this process up, until you have written, and analyzed, seven stories.

4. Patterns and Priorities

When you've finished this whole Inventory, for all seven of your accomplishments/achievements/jobs/roles or whatever, you want to look for PATTERNS and PRIORITIES.

a) For Patterns, because it isn't a matter of whether you used a skill once only, but rather whether you used it again and again. "Once" proves nothing; "again and again" is very convincing.

"RUN, SPOT, RUN."

b) For Priorities (that is, Which Skills Are Most Important to You?), because the job you eventually choose may not be able to use all of your skills. You need to know *what you are willing to trade off, and what you are not.* This requires that you know which skills, or family of skills, are most important to you.

Double-Color, Prioritize

When you are done filling out the Transferable Skills Inventory, it will help you greatly in deciding Patterns and Priorities if you cut or tear out the preceding four pages of the Skills Inventory and spread them all out on a table or on the floor. Now you have a complete "aerial view" of all the skills you have.

At this point I suggest you use a second color (like red) and look back over all the "squares" you colored in. Sure, you *have* the skill. But now you want to ask yourself: do I still enjoy this skill/these skills today? If the answer is "Yes," DOUBLE-COLOR that particular square. And DOUBLE-UNDERLINE, in red, the particular skills you *enjoy,* in each corresponding Skill Paragraph.

When you are all done, look at the total "aerial view" of your skills, to see which family of skills has the most DOUBLE-COLOR (say, red); put it up at the top of the table or floor layout. Which family of skills has the next most DOUBLE-COLOR? Put it next. Thus, you will quickly see which skills are most important to you.

Choose the top ten—the ten that are your absolute favorites—and prioritize them, using the grid on the next page; or if you prefer, the electronic version described on page 170.

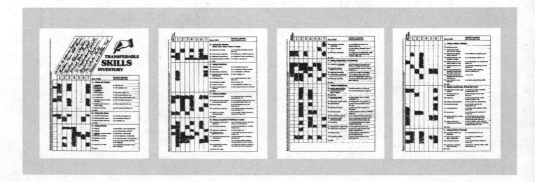

Chapter Eleven

PRIORITIZING GRID FOR 10 ITEMS OR LESS

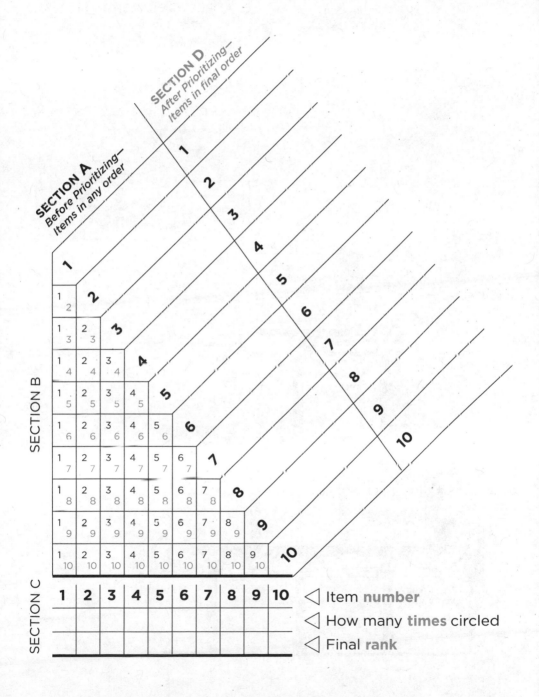

SECTION D
After Prioritizing—
Items in final order

SECTION A
Before Prioritizing—
Items in any order

SECTION B

SECTION C

◁ Item **number**

◁ How many **times** circled

◁ Final **rank**

Then list the top six or ten, in order of priority, on the diagram below.

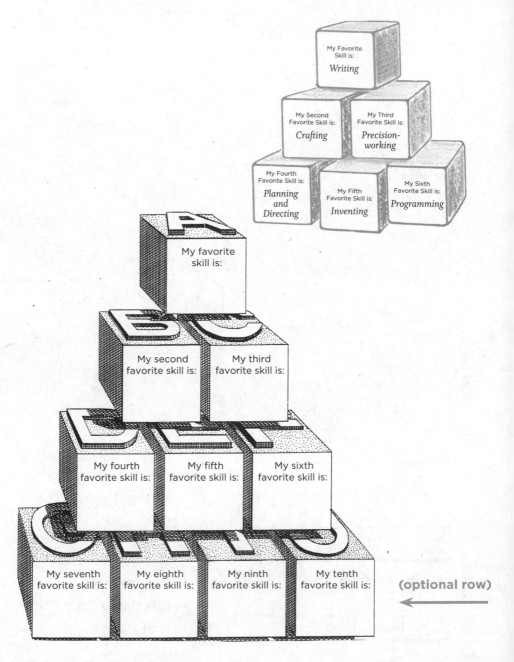

EXAMPLE (SIX FAVORITE SKILLS)

My Favorite Skill is:
Writing

My Second Favorite Skill is:
Crafting

My Third Favorite Skill is:
Precision-working

My Fourth Favorite Skill is:
Planning and Directing

My Fifth Favorite Skill is:
Inventing

My Sixth Favorite Skill is:
Programming

My favorite skill is:

My second favorite skill is:

My third favorite skill is:

My fourth favorite skill is:

My fifth favorite skill is:

My sixth favorite skill is:

My seventh favorite skill is:

My eighth favorite skill is:

My ninth favorite skill is:

My tenth favorite skill is:

(optional row)

5. "Flesh Out" Your Favorite Transferable Skills with Your Traits

We discussed traits earlier. In general, traits describe:

How you deal with time, and promptness.

How you deal with people and emotions.

How you deal with authority, and being told what to do at your job.

How you deal with supervision, and being told how to do your job.

How you deal with impulse vs. self-discipline, within yourself.

How you deal with initiative vs. response, within yourself.

How you deal with crises or problems.

A CHECKLIST OF MY STRONGEST TRAITS

I am very . . .

- ❏ Accurate
- ❏ Achievement-oriented
- ❏ Adaptable
- ❏ Adept
- ❏ Adept at having fun
- ❏ Adventuresome
- ❏ Alert
- ❏ Appreciative
- ❏ Assertive
- ❏ Astute
- ❏ Authoritative
- ❏ Calm
- ❏ Cautious
- ❏ Charismatic
- ❏ Competent
- ❏ Consistent
- ❏ Contagious in my enthusiasm
- ❏ Cooperative
- ❏ Courageous
- ❏ Creative
- ❏ Decisive
- ❏ Deliberate
- ❏ Dependable/have dependability
- ❏ Diligent
- ❏ Diplomatic

- ❏ Discreet
- ❏ Driving
- ❏ Dynamic
- ❏ Extremely economical
- ❏ Effective
- ❏ Energetic
- ❏ Enthusiastic
- ❏ Exceptional
- ❏ Exhaustive
- ❏ Experienced
- ❏ Expert
- ❏ Firm
- ❏ Flexible
- ❏ Humanly oriented
- ❏ Impulsive
- ❏ Independent
- ❏ Innovative
- ❏ Knowledgeable
- ❏ Loyal
- ❏ Methodical
- ❏ Objective
- ❏ Open-minded
- ❏ Outgoing
- ❏ Outstanding
- ❏ Patient
- ❏ Penetrating
- ❏ Perceptive
- ❏ Persevering

- ❏ Persistent
- ❏ Pioneering
- ❏ Practical
- ❏ Professional
- ❏ Protective
- ❏ Punctual
- ❏ Quick/work quickly
- ❏ Rational
- ❏ Realistic
- ❏ Reliable
- ❏ Resourceful
- ❏ Responsible
- ❏ Responsive
- ❏ Safeguarding
- ❏ Self-motivated
- ❏ Self-reliant
- ❏ Sensitive
- ❏ Sophisticated, very sophisticated
- ❏ Strong
- ❏ Supportive
- ❏ Tactful
- ❏ Thorough
- ❏ Unique
- ❏ Unusual
- ❏ Versatile
- ❏ Vigorous

You need to flesh out your skill-description for each of your six or more favorite skills so that you are able to describe each of your talents or skills with more than just a one-word verb or gerund, like organizing.

Let's take organizing as our example. You tell us proudly: "I'm good at organizing." That's a fine start at defining your skills, but unfortunately it doesn't yet tell us much. Organizing WHAT? People, as at a party? Nuts and bolts, as on a workbench? Or lots of information, as on a computer? These are three entirely different skills. The one word *organizing* doesn't tell us which one is yours.

So, please flesh out each of your favorite transferable skills with an object—some kind of Data/Information, or some kind of People, or some kind of Thing, and then add an adverb or adjective, too.

Why adjectives? Well, "I'm good at organizing information painstakingly and logically" and "I'm good at organizing information in a flash, by intuition," are two entirely different skills. The difference between them is spelled out not in the verb, nor in the object, but in the adjectival or adverbial phrase there at the end. So, expand each definition of your six or more favorite skills, in the fashion I have just described.

> When you are face-to-face with a person-who-has-the-power-to-hire-you, you want to be able to explain what makes you different from nineteen other people who can basically do the same thing that you can do. It is often the adjective or adverb that will save your life, during that explanation.

A Picture Is Worth a Thousand Words

When you have your top favorite skills, and *fleshed them out*, it is time to put them on the central petal of the Flower Diagram. Copy this diagram (from here or pages 160–61) on a larger piece of paper (or cardboard) if you need to.

The Flower

"THAT ONE PIECE OF PAPER"

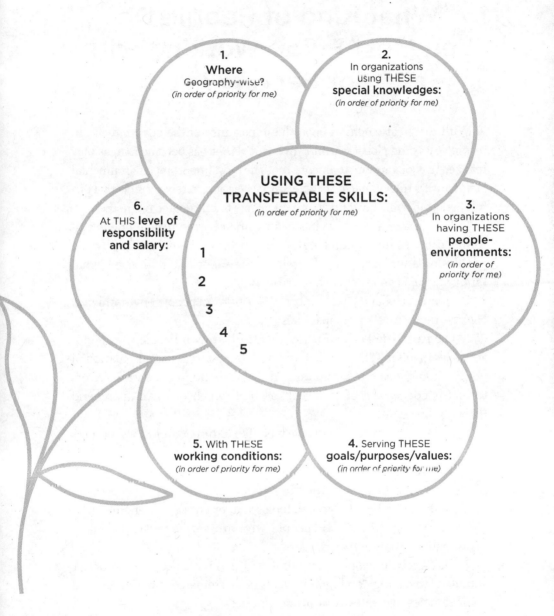

STEP 4

What Kind of People Do You Most Enjoy Working with or Serving?

With the great emphasis upon the importance of the environment, in recent years, and global warming in particular, it has become increasingly realized that jobs are environments, too. The most important environmental factor always turns out to be people, since every job, except possibly that of a full-fledged hermit, surrounds us with people to one degree or another.

Indeed, many a good job has been ruined by the people one is surrounded by. Many a mundane job has been made delightful, by the people one is surrounded by. Therefore, it is important to think out what kinds of people you want to be surrounded by.

Dr. John L. Holland offers the best description of people-environments. He says there are six principal ones:

1. The **Realistic** People-Environment: filled with people who prefer activities involving "the explicit, ordered, or systematic manipulation of objects, tools, machines, and animals." "Realistic," incidentally, refers to Plato's conception of "the real" as that which one can apprehend through the senses.

I summarize this as: R = people who like nature, or athletics, or tools and machinery.

2. The **Investigative** People-Environment: filled with people who prefer activities involving "the observation and symbolic, systematic, creative investigation of physical, biological, or cultural phenomena."

I summarize this as: I = people who are very curious, liking to investigate or analyze things.

3. The **Artistic** People-Environment: filled with people who prefer activities involving "ambiguous, free, unsystematized activities and competencies to create art forms or products."

I summarize this as: A = people who are very artistic, imaginative, and innovative.

4. The **Social** People-Environment: filled with people who prefer activities involving "the manipulation of others to inform, train, develop, cure, or enlighten."

I summarize this as: S = people who are bent on trying to help, teach, or serve people.

5. The **Enterprising** People-Environment: filled with people who prefer activities involving "the manipulation of others to attain organizational or self-interest goals."

I summarize this as: E = people who like to start up projects or organizations, and/or influence or persuade people.

6. The **Conventional** People-Environment: filled with people who prefer activities involving "the explicit, ordered, systematic manipulation of data, such as keeping records, filing materials, reproducing materials, organizing written and numerical data according to a prescribed plan, operating business and data processing machines." "Conventional," incidentally, refers to the "values" that people in this environment usually hold—representing the broad mainstream of the culture.

I summarize this as: C = people who like detailed work, and like to complete tasks or projects.

According to John's theory and findings, everyone has three preferred people-environments, from among these six. The letters for your three preferred people-environments gives you what is called your "Holland Code."

For those who don't have Internet access (or are in a hurry), I invented (many years ago) a quick and easy way to get an *approximation* of your "Holland Code," as it's called. I call it "The Party Exercise." Here is how the exercise goes (do it!):

> There is, incidentally, a relationship between the people you like to be surrounded by *and* your skills *and* your values. See John Holland's book, *Making Vocational Choices* (3rd ed., 1997). You can procure it by going to the Psychological Assessment Resources, Inc., website at www3.parinc.com or calling 1-800-331-8378. *The book is $50.00 at this writing.* PAR also has John Holland's instrument, called *The Self-Directed Search* (or SDS, for short), for discovering what your Holland Code is. PAR lets you take the test online for a small fee ($9.95) at www.self-directed-search.com.

On the next page is an aerial view of a room in which a two-day (!) party is taking place. At this party, people with the same or similar interests have (for some reason) all gathered in the same corner of the room.

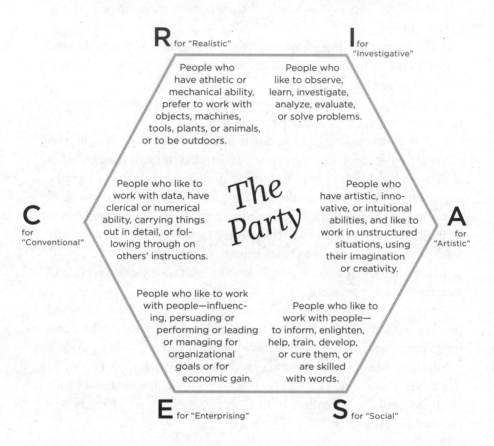

R for "Realistic"   **I** for "Investigative"

People who have athletic or mechanical ability, prefer to work with objects, machines, tools, plants, or animals, or to be outdoors.

People who like to observe, learn, investigate, analyze, evaluate, or solve problems.

The Party

C for "Conventional"   **A** for "Artistic"

People who like to work with data, have clerical or numerical ability, carrying things out in detail, or following through on others' instructions.

People who have artistic, innovative, or intuitional abilities, and like to work in unstructured situations, using their imagination or creativity.

People who like to work with people—influencing, persuading or performing or leading or managing for organizational goals or for economic gain.

People who like to work with people—to inform, enlighten, help, train, develop, or cure them, or are skilled with words.

E for "Enterprising"   **S** for "Social"

1) Which corner of the room would you instinctively be drawn to, as the group of people you would most enjoy being with for the longest time? (Leave aside any question of shyness, or whether you would have to talk to them.) Write the letter for that corner here: ☐

2) After fifteen minutes, everyone in the corner you have chosen leaves for another party crosstown, except you. Of the groups that still remain now, which corner or group would you be drawn to the most, as the people you would most enjoy being with for the longest time? Write the letter for that corner here: ☐

3) After fifteen minutes, this group too leaves for another party, except you. Of the corners, and groups, which remain now, which one would you most enjoy being with for the longest time? Write the letter for that corner here:

The three letters you just chose, in the three steps, are called your "Holland Code." Here is what you should now do:

1. Circle them on the People petal, on your Flower Diagram.

Put three circles around your favorite corner; two circles around your next favorite; and one circle around your third favorite.

2. Once the corners are circled, you may wish to write (for yourself and your eyes only) a temporary statement about your future job or career, using the descriptors on the Party Exercise, previous.

If your "Code" turned out to be IAS, for example, you might write: *"I would like a job or career best if I were surrounded by people who are very curious, and like to investigate or analyze things (I); who are also very innovative (A); and who are bent on trying to help or serve people (S)."*

3. See what clues the Internet has to offer.

Back on April 11 to 14, 1977, I conducted a workshop at the University of Missouri-Columbia, introducing "The Party Exercise." Subsequently, some unknown genius there did a rhapsody on this, calling it "The Career Interests Game." It is brilliant, and can be found on that University's Career Center's website, at: http://career.missouri.edu/students/explore/thecareerinterestsgame.php. You play the "Game" the same way, but afterward you can click on each letter of RIASEC (in color!) and find out what skills, interests, hobbies, and career possibilities go with each letter. For a complete *Holland Code*, of course, you need the *combination* of all three letters in your Code; but this at least offers a good beginning, taking one letter at a time. It is free.

Another Holland website is Lawrence Jones's *Career Key*, found at http://careerkey.org/asp/your_personality/take_test.asp. It costs $9.95 to take it, but offers suggestions as to related college majors, possible careers, etc., when you are done. Great test!

The final *Holland*-related site I want to mention is CareerPlanner .com's *Career Test*, invented by Michael T. Robinson, and found at http:// www.careerplanner.com. I recommend it; it will cost you $29.95 to take this test, so you must decide if it's worth the cost. You get a listing of thirty to one hundred careers related to the results of your test. As in all test results, treat these as starting points, only, for your subsequent research and informational interviewing. Please. Write the code on the Favorite People petal on the Flower Diagram, pages 160–61.

The Seven Steps to Finding a Life That Has Meaning and Purpose

What Are Your Favorite Working Conditions?

Plants that grow beautifully at sea level, often perish if they're taken ten thousand feet up the mountain. Likewise, we do our best work under certain conditions, but not under others. Thus, the question: "What are your favorite working conditions?" actually is a question about "Under what circumstances do you do your most effective work?"

The best way to approach this is by starting with the things you *disliked* about all your previous jobs, using the chart on the facing page to list these. You may copy this chart onto a larger piece of paper if you wish, before you begin filling it out. *Column A may begin with such factors as: "too noisy," "too much supervision," "no windows in my workplace," "having to be at work by 6 a.m.," etc.*

Of course, when you get to Column B, you must rank these factors that are in Column A, in their exact order of importance, to you.

As always, if you are baffled as to how to prioritize these factors in exact order, use the Prioritizing Grid on page 199.

The question to ask yourself, there, as you confront each "pair" is: "If I were offered two jobs, and in the first job I would be rid of this first distasteful working condition, but not the second, while in the second job, I would be rid of the second distasteful working condition, but not the first, which distasteful working condition would I choose to get rid of?"

Note that when you later come to Column C, the factors will already be prioritized. Your only job, there, is to think of the "positive" form of that factor that you hated so much (in Column B). (It is not always "the exact opposite." For example, *too much supervision*, listed in Column B, does not always mean *no supervision*, in Column C. It *might* mean: *a moderate amount of supervision, once or twice a day*.)

Once you've finished Column C, enter the top five factors from there on the Working Conditions petal of the Flower Diagram, pages 160–61.

DISTASTEFUL WORKING CONDITIONS

	Column A — Distasteful Working Conditions	Column B — Distasteful Working Conditions Ranked	Column C + The Keys to My Effectiveness at Work
Places I Have Worked Thus Far in My Life	I Have Learned from the Past That My Effectiveness at Work Is Decreased When I Have to Work Under These Conditions	Among the Factors or Qualities Listed in Column A, These Are the Ones I Dislike Absolutely the Most (in Order of Decreasing Dislike)	The Opposite of These Qualities, in Order: I Believe My Effectiveness Would Be at an Absolute Maximum, If I Could Work Under These Conditions

STEP 6

What Level Would You Like to Work at, and What Salary Would You Be Satisfied With?

Salary is something you must think out ahead of time, when you're contemplating your ideal job or career. Level goes hand-in-hand with salary, of course.

1. The first question here is at what level would you like to work, in your ideal job?

Level is a matter of how much responsibility you want, in an organization:

- ❑ Boss or CEO (this may mean you'll have to form your own business)
- ❑ Manager or someone under the boss who carries out orders
- ❑ The head of a team
- ❑ A member of a team of equals
- ❑ One who works in tandem with one other partner
- ❑ One who works alone, either as an employee or as a consultant to an organization, or as a one-person business

Enter a two- or three-word summary of your answer, on the Salary and Level of Responsibility petal of your Flower Diagram, pages 160–61.

2. The second question here is what salary would you like to be aiming for?

Here you have to think in terms of minimum or maximum. **Minimum** is what you would need to make, if you were just barely "getting by." And you need to know this *before* you go in for a job interview with anyone (*or before you form your own business, and need to know how much profit you must make, just to survive*).

Maximum could be any astronomical figure you can think of, but it is more useful here to put down the salary you realistically think you could make, with your present competency and experience, were you working for a real, *but generous*, boss. (If this maximum figure is still depressingly low, then put down the salary you would like to be making five years from now.)

Make out a detailed outline of your estimated expenses *now*, listing what you need *monthly* in the following categories[3]:

Housing
    Rent or mortgage payments.................. $ _____
    Electricity/gas........................... $ _____
    Water.................................... $ _____
    Telephone................................ $ _____
    Garbage removal.......................... $ _____
    Cleaning, maintenance, repairs[4]........ $ _____
Food
    What you spend at the supermarket
    and/or meat market, etc. .... $ _____
    Eating out .... $ _____
Clothing
    Purchase of new or used clothing .... $ _____
    Cleaning, dry cleaning, laundry............. $ _____
Automobile/transportation[5]
    Car payments .... $ _____
    Gas (who knows?) .... $ _____
    Repairs .... $ _____
    Public transportation (*bus, train, plane*) .... $ _____

---

3. If this kind of financial figuring is not your cup of tea, find a buddy, friend, relative, family member, or anyone, who can help you do this. If you don't know anyone who could do this, go to your local church, synagogue, religious center, social club, gym, or wherever you hang out, and ask the leader or manager there, to help you find someone. If there's a bulletin board, put up a notice on the bulletin board.

4. If you have extra household expenses, such as a security system, be sure to include the quarterly (or whatever) expenses here, divided by three.

5. Your checkbook stubs and/or online banking records will tell you a lot of this stuff. But you may be vague about your cash or credit card expenditures. For example, you may not know how much you spend at the supermarket, or how much you spend on gas, etc. But there is a simple way to find out. Just carry a little notepad and pen around with you for two weeks or more, and jot down everything you pay cash (or use credit cards) for—on the spot, right after you pay it. At the end of those two weeks, you'll be able to take that notepad and make a realistic guess of what should be put down in these categories that now puzzle you. (Multiply the two-week figure by two, and you'll have the monthly figure.)

Insurance

    Car. . . . . $ _____

    Medical or health care . . . . $ _____

    House and personal possessions . . . . $ _____

    Life . . . . $ _____

Medical expenses

    Doctors' visits . . . . $ _____

    Prescriptions. . . . . $ _____

    Fitness costs . . . . $ _____

Support for other family members

    Child-care costs *(if you have children)* . . . . $ _____

    Child-support *(if you're paying that)*. . . . . $ _____

    Support for your parents *(if you're helping out)* . . $ _____

Charity giving/tithe *(to help others)* . . . . $ _____

School/learning

    Children's costs *(if you have children in school)* . . $ _____

    Your learning costs *(adult education,*

    job-hunting classes, etc.) . . . . $ _____

Pet care *(if you have pets)* . . . . $ _____

Bills and debts *(usual monthly payments)*

    Credit cards . . . . $ _____

    Local stores. . . . . $ _____

    Other obligations you pay off monthly . . . . $ _____

Taxes

    Federal[6] *(next April's due, divided by*

    months remaining until then). . . . . $ _____

    State *(likewise)* . . . . $ _____

    Local/property *(next amount due, divided by*

    months remaining until then). . . . . $ _____

    Tax-help *(if you ever use an accountant,*

    pay a friend to help you with taxes, etc.). . . . . $ _____

Savings . . . . $ _____

---

6. Incidentally, for U.S. citizens, looking ahead to next April 15, be sure to check with your local IRS office or a reputable accountant to find out if you can deduct the expenses of your job-hunt on your federal (and state) income tax returns. At this writing, some job-hunters can, if—big IF—this is not your first job that you're looking for, if you haven't been unemployed too long, and if you aren't making a career-change. Do go find out what the latest "ifs" are. If the IRS says you are eligible, keep careful receipts of everything related to your job-hunt, as you go along: telephone calls, stationery, printing, postage, travel, etc.

Retirement (Keogh, IRA, SEP, etc.)............ $ _____
Amusement/discretionary spending
    Movies, video rentals, etc. .... $ _____
    Other kinds of entertainment .... $ _____
    Reading, newspapers, magazines, books .... $ _____
    Gifts (birthday, Christmas, etc.) .... $ _____
    Vacations .... $ _____

Total Amount You Need Each Month .... $ _____

Multiply the total amount you need each month by 12, to get the yearly figure. Divide the yearly figure by 2,000, and you will be reasonably near the *minimum* hourly wage that you need. Thus, if you need $3,333 per month, multiplied by 12 that's $40,000 a year, and then divided by 2,000, that's $20 an hour.

Parenthetically, you may want to prepare two different versions of the above budget: one with the expenses you'd ideally *like* to make, and the other a minimum budget, which will give you what you are looking for, here: the floor, below which you simply cannot afford to go.

Enter the maximum, and minimum, on your Salary and Level of Responsibility petal on the Flower Diagram, pages 160–61.

Optional Exercise: You may wish to put down other rewards, besides money, that you would hope for, from your next job or career. These might be:

❑ Adventure   ❑ Challenge   ❑ Respect   ❑ Influence
❑ Popularity   ❑ Fame   ❑ Power
❑ Intellectual stimulation from the other workers there
❑ A chance to be creative
❑ A chance to help others
❑ A chance to exercise leadership
❑ A chance to make decisions
❑ A chance to use your expertise
❑ A chance to bring others closer to God
❑ Other: _____

If you do check off things on this list, arrange your answers in order of importance to you, and then add them to the Salary and Level of Responsibility petal.

STEP 7

Where Would You Most Like to Live, If You Have a Choice?

The Point of This Step: To answer this question: *to the degree you have a choice—now or down the line—where would you most like to live?*

Why This Is Important for You to Know: Human beings are like flowers. Our soul flourishes in some environs, but withers and dies—or at least becomes extremely unhappy—in others.

What You Want to Beware Of: Thinking that where you live is not important. Or thinking, if you have a partner, and you each want to live in different places, that one of you can get their way, but the other is going to have to give up *their* dream. Nonsense! If this were part of a course about Thinking, what would the Lesson be? The subject of the Lesson would be: how can two partners, who initially disagree, learn to agree on a place where both get what they want?

In case you haven't got a clue, there is an interesting exercise you can do. It begins with your past *(the places where you used to live)*, and extracts from it some information that is tremendously useful in plotting your future.

It is particularly useful when you have a partner, and the two of you haven't yet been able to agree on where you want to live.

DIRECTIONS FOR DOING THIS EXERCISE:

1. Copy the chart that is on the next two pages, onto a larger (*e.g., 24″ x 36″*) piece of paper or cardboard, which you can obtain from any arts and crafts store or supermarket, in your town or city. If you are doing this exercise with a partner, make a copy for them too, so that each of you is working on a clean copy of your own, and can follow these instructions independently.

2. In *Column 1*, each of you should list all the places where you have ever lived.

3. In *Column 2,* each of you should list all the factors you disliked (and still dislike) about each place. The factors do not have to be put exactly opposite the name in *Column 1.* The names in *Column 1* exist simply to jog your memory.

   If, as you go, you remember some good things about any place, put *those* factors at the bottom of the next column, *Column 3.*

   If the same factors keep repeating, just put a checkmark after the first listing of that factor, every time it repeats.

   Keep going until you have listed all the factors you disliked or hated about each and every place you named in *Column 1.* Now, in effect, throw away *Column 1;* discard it from your thoughts. The negative factors were what you were after. *Column 1* has served its purpose.

4. In *Column 3,* you look at the negative factors you listed in *Column 2* and try to list each one's opposite. For example, "the sun never shone, there" would, in *Column 3,* be turned into "mostly sunny, all year 'round." It will not always be *the exact opposite.* For example, the negative factor "rains all the time" does not necessarily translate into the positive "sunny all the time." It might be something like "sunny at least 200 days a year." It's your call. Keep going, until every negative factor in *Column 2* is turned into its opposite, a positive factor, in *Column 3.* At the bottom, note the positive factors you already listed there, when you were working on *Column 2.*

5. In *Column 4,* now, list the positive factors in *Column 3,* in the order of most important (to you), down to least important (to you). For example, if you were looking at, and trying to name a new town, city, or place where you could be happy and flourish, what is the first thing you would look for? Would it be, good weather? or lack of crime? or good schools? or access to cultural opportunities, such as music, art, museums, or whatever? or would it be inexpensive housing? etc., etc. Rank all the factors in *Column 4.* Use the Prioritzing Grid on page 219 if you need to.

6. If you are doing this by yourself, list on a *scribble sheet* the top ten factors, in order of importance to you, and show it to everyone you meet for the next ten days, with the ultimate question: "Can

My Geographical Preferences
Decision Making for Just You

Column 1 Names of Places I Have Lived	Column 2 From the Past: Negatives	Column 3 Translating the Negatives into Positives	Column 4 Ranking of My Positives
	Factors I Disliked and Still Dislike about Any Place		1. 2. 3. 4. 5. 6. 7. 8. 9. 10. 11. 12.
		Factors I Liked and Still Like about Any Place	13. 14. 15.

Our Geographical Preferences
Decision Making for You and a Partner

Column 5 Places That Fit These Criteria	Column 6 Ranking of His/Her Preferences	Column 7 Combining Our Two Lists (Columns 4 & 6)	Column 8 Places That Fit These Criteria
	a.	a. 1.	
	b.	b. 2.	
	c.	c. 3.	
	d.	d. 4.	
	e.	e. 5.	
	f.	f. 6.	
	g.	g. 7.	
	h.	h. 8.	
	i.	i. 9.	
	j.	j. 10.	
	k.	k. 11.	
	l.	l. 12.	
	m.	m. 13.	
	n.	n. 14.	
	o.	o. 15.	

you think of places that have these ten factors, or at least the top five?" Jot down their suggestions on the back of the *scribble sheet.* When the ten days are up, look at the back of your sheet and circle the three places that seem the most interesting to you. If there is only a partial overlap between your dream factors and the places your friends and acquaintances suggested, *make sure the overlap is in the factors that count the most.* Now you have some names that you will want to find out more about, until you are sure which is your absolute favorite place to live, and then your second, and third, as backups.

Put the names of the three places, and/or your top five geographical factors, on the Flower Diagram, on the Where I Would Like to Live petal, pages 160–61.

7. If you are doing this with a partner, skip *Column 5.* Instead, when you have finished your *Column 4,* look at your partner's *Column 4,* and copy it into *Column 6.* The numbering of *your* list in *Column 4* was 1, 2, 3, 4, etc. Number your partner's list, as you copy it into *Column 6,* as a, b, c, d, etc.

8. Now, in *Column 7,* combine your *Column 4* with *Column 6* (your partner's old *Column 4,* renumbered). Both of you can work now from just one person's chart. Combine the two lists as illustrated on the chart. First your partner's top favorite geographical factor ("a"), then *your* top favorite geographical factor ("1"), then your partner's second most important favorite geographical factor ("b"), then *yours* ("2"), etc., until you have ten or fifteen favorite geographical factors *(yours and your partner's)* listed, in order, in *Column 7.*

9. List on a *scribble sheet* the top ten factors, and both of you should show it to everyone you meet, for the next ten days, with the same question as above: "Can you think of any places that have these ten factors, or at least the top five?" Jot down their suggestions on the back of the *scribble sheet.* When the ten days are up, you and your partner should look at the back of your sheet and circle the three places that look the most interesting to the two of you. If there is only a partial overlap between your dream factors and the places your friends and acquaintances suggested, make sure the

PRIORITIZING GRID FOR 10 ITEMS OR LESS

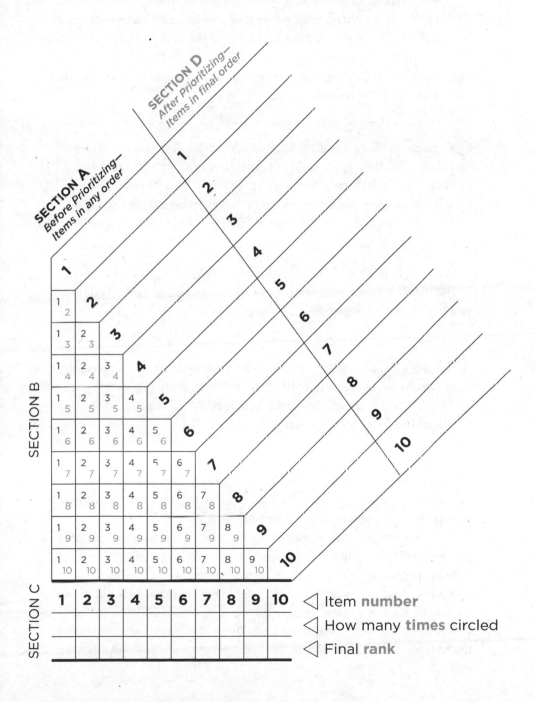

The Parachute Workbook (Updated 2010)   219

overlap is in the factors that matter the most to the two of you, i.e., the ones that are at the top of your list in *Column 7*. Now you have some names of places that you will want to find out more about, until you are sure which is the absolute favorite place to live for both of you, and then your second, and third, as backups.

Put the names of the top three places, and/or your top five geographical factors, on the Flower Diagram, on the Where I Would Most Like to Live petal, pages 160–61.

Conclusion: Was all of this too much work? Then do what one family did: they put a map of the U.S. up on a corkboard, and then they each threw a dart at the map from across the room, and when they were done they asked themselves where the most darts landed. It turned out to be around "Denver." So, *Denver* it was!

Well you're done with The Flower. Now what?

Put that sheet on a wall, or on the door of your refrigerator. And there you have it: a simple picture (as it were) of You.

A Lightbulb Goes On

But, it's not *just* a picture of You. Just as important, it's a picture of Your Dream Job as well. It's both of these things at once, because you're looking for a dream job or career *that matches you*. You match it. It matches you. Bingo! Mirror images.

And now what should happen? Well, for some of you there will be a big *Aha!* as you look at your Flower Diagram. A lightbulb will go on, over your head, and you will say, "My goodness, I see *exactly* what sort of career this points me to." This happens particularly with intuitive people. And people who hum. (Don't ask why.)

If you are one of those intuitive people, I say, "Good for you!" Just two gentle warnings, if I may:

Don't prematurely close out *other* possibilities.

And *don't* say to yourself: "Well, I see what it is that I would die to be able to do, but I *know* there is no job in the world like that, that *I* would be able to get." Dear friend, you don't know any such thing. You haven't done your research yet. Of course, it is always possible that when you've completed all that research, and conducted your search, you still may not be able to find *all* that you want—down to the last detail. But you'd be surprised at how much of your dream you may be able to find.

Sometimes it will be found in *stages*. One retired man I know, who had been a senior executive with a publishing company, found himself bored to death in retirement, after he turned 65. He contacted a business acquaintance, who said apologetically, "We just don't have anything open that matches or requires your abilities; right now all we need is someone in our mail room." The 65-year-old executive said, "I'll take that job!" He did, and over the ensuing years steadily advanced once again, to just the job he wanted: as a senior executive in that organization, where he utilized all his prized skills, for some time. He retired as senior executive for the second time, at the age of 85. Like him, you may choose to go by stages.

Other times, it may be that you will be able to find your dream directly without having to go through stages.

THE VIRTUE OF "PASSION" IN YOUR JOB-HUNT

Whether in stages or directly, it is amazing how often people do get their dream job or career. The more you don't cut the dream down, because of what you think you know about *the real world*, the more likely you are to find what you are looking for.

Hold on to *all* of your dream. Most people don't find their heart's desire, because they decide to pursue just half their dream— and consequently they hunt for it with only *half a heart*.

If you decide to pursue your whole dream, your best dream, the one you would die to do, I guarantee you that you will hunt for it *with all your heart*. It is this *passion* that often is the difference between successful career-changers, and unsuccessful ones.

Other Possibility, You Look at Your Flower Diagram and . . . a Lightbulb *Doesn't* Go On

In contrast to what I just said, many of you will look at your completed Flower Diagram, and you won't have *a clue* as to what job or career it points to. Soooo, we need a "fallback" strategy. Of course it involves more "step-by-step-by-step" stuff.

Here's how it goes. Take a piece of paper, with pen or pencil, or go to your computer, and keyboard in hand, make some notes:

1. First, look at your Flower Diagram, and from the center petal choose your three to five most *favorite* skills.

2. Then, look at your Flower Diagram and write down your three *top* interests or *favorite* fields.

3. Now, take these notes, and show them to at least five friends, family members, or professionals whom you know.

4. Jot down *everything* these five people suggest or recommend to you.

5. After you have finished talking to them, you want to go home and look at all these notes. Anything helpful or valuable here? If not, if none of it looks valuable, then set it aside, and go talk to five more of your friends, acquaintances, or people you know in the business world or nonprofit sector. Repeat, as necessary.

6. When you finally have some worthwhile suggestions, sit down, look over their combined suggestions, and ask yourself some questions.

As you will recall, skills usually point toward a job-title or job-level, while interests or Fields of Fascination usually point toward a career field. So, you want to ask them, in the case of your skills, *What job-title or jobs do these skills suggest to you?*

Then ask them, in the case of your favorite Fields of Fascination, *What career fields do these suggest to you?*

- First, you want to look at what these friends suggested about your skills: *what job or jobs came to their mind?* It will help you to know that most jobs can be classified under nineteen headings or families, as below. Which of these nineteen do your friends' suggestions predominantly point to? Which of these nineteen grabs you?

JOB FAMILIES

1. Executive, Administrative, and Managerial Occupations
2. Engineers, Surveyors, and Architects
3. Natural Scientists and Mathematicians
4. Social Scientists, Social Workers, Religious Workers, and Lawyers
5. Teachers, Counselors, Librarians, and Archivists
6. Health Diagnosing and Treating Practitioners
7. Registered Nurses, Pharmacists, Dieticians, Therapists, and Physician Assistants
8. Health Technologists and Technicians
9. Technologists and Technicians in Other Fields: Computer Specialists, Programmers, Information Technicians, Information Specialists, etc.
10. Writers, Artists, Digital Artists, and Entertainers
11. Marketing and Sales Occupations
12. Administrative Support Occupations, including Clerical
13. Service Occupations
14. Agricultural, Forestry, and Fishing Occupations
15. Mechanics and Repairers
16. Construction and Extractive Occupations
17. Production Occupations
18. Transportation and Material Moving Occupations
19. Handlers, Equipment Cleaners, Helpers, and Laborers

- Next, you want to look at what your friends suggested about your interests or Fields of Fascination: *what fields or careers came to their minds?* It will help you to know that most of the job families above can be classified under four broad headings: *Agriculture, Manufacturing, Information Industries, and Service Industries.* Which

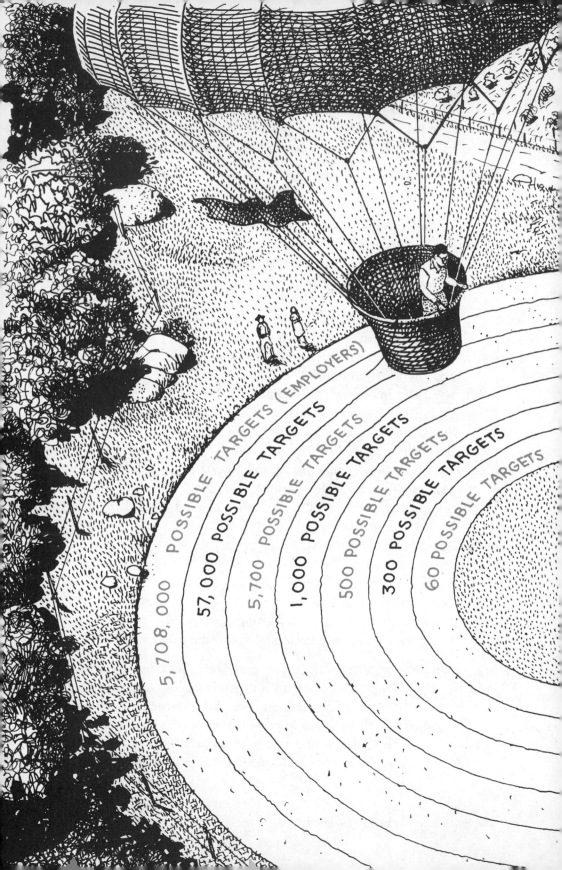

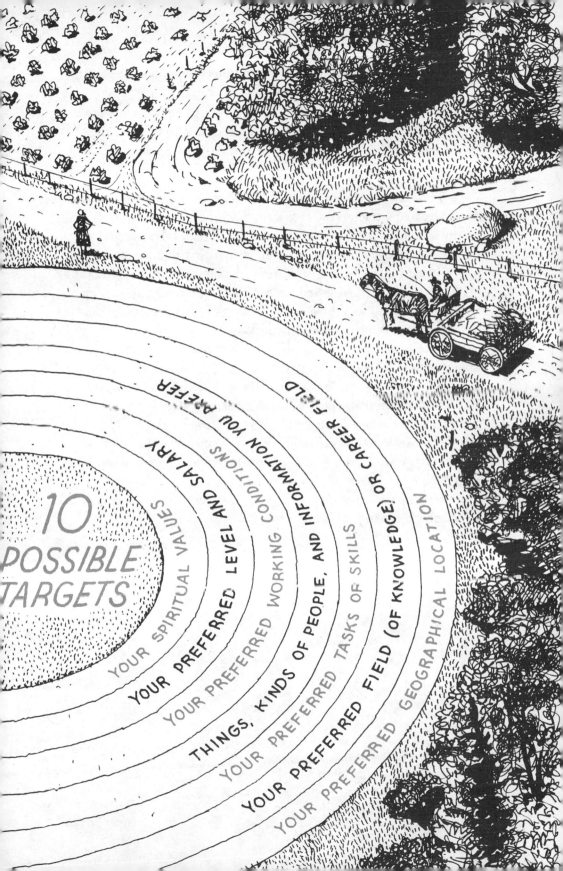

of these four do your friends' suggestions predominantly *point to?* Which of these four grabs you?

- The next question you want to ask yourself is: job-titles and career-fields can be broken down further, according to whether you like to work primarily with *people* or primarily with *information/data* or primarily with *things*.

Let's take the field of agriculture as an example. Within this field, you could be driving tractors or other farm machinery—and thus work primarily with *things;* or you could be gathering statistics about crop growth for some state agency—and thus work primarily with *information/data;* or you could be teaching agriculture in a college classroom—and thus work primarily with *people* and *ideas.* Almost all fields as well as career families offer you these three choices, though *of course* many jobs combine two of the three in some intricate way.

Still, you do want to tell yourself what your *preference* is, and what you *primarily* want to work with. Otherwise your job-hunt or career-change is going to leave you very frustrated at the end. In this matter, it is often your favorite skill that will give you the clue. If it *doesn't,* then go back and look at the whole Skills petal, on your Flower Diagram. What do you think? Are your favorite skills weighted more toward working with *people,* or toward working with *information/data,* or toward working with *things?*

And, no matter what that *petal* suggests, which of the three do you absolutely prefer, in your heart of hearts?

Giving Your Flower a Name

Once you have these *clues* from your friends, you need to go name your Flower. To do this, you need to answer three questions for yourself, in the order indicated below:

QUESTION #1

What are the names of jobs or careers that would give me a chance to use my most enjoyable skills, in a field that is based on my favorite subjects?

Just make sure that you get the names of at least *two* careers, or jobs, that you think you could be happy doing. Never, ever, put all your eggs in one basket. The secret of surviving out there in the jungle is *having alternatives.*

Be careful. Be thorough. Be persistent. This is your life you're working on, and your future. Make it glorious. Whatever it takes, find out the name of your ideal career, your ideal occupation, your ideal job—*or jobs.*

QUESTION #2

What kinds of organizations would and/or do employ people in these careers?

Before you think of individual places where you might like to work, it is necessary to stop and think of all the *kinds* of places where one might get hired.

Let's take an example. Suppose in your new career you want to be a teacher. You must then ask yourself: *what kinds of places hire teachers?* You might answer, *"just schools"*—and finding that schools in your geographical area have no openings, you might say, *"Well, there are no jobs for people in this career."*

But wait a minute! There are countless other *kinds* of organizations and agencies out there, besides schools, that employ *teachers*. For example, corporate training and educational departments, workshop sponsors, foundations, private research firms, educational consultants, teachers' associations, professional and trade societies, military bases, state and local councils on higher education, fire and police training academies, and so on and so forth.

"*Kinds* of places" also means places with different *hiring options*, besides full-time, such as:

- places that would employ you part-time (maybe you'll end up deciding to hold down two or even three part-time jobs, which altogether would add up to one full-time job, in order to give yourself more variety);

- places that take temporary workers, on assignment for one project at a time;

- places that take consultants, one project at a time;

- places that operate primarily with volunteers, etc.;

- places that are nonprofit;

- places that are for-profit;

- and, don't forget, places that you yourself could start up, should you decide to be your own boss (see chapter 9).

Don't forget that as you talk to workers about their jobs or careers (in the previous section), they may accidentally volunteer information about hiring options. Listen keenly, and take notes.

QUESTION #3

Among the kinds of organizations uncovered in the previous question, what are the names of particular places that I especially like?

As you interview workers about their jobs or careers, they will probably innocently mention actual names of organizations that have such jobs—plus what's good or bad about the place. This is important information for you. Jot it all down. Keep notes *as though it were part of your religion.*

Now when this name-gathering is all done, what do you have? Well, either you'll have *too few names* of places to work, or you'll end up with *too much information*—too many names of places that hire people in the career that interests you. There are ways of dealing with either of these eventualities. We'll take this last scenario, first.

Cutting Down the Territory

To avoid ending up with the names of too many places, you will want to cut down the territory, so you are left with *a manageable number* of "targets" to research and visit.[7]

Let's take an example. Suppose you discover that the career that interests you the most is *welding.* You want to be a welder. Well, that's a beginning. You've cut the 23 million U.S. job-markets down to:

• I want to work in a place that hires welders.

But the territory is still too large. There might be thousands of places in the country, that use welders. You can't go visit them all. So, you've got to cut down the territory, further. Suppose that on your geography petal you said that you really want to live and work in the San Jose area of California. That's helpful: that cuts down the territory further. Now your goal is:

• I want to work in a place that hires welders, within the San Jose area.

---

7. If you resist this idea of *cutting down the territory*—if you feel you could be happy anywhere just as long as you were using your favorite skills—then you'll have to go visit them all. Good luck! We'll see you in about forty-three years.

But, the territory is still too large. There could be 100, 200, 300 organizations that fit that description. So you look at your Flower Diagram for further help, and you notice that under *preferred working conditions* you said you wanted to work for an organization with fifty or fewer employees. Good, now your goal is:

• I want to work in a place that hires welders, within the San Jose area, that has fifty or fewer employees.

This territory may still be too large. So you look again at your Flower Diagram for further guidance, and you see that you said you wanted to work for an organization that works with, or produces, wheels. So now your statement of what you're looking for, becomes:

• I want to work in a place that hires welders, within the San Jose area, has fifty or fewer employees, and makes wheels.

Using your Flower Diagram, you can thus keep cutting down the territory, until the *"targets"* of your job-hunt are no more than ten places. That's a manageable number of places for you to *start with*. You can always expand the list later, if none of these ten turns out to be promising or interesting.

Expanding the Territory

Sometimes your problem will be just the opposite. We come here to the second possibility: if your Informational Interviewing doesn't turn up enough names of places where you could get hired in your new career, then you're going to have to expand your list. You're going to have to consult some directories.

Your salvation is going to be, first of all, the Yellow Pages of your local phone book. Look under every heading that is of any interest to you. Also, see if the local chamber of commerce publishes a business directory; often it will list not only small companies but also local divisions of larger companies, with names of department heads; sometimes they will even include the North American Industry Classification System

(NAICS) codes, should you care. If you are diligent here, you won't lack for names, believe me—unless it's a very small town you live in, in which case you'll need to cast your net a little wider, to include other towns, villages, or cities that are within commuting distance.

Informational Interviewing

There is a name for this process I have just described. It is called *Informational Interviewing*—a term I invented many many years ago. But it is sometimes, incorrectly, called *by other names*. Some even call this gathering of information *Networking*, which it is not.

To avoid this confusion, I have summarized in the chart on pages 232–33 just exactly what *Informational Interviewing* is, and how it differs from the other ways in which *people* can help and support you, during your job-hunt or career-change—namely, *Networking, Support Groups,* and *Contacts*. I have also thrown in, at no extra charge, a *first* column in that chart, dealing with an aspect of the job-hunt that *never* gets talked about: namely, the importance before your job-hunt ever begins, of *reestablishing friendships you have let slip*—by calling or visiting them early on in your job-hunt—*before* you ever need anything from them, as you most certainly will, later on in your job-hunt. The first column in the chart explains this further.

Talking to Workers, "Trying on" Jobs

When you go talk to people, you are hoping they will give you ideas, as we saw, about *which careers* will use your skills and *languages* or Fields of Fascination and interests.

That's the first step.

The second step is that you want also to get some idea of *what that work feels like, from the inside.*

Therefore, during Informational Interviewing, you want to talk to people who are actually doing the work you think you'd love to do. Why? In effect, you are mentally *trying on jobs* to see if they fit you.

It is exactly analogous to your going to a clothing store and trying on different suits (or dresses) that you see in their window or on their racks. Why try them on? Well, the suits or dresses that look *terrific* in the window don't always look so hot when you see them on *you*. The clothes don't hang quite right, etc.

The Process	1. Valuing Your Community Before the Job-Hunt	2. Networking
What Is Its Purpose?	To make sure that people whom you may someday need to do you a favor, or lend you a hand, know long beforehand that you value and prize them *for themselves.*	To gather a list of contacts now who might be able to help you with your career, or with your job-hunting, at some future date. And to go out of your way to regularly add to that list. *Networking is a term often reserved only for the business of **adding** to your list; but, obviously, this presupposes you first listed everyone you already know.*
Who Is It Done With?	Those who live with you, plus your family, relatives, friends, and acquaintances, however near (geographically) or far.	People in your present field, or in a field of future interest that you yourself meet; also, people whose names are given to you by others.
When You're Doing This Right, How Do You Go about It? (Typical Activities)	You make time for them in your busy schedule, long before you find yourself job-hunting. You do this by: 1. Spending "quality time" with those you live with, letting them know you really appreciate who they are, and what kind of person they are. 2. Maintaining contact (phone, lunch, a thank-you note) with those who live nearby. 3. Writing friendly notes, regularly, to those who live at a distance—*thus letting them all know that you appreciate them* for themselves.	You deliberately attend, for this purpose, meetings or conventions in your present field, or the field/career you are thinking of switching to, someday. You talk to people at meetings and at "socials," exchanging calling cards after a brief conversation. Occasionally, someone may suggest a name to you as you are about to set off for some distant city or place, recommending that while you are there, you contact them. A phone call may be your best bet, with a follow-up letter after you return home, unless *they* invite *you* to lunch during the phone call. Asking *them* to lunch sometimes "bombs." (See below.)
When You've Really Botched This Up, What Are the Signs?	You're out of work, and you find yourself having to contact people that you haven't written or phoned in ages, suddenly asking them out of the blue for their help with your job-hunt. *The message inevitably read from this is that you don't really care about them at all, except when you can use them. Further, you get perceived as one who sees others only in terms of what they can do for you, rather than in a relationship that is "a two-way street."*	It's usually when you have approached a very busy individual and asked them to have lunch with you. If it is an aimless lunch, with no particular agenda—they ask during lunch what you need to talk about, and you lamely say, "Well, uh, I don't know, So-and-So just thought we should get to know each other"—you will not be practicing *Networking.* You will be practicing *Antagonizing.*

3. Developing a Support Group	4. Informational Interviewing	5. Using Contacts
To enlist some of your family or close friends specifically to help you with your emotional, social, and spiritual needs, when you are going through a difficult transition period, such as a job-hunt or career-change—so that you do not have to face this time all by yourself.	To screen careers *before* you change to them. To screen jobs *before* you take them, rather than afterward. To screen places *before* you decide you want to seek employment there. To find answers to *very specific questions* that occur to you during your job-hunt.	It takes, let us say, 77 pairs of eyes and ears to find a new job or career. Here you recruit those 76 other people (don't take me literally—it can be any number you choose) to be your eyes and ears—once you know what kind of work, what kind of place, what kind of job you are looking for, and *not before*.
You try to enlist people with one or more of the following qualifications: you feel comfortable talking to them; they will take initiative in calling you, on a regular basis; they are wiser than you are; and they can be a hard taskmaster, when you need one.	Workers, workers, workers. You *only* do Informational Interviewing with people actually doing the work that interests you as a potential new job or career for yourself.	Anyone and everyone who is on your "networking list." (See column 2.) It includes family, friends, relatives, high school alumni, college alumni, former co-workers, church/synagogue members, places where you shop, etc.
There should be four of them, at least. They may meet with you regularly, once a week, as a group, for an hour or two, to check on how you are doing. One or more of them should also be available to you on an "as needed" basis: the Listener, when you are feeling "down," and need to talk; the Initiator, when you are tempted to hide; the Wise One, when you are puzzled as to what to do next; and the Taskmaster, when your discipline is falling apart, and you need someone to encourage you to "get at it." It helps if there is also a Cheerleader among them, whom you can tell your victories to.	You get names of workers from your co-workers, from departments at local community colleges, or career offices. Once you have names, you call them and ask for a chance to talk to them *for twenty minutes*. You make a list, ahead of time, of all the questions you want answers to. If nothing occurs to you, try these: 1. How did you get into this line of work? Into this particular job? 2. What kinds of things do you like the most about this job? 3. What kinds of things do you like the least about this job? 4. Who else, doing this same kind of work, would you recommend I go talk to?	Anytime you're stuck, you ask your contacts for help *with specific information*. For example: When you can't find workers who are doing the work that interests you. When you can't find the names of places that do that kind of work. When you have a place in mind, but can't figure out the name of "the-person-who-has-the-power-to-hire-you." When you know that name, but can't get in to see that person. At such times, you call every contact you have on your Networking list, if necessary, until someone can tell you the specific answer you need.
You've "botched it" when you have no support group, no one to turn to, no one to talk to, and you feel that you are in this, all alone. You've "botched it" when you are waiting for your friends and family to notice how miserable you are, and to prove they love you by taking the initiative in coming after you; rather than, as is necessary with a support group, *your* choosing and recruiting them—asking them for their help and aid.	You're trying to use this with people-who-have-the-power-to-hire-you, rather than with workers. You're claiming you want information when really you have some other hidden agenda, with this person. (*P.S. They usually can smell the hidden agenda, a mile away.*) You've botched it, whenever you're telling a lie to someone. The whole point of Informational Interviewing is that it is a search for Truth.	Approaching your "contacts" too early in your job-hunt, and asking them for help only in the most general and vague terms: "John, I'm out of work. If you hear of anything, please let me know." *Any what thing?* You must do all your own homework *before* you approach your contacts. They will not do your homework for you.

Likewise, careers that *sound* terrific in books or in your imagination don't always look so great when you see them up close and personal.

What you're ultimately trying to find is a career that looks terrific inside and out—in the window, *and* also on you. Here are some questions that will help *with workers who are actually doing the career you think you might like to do*:

- How did you get into this work?
- What do you like the most about it?
- What do you like the least about it?
- And, where else could I find people who do this kind of work? *(You should always ask them for more than one name, here, so that if you run into a dead end at any point, you can easily go visit the other names they suggested.)*

If it becomes apparent to you, during the course of any of these Informational Interviews, that this career, occupation, or job you were exploring definitely *doesn't* fit you, then the last question (above) gets turned into a different kind of inquiry:

- Do you have any ideas as to who else I could talk to, about my skills and Fields of Fascination or interests—so I can find out how they all might fit together, in one job or career?

Then go visit the people they suggest.

If they can't think of *anyone*, ask them if they know who *might* know.

"They Say I Have to Go Back to School, but I Haven't the Time or the Money"

Next step: having found the names of jobs or careers that interest you, having mentally *tried them on* to see if they fit, you next want to find out *how much training, etc., it takes, to get into that field or career*. You ask the same people you have been talking to, previously.

More times than not, you will hear *bad news*. They will tell you something like: "In order to be hired for this job, you have to have a master's degree and ten years' experience at it."

If you have the time, and the money, fine! But what if you don't? Then you search for *exceptions*:

"Yes, but do you know of anyone in this field who got into it without that master's degree, and ten years' experience?

And where might I find him or her?

And if you don't know of any such person, who might know?"

Throughout Informational Interviewing, don't assume anything ("But I just assumed that . . ."). Question *all* assumptions, no matter how many people tell you that "this is just the way things are."

Keep in mind that there are people *out there* who will tell you something that absolutely *isn't* so, with every conviction in their being—because they *think* it's true. Sincerity they have, 100 percent. Accuracy is something else again. You will need to check and cross-check any information that people tell you or that you read in books (even this one).

No matter how many people tell you that such-and-so are the rules about getting into a particular occupation, and there are no exceptions— believe me there *are* exceptions, to almost *every* rule, except where a profession has rigid entrance examinations, as in, say, medicine or law.

Rules are rules. But what you are counting on is that somewhere in this country, somewhere in this vast world, *somebody* found a way to get into this career you dream of, without going through all the hoops that everyone else is telling you are *absolutely essential.*

You want to find out who these people are, and go talk to them, to find out *how they did it.*

Okay, but suppose you are determined to go into a career that takes *years* to prepare for, and you can't find *anyone* who took a shortcut? What then?

Every professional speciality has one or more *shadow* professions, which require much less training. For example, instead of becoming a doctor, you can go into paramedical work; instead of becoming a lawyer, you can go into paralegal work, instead of becoming a licensed career counselor, you can become a career coach.

Have a "Plan B"

Sooner or later, as you interview one person after another, you'll begin to get some definite ideas about a career that is of interest to you. It uses your favorite skills. It employs your favorite Fields of Fascination or fields of interest. You've interviewed people *actually doing that work*, and it all sounds fine. This part of your Informational Interviewing is over.

As I mentioned earlier, just make sure that you get the names of at least *two* careers, or jobs, that you think you could be happy doing. Never, ever, put all your eggs in one basket. The secret of surviving out there in the jungle is *having alternatives*.

Eventually, you will get the names of careers that attract you, and after that, you will find the names of particular organizations that employ "people who can do *that*." Do you rush right over? No. You research those places, first.

Researching Places Before You Approach Them

Why should you research places, before you approach them for a hiring-interview? Well, first of all, you want to know something about the organization from the inside: what kind of work they do there. And what their needs or problems or challenges are. And what kind of goals they are trying to achieve, what obstacles they are running into, and how your skills and knowledges can possibly help them. *(When you do at last go in for a hiring-interview, you want above all else to be able to show them that you have something they need.)*

Second, you want to find out if you would enjoy working there. You want to take the measure of that organization or organizations. Everybody takes the measure of an organization, but the problem with most job-hunters or career-changers is it's *after* they are hired there.

In the U.S., for example, a survey of the federal/state employment service once found that 57 percent of those who found a job through that service were not working at that job just thirty days later, and this was *because* they used the first ten or twenty days *on the job* to screen out that job.

You, by doing this research ahead of time, are choosing a better path, by far. Essentially, you are *screening out* careers, jobs, places *before* you commit to them. How intelligent!

So, try to think of every way in the world that you can find out more about those organizations *(plural, not singular)* that interest you, *before you go to see if you can get hired there.* There are several ways you can do this research ahead of time.

- **What's on the Internet.** Many job-hunters or career-changers think that every organization, company, or nonprofit, has its own website, these days. Not true. Maybe they do, and maybe they don't. It often has to do with the size of the place, its access to a good Web designer, its desperation for customers, etc. Easy way to find out: if you have access to the Internet, type the name of the place into your favorite search engine (*Google, Yahoo, or whatever*) and see what it turns up. Try more than one search engine.[8] Sometimes one knows things the others don't.

- **What's in Print.** The organization itself may have stuff in print, or on its website, about its business, purpose, etc. The CEO or head of the organization may have given talks. The organization may have copies of those talks. In addition, there may be brochures, annual reports, etc., that the organization has put out, about itself. How do you get ahold of these? The person who answers the phone there, when you call, will know, or know who to refer you to. Also, if it's a decent-sized organization that you are interested in, public libraries may have files on the organization— newspaper clippings, articles, etc. You never know; and it never hurts to ask your friendly neighborhood research librarian.

- **Friends and Neighbors.** Ask *everyone* you know, if they know anyone who works at the places that interest you. And, if they do, ask them if they could arrange for you and that person to get together, for lunch, coffee, or tea. At that time, tell them why the place interests you, and indicate you'd like to know more about it. (*It helps if your mutual friend is sitting there with the two of you, so the purpose of this little chat won't be misconstrued.*) This is the vastly preferred way to find out about a place. However, obviously you need a couple of additional alternatives up your sleeve, in case you run into a dead end here.

- **People at the Organizations in Question, or at Similar Organizations.** You can also go directly to organizations and ask questions about the place, but here I must caution you about several *dangers.*

  First, make sure you're not asking them questions that are in print somewhere, which you could easily have read for yourself instead of bothering *them.* This irritates people.

---

8. For more names of search engines, see Danny Sullivan's *SearchEngineWatch,* at http://searchenginewatch.com/links. For tips on how to search, see http://searchengine watch.com/facts.

Second, make sure that you approach the people at that organization *whose business it is to give out information*—receptionists, public relations people, "the personnel office," "the human relations department," etc.—*before* you ever approach people higher up in that organization.

Third, make sure that you approach *subordinates* rather than the top person in the place, if the subordinates would know the answer to your questions. Bothering the boss there with some simple questions that someone else could have answered is committing *job-hunting suicide*.

Fourth, make sure you're not using this approach simply as a sneaky way to get in to see the boss, and make a pitch for them to hire you. You said this was just information gathering. Keep it at that.

- **Temporary Agencies.** Many job-hunters and career-changers have found that a useful way to explore organizations is to go and work at a temporary agency. Employers turn to such agencies in order to find: a) job-hunters who can work part-time for a limited number of days; and b) job-hunters who can work full-time for a limited number of days. The advantage to you of temporary work is that if there is an agency that loans out people with your particular skills and expertise, you get a chance to be sent to a number of different employers over a period of several weeks, and see each one from the inside. Maybe the temp agency won't send you to exactly the place you hoped for; but sometimes you can develop contacts in the place you love, even while you're temporarily working somewhere else— if both organizations are in the same field.

  Some of you may balk at the idea of enrolling with a temporary agency, because you remember the old days when such agencies were solely for clerical workers and secretarial help. But the field has seen an explosion of services in the last decade, and there are temporary agencies these days (*at least in the larger cities*) for many occupations. In your city you may find temporary agencies for: accountants, industrial workers, assemblers, drivers, mechanics, construction people, engineering people, software engineers, programmers, computer technicians, production workers, management/executives, nannies (for young and old), health care/

dental/medical people, legal specialists, lawyers, insurance specialists, sales/marketing people, underwriting professionals, financial services, and the like, as well as for the old categories: data processing, secretarial, and office services. See your local phone book, under "Temporary Agencies."

- Volunteer Work. Another useful way to research a place before you ever ask them to hire you there, is to volunteer your services at that place that interests you. Of course, some places will turn your offer down, cold. But others will be interested. If they are, it will be relatively easy for you to talk them into letting you work there for a while, because you offer your services *without pay*, and for a brief, limited, agreed upon, period of time. In other words, from their point of view, if you turn out to be a *pain*, they won't have to endure you for long.

In this fashion, you get a chance to learn about organizations from the inside. Not so coincidentally, if you do decide you would really like to work there, and permanently, they've had a chance to see you in action, and when you are about to end your volunteer time there, *may* want to hire you permanently. I say *may*. Don't be mad if they simply say, "Thanks very much for helping us out. Goodbye." (That's what *usually* happens.) Even so, you've learned a lot, and this will stand you in good stead, in the future—as you approach other organizations.

Send a Thank-You Note

After *anyone* has done you a favor, during this Informational Interviewing phase of your job-hunt, you must *be sure* to send them a thank-you note by the very next day, at the latest. Such a note goes to *anyone* who helps you, or who talks with you. That means friends, people at the organization in question, temporary agency people, secretaries, receptionists, librarians, workers, or whomever.

Ask them, at the time you are face-to-face with them, for their business card (if they have one), or ask them to write out their name and work address, on a piece of paper, for you. You *don't* want to misspell their name. It is difficult to figure out how to spell people's names, these days, simply from the sound of it. What sounds like "Laura" may actually be "Lara." What sounds like "Smith" may actually be "Smythe," and so on. Get that name and address, *but get it right*, please. And let me reiterate: thank-you notes must be prompt. E-mail the thank-you note that same night, or the very next day at the latest.

Follow it with a lovely printed copy, nicely formatted, and sent through the mail. (Most employers these days prefer a printed letter to a handwritten one, unless your handwriting is beautiful.)

Your thank-you note can be just two or three sentences. Something like: "*I wanted to thank you for talking with me yesterday. It was very helpful to me. I much appreciated your taking the time out of your busy schedule to do this. Best wishes to you,*" and then your signature. *Do* sign it, particularly if the thank-you note is printed. Printed letters sent through the mail without any signature seem to be multiplying like rabbits in the world of work, these days; the absence of a written signature is usually perceived as making your letter *tremendously* impersonal. You don't want to leave that impression.

What If I Get Offered a Job Along the Way, While I'm Just Gathering Information?

You probably won't. Let me remind you that during this information gathering, you are *not* talking primarily to *employers.* You're talking to *workers.*

Nonetheless, an occasional employer *may* stray across your path during your Informational Interviewing. And that employer *may* be so impressed with the carefulness you're showing, in going about your career-change and job-search, that they want to hire you, on the spot. So, it's *possible* that you'd get offered a job while you're still doing your information gathering. Not *likely,* but *possible.* And if that happens, what should you say?

Well, if you're desperate, you will of course say *yes.* I remember one wintertime when I had just gone through the knee of my last pair of pants, we were burning old pieces of furniture in our fireplace to stay warm, the legs on our bed had just broken, and we were eating spaghetti until it was coming out our ears. In such a situation, *of course* you say yes.

But if you're not *desperate,* if you have time to be more careful, then you respond to the job-offer in a way that will buy you some time. You tell them what you're doing: that the average job-hunter tries to screen a job *after* they take it. But you are doing what you are *sure* this employer would do if they were in your shoes: you are examining careers, fields, industries, jobs, organizations *before* you decide where you would do your best and most effective work.

And you tell them that since your Informational Interviewing isn't finished yet, it would be premature for you to accept their job offer, until you're *sure* that this is the place where you could be most effective, and do your best work.

Then, you add: "Of course, I'm tickled pink that you would want me to be working here. And when I've finished my personal survey, I'll be glad to get back to you about this, as my preliminary impression is that this is the kind of place I'd like to work in, and the kind of people I'd like to work for, and the kind of people I'd like to work with."

In other words, *if you're not desperate yet*, you don't walk immediately through any opened doors; but neither do you allow them to be shut.

CONCLUSION:

When a Dream Job Isn't Enough:
The Search for a Deeper Sense of Mission

The search for a *dream job* is, on its surface, a search for greater happiness. Most of us embark on this search because we want to be happier. We want to be happier in both our *work* and our *life*.

But some of us want even more.

We want deep contentment in our *soul*.

Though others may not believe, we do. And we want our faith to be a part of our *dream*. Hence, no discussion of *work happiness* can be complete—for us—unless we also find *soul happiness*. Unless we find some sense of *mission* for our life.

That is the subject of our first Appendix.

The Green Pages

NOTE

As I started writing this section, I toyed at first with the idea of following what might be described as an "all-paths approach" to religion: trying to stay as general and nonspecific as I could. But, after much thought, I decided not to try that. This, because I have read many other writers who tried, and I felt the approach failed miserably. An "all-paths" approach to religion ends up being a "no-paths" approach, even as a woman or man who tries to please everyone ends up pleasing no one. It is the old story of the "universal" vs. the "particular."

Those of us who do career counseling could predict, ahead of time, that trying to stay universal is not likely to be helpful, in writing about faith. We know well from our own field that truly helpful career counseling depends upon defining the **particularity** or uniqueness of each person we try to help. No employer wants to know what you have in common with everyone else. He or she wants to know what makes you unique and individual. As I have argued throughout this book, the inventory of your uniqueness or *particularity* is crucial if you are ever to find meaningful work.

This particularity invades *everything* a person does; it is not suddenly "jettisonable" when he or she turns to matters of faith. Therefore, when I or anyone else writes about faith I believe we **must** write out of our own particularity—which *starts,* in my case, with the fact that I write, and think, and breathe as a Christian—as you might expect from the fact that I was an ordained Episcopalian minister for many years. Understandably, then, this chapter speaks from a Christian perspective. I want you to be aware of that, at the outset.

Balanced against this is the fact that I have always been acutely sensitive to the fact that this is a pluralistic society in which we live, and that I in particular owe a great deal to my readers who have religious convictions quite different from my own. It has turned out that the people who work or have worked here in my office with me, over the years, have been predominantly of other faiths. Furthermore, *Parachute*'s more than ten million readers have not only included Christians of every variety and persuasion, Christian Scientists, Jews, Hindus, Buddhists, and adherents of Islam, but also believers in "new age" religions, secularists, humanists, agnostics, atheists, and many others. I have therefore tried to be very courteous toward the feelings of all my readers, *while at the same time* counting on them to translate my Christian thought forms into their own. This ability to thus translate is the indispensable *sine qua non* of anyone who wants to communicate helpfully with others in this pluralistic society of ours.

In the Judeo-Christian tradition from which I come, one of the indignant Biblical questions was, "Has God forgotten to be gracious?" The answer was a clear "No." I think it is important *for all of us* also to seek the same goal. I have therefore labored to make this chapter gracious as well as thought-provoking.

R.N.B.

Appendix A
Finding Your Mission in Life

Turning Point

For many of us, the job-hunt offers a chance to make some fundamental changes in our whole life. It marks a turning point in how we live our life.

It gives us a chance to ponder and reflect, to extend our mental horizons, to go deeper into the subsoil of our soul.

It gives us a chance to wrestle with the question, "Why am I here on Earth?" We don't want to feel that we are just another grain of sand lying on the beach called humanity, unnumbered and lost in the billions of other human beings.

We want to do more than plod through life, going to work, coming home from work. We want to find that special joy, "that no one can take from us," which comes from having a sense of Mission in our life.

We want to feel we were put here on Earth for some special purpose, to do some unique work that only we can accomplish.

We want to know what our Mission is.

The Meaning of the Word "Mission"

When used with respect to our life and work *Mission* has always been a religious concept, from beginning to end. It is defined by *Webster's* as "a continuing task or responsibility that one is destined or fitted to do or specially called upon to undertake," and historically has had two

245

major synonyms: *Calling* and *Vocation*. These, of course, are the same word in two different languages, English and Latin. Both imply God. To be given a Vocation or Calling implies *Someone who* calls. To have a Destiny implies *Someone who determined the destination for us*. Thus, the concept of Mission lands us inevitably in the lap of God, before we have hardly begun.

I emphasize this, because there is an increasing trend in our culture to try to speak about religious subjects without reference to God. This is true of "spirituality," "soul," and "Mission," in particular. More and more books talk about Mission as though it were simply "a purpose you choose for your own life, by identifying your enthusiasms."

This attempt to obliterate all reference to God from the originally religious concept of Mission, is particularly ironic because the proposed substitute word—enthusiasms—is derived from two Greek words, "en theos," and means "God in us."

In the midst of this increasingly secular culture, we find an oasis that—along with athletics—is very hospitable toward belief in God. That oasis is *job-hunting*. Most of the leaders who have evolved creative job-hunting ideas were—from the beginning—people who believed firmly in God, and said so: Sidney Fine, Bernard Haldane, and John Crystal (all of whom have departed this life), plus Arthur and Marie Kirn, Arthur Miller, Tom and Ellie Jackson, Ralph Matson, and of course myself.

Nor are we alone. In the U.S., anyway. This country is one of the most religious-in-belief, at least, on the face of the Earth. Back in 1989 the Gallup Organization found that 94 percent of us believe in God, 90 percent of us pray, 88 percent of us believe God loves us, and 33 percent of us report we have had a life-changing religious experience. And that these figures had remained virtually unchanged for the previous fifty years. (This was reported in George Gallup Jr. and Jim Castelli's *The People's Religion: American Faith in the '90s*, Macmillan & Co., 1989.) Ninety-two percent of us, according to the Pew Forum polls conducted in 2008, still believe in God.

However, it is not clear that we have made much connection between our belief in God and our work. Often our spiritual beliefs and our attitude toward our work live in separate mental ghettos, within our mind.

A dialogue between these two *is* opened up inside our head, and heart, when we are out of work. Unemployment, particularly in this brutal economy, gives us a chance to contemplate why we are here on Earth, and what our Calling, Vocation, or Mission is, uniquely, for each of us.

Unemployment becomes *life transition*, when we can't find a job doing the same work we've always done. Since we have to rethink one thing, many of us elect to rethink *everything.*

Something awakens within us. Call it *yearning.* Call it *hope.* We come to realize the dream we dreamed has never died. And we go back to get it. We decide to resume our search . . . for the life we know within our heart that we were meant to live.

Now we have a chance to marry our work and our religious beliefs, to talk about Calling, and Vocation, and Mission in life—to think out why we are here, and what plans God has for us.

That's why a period of unemployment can absolutely change our life.

The Secret of Finding Your Mission in Life: Taking It in Stages

I will explain the steps toward finding your Mission in life that I have learned in all my years on Earth. Just remember two things. First, I speak from a lifelong Christian perspective, and trust you to translate this into your own thought-forms.

Second, I know that these steps are not the only Way. Many people have discovered their Mission by taking other paths. And you may, too. But hopefully what I have to say may shed some light upon whatever path you take.

I have learned that if you want to figure out what your Mission in life is, it will likely take some time. It is not a *problem* to be solved in a day and a night. It is a *learning process* that has steps to it, much like the process by which we all learned to eat. As a baby, we did not tackle adult food right off. As we all recall, there were three stages: first there had to be the mother's milk or bottle, then strained baby foods, and finally—after teeth and time—the stuff that grown-ups chew. Three stages—and the two earlier stages were not to be disparaged. It was all

Eating, just different forms of Eating—appropriate to our development at the time. But each stage had to be mastered, in turn, before the next could be approached.

There are usually three stages also to learning what your Mission in life is, and the two earlier stages are likewise not to be disparaged. It is all "Mission"—just different forms of Mission, appropriate to your development at the time. But each stage has to be mastered, in turn, before the next can be approached.

Of course, there is a sense in which you never master any of these stages, but are always growing in understanding and mastery of them, throughout your whole life here on Earth.

As it has been impressed on me by observing many people over the years (admittedly through *Christian spectacles*), it appears that the three parts to your Mission here on Earth can be defined generally as follows:

1. *Your first Mission here on Earth* is one that you share with the rest of the human race, but it is no less your individual Mission for the fact that it is shared: and it is, **to seek to stand hour by hour in the conscious presence of God, the One from whom your Mission is derived.** *The Missioner before the Mission*, is the rule. In religious language, your Mission here is: *to know God, and enjoy Him forever, and to see His hand in all His works.*

2. Second, once you have begun doing that in an earnest way, *your second Mission here on Earth* is also one that you share with the rest of the human race, but it is no less your individual mission for the fact that it is shared: and that is, **to do what you can, moment by moment, day by day, step by step, to make this world a better place, following the leading and guidance of God's Spirit within you and around you.**

3. Third, once you have begun doing that in a serious way, *your third Mission here on Earth* is one that is uniquely yours, and that is:

   a) **to exercise the Talent that you particularly came to Earth to use—your greatest gift, which you most delight to use,**

   b) **in the place(s) or setting(s) that God has caused to appeal to you the most,**

   c) **and for those purposes that God most needs to have done in the world.**

When fleshed out, and spelled out, I think you will find that there you have the definition of your Mission in life. Or, to put it another way, these are the three Missions that you have in life.

The Two Rhythms of the Dance of Mission: Unlearning, Learning, Unlearning, Learning

The distinctive characteristic of these three stages is that in each we are forced to *let go* of some fundamental assumptions that our culture has taught us, about the nature of Mission. In other words, throughout this quest and at each stage we find ourselves engaged not merely in a process of *Learning*. We are also engaged in a process of *Unlearning*. Thus, we can restate the above three Learnings, in terms of what we also need to *unlearn* at each stage:

• We need in the first stage to *unlearn* the idea that our Mission is primarily to keep busy *doing* something (here on Earth), and learn instead that our Mission is first of all to keep busy *being* something (here on Earth). In Christian language (and others as well), we might say that we were sent here to learn how *to be* sons of God, and daughters of God, before anything else. *"Our Father, who art in heaven . . ."*

• In the second stage, "Being" issues into "Doing." At this stage, we need to *unlearn* the idea that everything about our Mission must be *unique* to us, and learn instead that some parts of our Mission here on Earth are *shared* by all human beings: e.g., we were all sent here to bring more gratitude, more kindness, more forgiveness, and more love, into the world. We share this Mission because the task is too large to be accomplished by just one individual.

• We need in the third stage to *unlearn* the idea that the part of our Mission that is truly unique, and most truly ours, is something Our Creator just *orders* us to do, without any agreement from our spirit, mind, and heart. (On the other hand, neither is it something that each of us chooses and then merely asks God to bless.) We need to learn that God so honors our free will, that He has ordained that our unique Mission be something that we have some part in choosing.

• In this third stage we need also to *unlearn* the idea that our unique Mission must consist of some achievement for all the world to see—and learn instead that as the stone does not always know what ripples it has caused in the pond whose surface it impacts, so neither we nor those who watch our life will always know *what we have achieved* by our life and by our Mission. *It may be* that by the grace of God we helped bring about a profound change for the better in the lives of other souls around us, but it also may be that this takes place beyond our sight, or after we have gone on. And we may never know what we have accomplished, until we see Him face to face after this life is past.

• Most finally, we need to *unlearn* the idea that what we have accomplished is our doing, and ours alone. It is God's Spirit breathing in us and through us that helps us do whatever we do, and so the singular first-person pronoun is never appropriate, but only the plural. Not "*I* accomplished this" but "*We* accomplished this, God and I, working together. . . ."

That should give you a general overview. But I would like to add some random comments on my part about each of these three Missions of ours here on Earth.

Some Random Comments about Your First Mission in Life

Your first Mission here on Earth is one that you share with the rest of the human race, but it is no less your individual Mission for the fact that it is shared: and that is, **to seek to stand hour by hour in the conscious presence of God, the One from whom your Mission is derived.** The Missioner before the Mission, is the rule. In religious language, your Mission is: to know God, and enjoy Him forever, and to see His hand in all His works.

Comment 1:
How We Might Think of God

Each of us has to go about this primary Mission according to the tenets of his or her own particular religion. But I will speak what I know out of the context of my own particular faith, and you may perhaps translate and apply it to yours. I will speak as a Christian, who believes (passionately) that Christ is the Way and the Truth and the Life. But I also believe, with St. Peter, "that God shows no partiality, but in every nation any one who fears Him and does what is right is acceptable to Him" (Acts 10:34–35).

Now, Jesus claimed many unique things about Himself and His Mission; but He also spoke of Himself as the great prototype for us all. He called Himself "the Son of Man," and He said, "I assure you that the man who believes in me will do the same things that I have done, yes, and he will do even greater things than these. . . ." (John 14:12).

Emboldened by His identification of us with His Life and His Mission, we might want to remember how He spoke about His Life here on Earth. He put it in this context: **"I came from the Father and have come into the world; again, I am leaving the world and going to the Father"** (John 16:28).

If there is a sense in which this is, in even the faintest way, true also of our lives (and I shall say in a moment in what sense I think it is true), then instead of calling our great Creator "God" or "Father" right off, we might begin our approach to the subject of religion by referring to the One Who gave us our Mission and sent us to this planet not as "God" or "Father" but—*just to help our thinking*—as: **"The One From Whom We Came and The One To Whom We Shall Return,"** when this life is done.

If our life here on Earth is to be at all like Christ's, then this is a true way to think about the One Who gave us our Mission. We are not some kind of eternal, preexistent *being.* We are **creatures,** who once did not exist, and then came into Being, and continue to have our Being, only at the will of our great Creator. But as creatures we are both body and soul; although we know our body was created in our mother's womb, our soul's origin is a great mystery. Where it came from, at what moment the Lord created it, is something we cannot know. It is not unreasonable to suppose, however, that the great God created our *soul* before it entered our body, and in that sense we did indeed stand before God before we were born; and He is indeed **"The One From Whom We Came and The One To Whom We Shall Return."**

Therefore, before we go searching for "what work was I sent here to do?" we need to establish—or in a truer sense *reestablish*—contact with **"The One From Whom We Came and The One To Whom We Shall Return."** Without this reaching out of the creature to the great Creator, without this reaching out of *the creature with a Mission* to *the One Who Gave Us That Mission,* the question *what is my Mission in life?* is void and null. The *what* is rooted in the *Who;* absent the Personal, one cannot meaningfully discuss The Thing. It is like the adult who cries, "I want to get married," without giving any consideration to *who* it is they want to marry.

Comment 2:
How We Might Think of Religion or Faith

In light of this larger view of our creatureliness, we can see that *religion* or *faith* is not a question of whether or not we choose to (*as it is so commonly put*) "have a relationship with God." Looking at our life in a larger context than just our life here on Earth, it becomes apparent that some sort of relationship with God is a given for us, about which we have absolutely no choice. God and we **were** and **are** related, during the time of our soul's existence before our birth and in the time of our soul's continued existence after our death. The only choice we have is what to do about **The Time In Between,** i.e., what we want the nature of our relationship with God to be during our time here on Earth and how that will affect the *nature* of the relationship, then, after death.

One of the corollaries of all this is that by the very act of being born into a human body, it is inevitable that we undergo a kind of *amnesia*—an amnesia that typically embraces not only our nine months in the womb, our baby years, and almost one-third of each day (sleeping), but more important any memory of our origin or our destiny. We wander on Earth as an amnesia victim. To seek after Faith, therefore, is to seek to climb back out of that amnesia. Religion or Faith is **the hard reclaiming of knowledge we once knew as a certainty.**

Comment 3:
The First Obstacle to Executing This Mission

This first Mission of ours here on Earth is not the easiest of Missions, simply because it is the first. Indeed, in many ways, it is the most difficult. All can see is that our life here on Earth is a very physical life. We eat, we drink, we sleep, we long to be held, and to hold. We inherit a physical body, with very physical appetites, we walk on the physical earth, and we acquire physical possessions. It is the most alluring of temptations, *in our amnesia*, to come up with just a *Physical* interpretation of this life: to think that the Universe is merely interested in the survival of species. Given this interpretation, the story of our individual life could be simply told: we are born, grow up, procreate, and die.

But we are ever recalled to do what we came here to do: that without rejecting the joy of the Physicalness of this life, such as the love of the blue sky and the green grass, we are to reach out beyond all this to **recall** and recover a *Spiritual* interpretation of our life. *Beyond* the physical and *within* the physicalness of this life, to detect a Spirit and a Person from beyond this Earth who is with us and in us—the very real and loving and awesome Presence of the great Creator from whom we came—and the One to whom we once again shall go.

Comment 4:
The Second Obstacle to Executing This Mission

It is one of the conditions of our earthly amnesia and our creature-liness that, sadly enough, some very *human* and very *rebellious* part of us *likes* the idea of living in a world where we can be our own god—and therefore loves the purely Physical interpretation of life, and finds it *anguish* to relinquish it. Traditional Christian vocabulary calls this "**sin**" and has a lot to say about the difficulty it poses for this first part of our Mission. All who live a thoughtful life know that it is true: our greatest enemy in carrying out this first Mission of ours is indeed *our own* heart and our own rebellion.

Comment 5:
Further Thoughts about What Makes Us
Special and Unique

As I said earlier, many of us come to this issue of our Mission in life, because we want to feel that we are unique. And what we mean by that, is that we hope to discover some "specialness" intrinsic to us, which is our birthright, and which no one can take from us. What we, however, discover from a thorough exploration of this topic, is that we are indeed special—but only because God thinks us so. Our specialness and uniqueness reside in Him, and His love, rather than in anything intrinsic to our own *being*. The proper appreciation of this distinction causes our feet to carry us in the end not to the City called Pride, but to the Temple called Gratitude.

> What is religion? Religion is the service of God out of grateful love for what God has done for us. The Christian religion, more particularly, is the service of God out of grateful love for what God has done for us in Christ.
>   PHILLIPS BROOKS, author of
>   *O Little Town of Bethlehem*

Comment 6:
The Unconscious Doing of the Work We Came to Do

You may have *already* wrestled with this first part of your Mission here on Earth. You may not have called it that. You may have called it simply "learning to believe in God." But if you ask what your Mission is in life, this one was and is the precondition of all else that you came here to do. Absent this Mission, it is folly to talk about the rest. So, if you have been seeking faith, or seeking to strengthen your faith, you have—willy-nilly—already been about *the doing of the Mission you were given.* Born into **This Time In Between,** you have found His hand again, and reclasped it. You are therefore ready to go on with His Spirit to tackle together what you came here to do—the other parts of your Mission.

Some Random Comments about
Your Second Mission in Life

Your second Mission here on Earth is also one that you share with the rest of the human race, but it is no less your individual Mission for the fact that it is shared: and that is, **to do what you can moment by moment, day by day, step by step, to make this world a better place—following the leading and guidance of God's Spirit within you and around you.**

Comment 1:
The Uncomfortableness of One Step at a Time

Imagine yourself out walking in your neighborhood one night, and suddenly you find yourself surrounded by such a dense fog, that you have lost your bearings and cannot find your way. Suddenly, a friend appears out of the fog, and asks you to put your hand in theirs, and they will lead you home. And you, not being able to tell where you are going, trustingly follow them, even though you can only see one step at a time. Eventually you arrive safely home, filled with gratitude. But as you reflect upon the experience the next day, you realize how unsettling it was to have to keep walking when you could see only one step at a time, even though you had guidance you knew you could trust.

Now I have asked you to imagine all of this, because this is the essence of the second Mission to which *you* are called—and *I* am called—in this life. It is all very different than we had imagined. When the question, *"What is your Mission in life?"* is first broached, and we have put our hand in God's, as it were, we imagine that we will be taken up to *some mountaintop*, from which we can see far into the distance. And that we will hear a voice in our ear, saying, "Look, look, see that distant city? That is the goal of your Mission; that is where everything is leading, every step of your way."

But instead of the mountaintop, we find ourself in *the valley*—wandering often in a fog. And the voice in our ear says something quite different from what we thought we would hear. It says, **"Your Mission is to take one step at a time, even when you don't yet see where it all is leading, or what the Grand Plan is, or what your overall Mission in life is. Trust Me; I will lead you."**

Comment 2:
The Nature of This Step-by-Step Mission

As I said, in every situation you find yourself, you have been sent here to do whatever you can—moment by moment—that will bring more gratitude, more kindness, more forgiveness, more honesty, and more love into this world.

There are dozens of such moments every day. Moments when you stand—as it were—at a spiritual crossroads, with two ways lying before you. Such moments are typically called **"moments of decision."** It does not matter what the frame or content of each particular decision is. It all devolves, in the end, into just two roads before you, *every time*. **The one** will lead to *less* gratitude, *less* kindness, *less* forgiveness, *less* honesty, or *less* love in the world. **The other** will lead to *more* gratitude, *more* kindness, *more* forgiveness, *more* honesty, or *more* love in the world.

Your Mission, each moment, is to seek to choose the latter spiritual road, rather than the former, *every time.*

Comment 3:
Some Examples of This Step-by-Step Mission

I will give a few examples, so that the nature of this part of your Mission may be unmistakably clear.

You are out on the freeway, in your car. Someone has gotten into the wrong lane, to the right of *your* lane, and needs to move over into the lane you are in. You *see* their need to cut in, ahead of you. **Decision time.** In your mind's eye you see two spiritual roads lying before you: the one leading to less kindness in the world (you speed up, to shut this driver out, and don't let them move over), the other leading to more kindness in the world (you let the driver cut in). **Since you know this is part of your Mission, part of the reason why you came to Earth, your calling is clear. You know which road to take, which decision to make.**

You are hard at work at your desk, when suddenly an interruption comes. The phone rings, or someone is at the door. They need something from you, a question of some of your time and attention. **Decision time.** In your mind's eye you see two spiritual roads lying before you: the one leading to less love in the world (you tell them you're just too busy to be bothered), the other leading to more love in the world (you put aside your work, decide that God may have sent this person to you, and say, "Yes, what can I do to help you?"). **Since you know this is part of your Mission, part of the reason why you came to Earth, your calling is clear. You know which road to take, which decision to make.**

Your mate does something that hurts your feelings. **Decision time.** In your mind's eye you see two spiritual roads lying before you: the one leading to less forgiveness in the world (you institute an icy silence between the two of you, and think of how you can punish them or otherwise get even), the other leading to more forgiveness in the world (you go over and take them in your arms, speak the truth about your hurt feelings, and assure them of your love). **Since you know this is part of your Mission, part of the reason why you came to Earth, your calling is clear. You know which road to take, which decision to make.**

You have not behaved at your most noble, recently. And now you are face to face with someone who asks you a question about what happened. **Decision time.** In your mind's eye you see two spiritual roads lying before you: the one leading to less honesty in the world (you lie about what happened, or what you were feeling, because you fear losing their respect or their love), the other leading to more honesty in the world (you tell the truth, together with how you feel about it, in retrospect). **Since you know this is part of your Mission, part of the reason why you came to Earth, your calling is clear. You know which road to take, which decision to make.**

Comment 4:
The Spectacle That Makes the Angels Laugh

It is necessary to explain this part of our Mission in some detail, because so many times you will see people wringing their hands, and saying, *"I want to know what my Mission in life is,"* all the while they are cutting people off on the highway, refusing to give time to people, punishing their mate for having hurt their feelings, and lying about what they did. And it will seem to you that the angels must laugh to see this spectacle. *For these people wringing their hands*, their Mission was right there, on the freeway, in the interruption, in the hurt, and at the confrontation.

Comment 5:
The Valley Versus the Mountaintop

At some point in your life your Mission may involve some grand *mountaintop experience*, where you say to yourself, "This, this, is why I came into the world. I know it. I know it." *But until then*, your Mission is here in *the valley*, and the fog, and the little callings moment by moment, day by day. More to the point, it is likely you cannot ever get to your mountaintop Mission unless you have first exercised your stewardship faithfully in the valley.

It is an ancient principle, to which Jesus alluded often, that if you don't use the information the Universe has already given you, you cannot expect it will give you any more. If you aren't being faithful in small things, how can you expect to be given charge over larger things? (Luke 16:10–12; 19:11–24). If you aren't trying to bring more gratitude, kindness, forgiveness, honesty, and love into the world each day, you can hardly expect that you will be entrusted with the Mission to help bring peace into the world or anything else large and important. If we do not live out our day-by-day Mission in the valley, we cannot expect we are yet ready for a larger *mountaintop* Mission.

Comment 6:
The Importance of Not Thinking of
This Mission as "Just a Training Camp"

The valley is not just a kind of "training camp." There is in your imagination even now an invisible *spiritual* mountaintop to which you may go, if you wish to see where all this is leading. And what will you see there, in the imagination of your heart, but the goal toward which all this is pointed: **that Earth might be more like heaven. That human life might be more like God's.** That is the large achievement toward which all our day-by-day Missions *in the valley* are moving. This is a *large* order, but it is accomplished by faithful attention to the doing of our great Creator's **will** in little things as well as in large. It is much like the building of the pyramids in Egypt, which was accomplished by the dragging of a lot of individual pieces of stone by a lot of individual men.

The valley, the fog, the going step by step, is no mere training camp. The goal is real, however large. **"Thy Kingdom come, Thy will be done, on Earth, as it is in heaven."**

Some Random Comments about Your Third Mission in Life

Your third Mission here on Earth is one that is uniquely yours, and that is:

a) **to exercise the Talent that you particularly came to Earth to use—your greatest gift that you most delightto use,**

b) **in those place(s) or setting(s) that God has caused to appeal to you the most,**

c) **and for those purposes that God most needs to have done in the world.**

It is customary in trying to identify this part of our Mission, to advise that we should ask God, in prayer, to speak to us—and **tell us** plainly what our Mission is. We look for a voice in the air, a thought in our head, a dream in the night, a sign in the events of the day, to reveal this thing that is otherwise *(it is said)* completely hidden. Sometimes, from just such answered prayer, people do indeed discover what their Mission is, beyond all doubt and uncertainty.

But having to wait for the voice of God to reveal what our Mission is, is not the truest picture of our situation. St. Paul, in Romans, speaks of a law "written in our members"—and this phrase has a telling application to the question of **how** God reveals to each of us our unique Mission in life. Read again the definition of our third Mission (above) and you will see: the clear implication of the definition is that God has **already** revealed His will to us concerning our vocation and Mission, by causing it to be **"written in our members."** We are to begin deciphering our unique Mission by studying our talents and skills, and more particularly which ones (or one) we most rejoice to use.

God actually has written His will *twice* in our members: *first in the talents* that He lodged there, and second *in His guidance of our heart*, as to which Talent gives us the greatest pleasure from its exercise **(it is usually the one that, when we use it, causes us to lose all sense of time).**

Even as the anthropologist can examine ancient inscriptions, and divine from them the daily life of a long-lost people, so we by examining **our talents** and **our heart** can *more often than we dream* divine the Will of the Living God. For true it is, our Mission is not something He **will** reveal; it is something He **has already** revealed. It is not to be found written in the sky; it is to be found written in our members.

Comment 2:
Career Counseling: We Need You

Arguably, our first two Missions in life could be learned from religion alone—without any reference whatsoever to career counseling, the subject of this book. Why then should career counseling claim that this question about our Mission in life is its proper concern, *in any way?*

It is when we come to this third Mission, which hinges so crucially on the question of our Talents, skills, and gifts, that we see the answer. If you've read the body of this book, before turning to this section, then you know without my even saying it, how much the identification of Talents, gifts, or skills is the province of career counseling. Its expertise, indeed its *raison d'être*, lies precisely in the identification, classification, and (forgive me) "prioritization" of Talents, skills, and gifts. To put the matter quite simply, career counseling knows how to do this better than any other discipline—**including** traditional religion. This is not a defect of religion, but the fulfillment of something Jesus promised: "When the Spirit of truth comes, He will guide you into all truth" (John 16:12). Career counseling is part (we may hope) of that promised late-coming truth. It can therefore be of inestimable help to the pilgrim who is trying to figure out what their greatest, and most enjoyable, Talent is, as a step toward identifying their unique Mission in life.

If career counseling needs religion as its helpmate in the first two stages of identifying our Mission in life, then religion repays the compliment by clearly needing career counseling as **its** helpmate here in the third stage.

And this place where you are in your life right now—facing the job-hunt and all its anxiety—is the perfect time to seek the union within your own mind and heart of both career counseling (as in the pages of this book) and your faith in God.

Comment 3:
How Our Mission Got Chosen:
A Scenario for the Romantic

It is a mystery that we cannot fathom, in this life at least, as to why one of us has this Talent, and the other one has that; why God chose to give one gift—and Mission—to one person, and a different gift—and Mission—to another. Since we do not know, and in some degree cannot know, we are certainly left free to speculate, and imagine.

We may imagine that before we came to Earth, our souls, *our Breath*, *our Light*, stood before the great Creator and volunteered for this Mission. And God and we, together, chose what that Mission would be and what particular gifts would be needed, which He then agreed to give us, after our birth. Thus, our Mission was not a command given preemptorily by an unloving Creator to a reluctant slave without a vote, but was a task jointly designed by us both, in which as fast as the great Creator said, **"I wish"** our hearts responded, **"Oh, yes."** As mentioned in an earlier comment, it may be helpful to think of the condition of our becoming human as that we became amnesiac about any consciousness our soul had before birth—and therefore amnesiac about the nature or manner in which our Mission was designed.

Appendix A

Our searching for our Mission now is therefore a searching to recover the memory of something we ourselves had a part in designing.

I am admittedly a hopeless romantic, so of course I like this picture. If you also are a hopeless romantic, you may like it, too. There's also the chance that it just may be true. We will not know until we see Him face to face.

Comment 4:
Mission as Intersection

There are all different kinds of voices calling you to all different kinds of work, and the problem is to find out which is the voice of God rather than that of society, say, or the superego, or self-interest. By and large a good rule for finding out is this: the kind of work God usually calls you to is the kind of work a) that you need most to do and b) the world most needs to have done. If you really get a kick out of your work, you've presumably met requirement a), but if your work is writing TV deodorant commercials, the chances are you've missed requirement b). On the other hand, if your work is being a doctor in a leper colony, you have probably met b), but if most of the time you're bored and depressed by it, the chances are you haven't only bypassed a) but probably aren't helping your patients much either. Neither the hair shirt nor the soft birth will do. **The place God calls you to is the place where your deep gladness and the world's deep hunger meet.**
     FRED BUECHNER
     Wishful Thinking—A Theological ABC

Excerpted from *Wishful Thinking—A Theological ABC* by Frederick Buechner, revised edition published by HarperOne. Copyright © 1973, 1993 by Frederick Buechner.

Comment 5:
Examples of Mission as Intersection

Your unique and individual Mission will most likely turn out to be a mission of Love, acted out in one or all of three arenas: either in the Kingdom of the Mind, whose goal is to bring more Truth into the world; or in the Kingdom of the Heart, whose goal is to bring more Beauty into the world; or in the Kingdom of the Will, whose goal is to bring more Perfection into the world, through Service.

Here are some examples:

"My mission is, out of the rich reservoir of love that God seems to have given me, to nurture and show love to others—most particularly to those who are suffering from incurable diseases."

"My mission is to draw maps for people to show them how to get to God."

"My mission is to create the purest foods I can, to help people's bodies not get in the way of their spiritual growth."

"My mission is to make the finest harps I can so that people can hear the voice of God in the wind."

"My mission is to make people laugh, so that the travail of this earthly life doesn't seem quite so hard to them."

"My mission is to help people know the truth, in love, about what is happening out in the world, so that there will be more honesty in the world."

"My mission is to weep with those who weep, so that in my arms they may feel themselves in the arms of that Eternal Love that sent me and that created them."

"My mission is to create beautiful gardens, so that in the lilies of the field people may behold the Beauty of God and be reminded of the Beauty of Holiness."

Comment 6:
Life as Long as Your Mission Requires

Knowing that you came to Earth for a reason, and knowing what that Mission is, throws an entirely different light upon your life from now on. You are, generally speaking, delivered from any further fear about how long you have to live. You may settle it in your heart that you are here until God chooses to think that you have accomplished your Mission, or until God has a greater Mission for you in another Realm. You need to be a good steward of what He has given you, while you are here; but you do not need to be an anxious steward or stewardess.

You need to attend to your health, *but you do not need to constantly worry about it.* You need to meditate on your death, *but you do not need to be constantly preoccupied with it.* To paraphrase the glorious words of

G. K. Chesterton: **"We now have a strong desire for living combined with a strange carelessness about dying. We desire life like water and yet are ready to drink death like wine."** We know that we are here to do what we came to do, and we need not worry about anything else.

Final Comment

A Job-Hunt Done Well

If you approach your job-hunt as an opportunity to work on this issue as well as the issue of how you will keep body and soul together, then hopefully your job-hunt will end with your being able to say: "Life has deep meaning to me, now. I have discovered more than my ideal job; I have found my Mission, and the reason why I am here on Earth."

Appendix B

A Guide to Choosing a Career Coach or Counselor

There are a lot of people out there, anxious to help you with your job-hunt or career-change, in case this book isn't sufficient for you. They're willing to help you, for a fee in most cases. (That is how they make their living.) They go by various names: career coach, career counselor, career development specialist, you name it.

I wish I could say that *everyone* who hangs out a sign saying they are now in this business could be completely depended upon. But—alas! and alack!—they can't all be. This career-coaching or career-counseling field is largely unregulated. And even where there is some kind of certification, resulting in their being able to put a lot of degree-soundin' initials after their name, that doesn't really tell you much. It means a lot *to them* of course; in many cases, they had to sweat blood in order to be able to put those initials after their name. (Or not. Some got their initials in little more than a long weekend.)

I used to try to explain what all those initials meant. There is a veritable alphabet-soup of them, with new ones born every year. But no more; I've learned, from more than thirty-five years of experience in this field, that 99.4 percent of all job-hunters and career-changers don't care a fig about these initials. All they want to know is: *do you know how to* help me find a job? Or, more specifically, *do you know how to help me find my dream job—one that matches the gifts, skills, and experience that I have, one that makes me excited to get up in the morning, and excited to go to bed at night, knowing I helped make this Earth a little better place to be in? If so, I'll hire you. If not, I'll fire you.*

How to Lose Your Shirt (or Save It)

Okay, then, *bye-bye initials!* Let us start in a simpler place, with this basic truth:

All coaches and counselors divide basically into three groups:

a) *those who are honest, compassionate, and caring, and know what they're doing;*

b) *those who are honest but don't know what they're doing; and*

c) *those who are dishonest, and merely want your money—large amounts, in a lump sum, and up front.*

In other words, you've got compassionate, caring people in the same field with crooks. And your job, if you want help, is to discern the one from the other.

It would help, of course, if someone could just give you a list of those who are firmly in the first category—honest and know what they're doing. But unfortunately, no one *(including me)* has such a list. You've got to do your own homework, or research here, and your own interviewing, in your own geographical area. And if you're too lazy to take the time and trouble to do this research, you will deserve what you get.

Why is it that *you* and only *you* can do this particular research? Well, let's say a friend tells you to go see so-and-so. He's a wonderful coach or counselor, but unhappily he reminds you of your Uncle Harry, whom you detest. Bummer! But, no one except you knows that you've always disliked your Uncle Harry. That's why no one else can do this research for you—because the real question is not "Who is best?" but "Who is best for you?" Those last two words demand that it be you who "makes the call."

Job-hunters and career-changers try to avoid this research, of course. One way to do that, is through overconfidence in your own intuition: *"Well, I'll just call up one place in my area, and if I like the sound of them, I'll sign up. I'm a pretty good judge of character."* Yeah, right! I've heard this refrain from so many job-hunters who called me only after they'd lost loads of money in a bad "pay-me-first" contract, because they had been *taken*, by slicker salespeople than they had ever run into before. *"But they seemed so sincere, and charming."*

They cry. I express, of course, my sympathy and empathy (I once got taken myself, the same way), but then I add a sobering note of caution, *"I'm terribly sorry to hear that you had such a heartbreaking experience, but—as the Scots would say—'Ya dinna do your homework.' Often you could easily have discovered whether a particular coach or counselor was any good, before you ever gave them any of your money, simply by doing the preliminary research that I urge upon everybody."*

The bottom line, for you: Intuition isn't enough.

Another way people try to avoid this research is by saying, "Well, I'll just see who Bolles recommends." That's pretty futile, because I never have recommended anyone. Some try to claim I do, including, in past years, some of the coaches or counselors listed in the *Sampler* at the end of this appendix, who claim that their very listing here constitutes a recommendation from me. Oh, come on! *This Sampler is more akin to the Yellow Pages, than it is to* Consumer Reports.

Let me repeat this, as I have for more than thirty-five years, and repeat it very firmly:

The listing of a firm or coach in this book does NOT constitute an endorsement or recommendation by me. Never has meant that. Never will. *(Anyone listed here who claims that it does—in their ads, brochures, or publicity—gets permanently removed from this Sampler the following year after I find out about it.)* This is not "a hall of fame"; it is just a *sampler* of names of those who have asked to be listed, and have answered some reasonable questions.

Consider them just a starting point for your search. You must check them out. You must do your own homework. You must do your own research.

A Guide to Choosing a Good Career Coach

So, how do you go about finding a good career coach or counselor, if you decide you need help? Well, you start by collecting three names of career coaches or counselors in your geographical area.

How do you find those names? Several ways:

First, you can get names from your friends: ask if any of them have ever used a career coach or counselor. And if so, did they like 'em? And if so, what is that coach's or counselor's name?

Second, you can get names from the Sampler in Appendix C (which begins on page 280). See if there are any career coaches or counselors who are near you. They may know how you can find still other names in your community. But I repeat what I said above: just because they're listed in the Sampler *doesn't* mean I recommend them. It only means they asked to be listed, and professed familiarity with the contents of this book (current edition, not way back—say, 2001). You've still got to research these people.

Need more names? Try your telephone book's Yellow Pages, under such headings as: *Aptitude and Employment Testing, Career and Vocational Counseling, Personnel Consultants,* and (if you are a woman) *Women's Organizations and Services.*

Once you have three names, you need to go do some comparison shopping. You want to talk with all three of them and decide which of the three (if any) you want to hook up with.

What will this initial interview cost you, with each of the three? The answer to that is easy: when first setting up an appointment, *ask.* You do have the right to inquire ahead of time how much they are going to have to charge you for the exploratory interview.

Some, a few, will charge you nothing for the initial interview. One of the brightest counselors I know says this: *I don't like to charge for the first interview because I want to be free to tell them I can't help them, if for some reason we just don't hit it off.*

However, do not expect that most individual coaches or counselors can afford to give you this exploratory interview for nothing! If they did that, and got a lot of requests like yours, they would never be able to make a living.

If this is not an individual counselor, but *a firm* trying to sell you a "pay-me-first" package *up front,* I guarantee they will give you the initial interview for free. They plan to use that "intake" interview (as they call it) to sell you a much more expensive program.

The Questions to Ask

When you are face to face with the individual coach or counselor (or firm), you ask each of them the same questions, listed on the form below. (Keep a little pad or notebook with you, or PDA, so you can write down their answers.)

After visiting the three places you chose for your comparison shopping, you can go home, sit down, put your feet up, look over your notes, and compare those places.

MY SEARCH FOR A GOOD CAREER COUNSELOR			
Questions I Will Ask Them	Answer from counselor #1	Answer from counselor #2	Answer from counselor #3
1. What is your program?			
2. Who will be counseling? And how long has this person been counseling?			
3. What is your success rate?			
4. What is the cost of your services?			
5. Is there a contract up front? If so, may I see it please, and take it home with me?			

You need to decide a) whether you want none of the three, or b) one of the three (and if so, which one). Remember, you don't have to choose *any* of the three coaches, if you didn't really care for any of them.

If that is the case, then go choose three new counselors out of the Yellow Pages or wherever, dust off the notebook, and go out again. It may take a few more hours to find what you want. But **the wallet, the purse, the job-hunt, the life, you save will be your own.**

As you look over your notes, you will soon realize there is no definitive way for you to determine a career coach's intentions. It's something you'll have to *smell out*, as you go along. But here are some clues.

These are primarily clues about large *firms*, most particularly *executive counseling firms*, and **rarely apply to individual coaches or counselors**, but read these anyway, for your own education.

Bad Vibes, on Up to Real Bad Vibes

If they give you the feeling that everything will be done for you, by them *(including interpretation of tests, and decision making about what this means you should do, or where you should do it)*—rather than asserting that you are going to have to do almost all the work, with their basically being your coach,

(Give them 15 bad points)

You want to learn how to do this for yourself; you're going to be job-hunting again, you know.

If they say they are not the person who will be doing the program with you, but deny you any chance to meet the coach or counselor you would be working with,

(Give them 75 bad points)

You're talking to a salesperson. My advice after talking to job-hunters for more than thirty-five years, is: avoid any firm that has a salesperson.

If you do get a chance to meet the counselor, but you don't like the counselor, period!,

(Give them 150 bad points)

I don't care what their expertise is, if you don't like them, you're going to have a rough time getting what you want. I guarantee it. Rapport is everything.

If you ask how long the counselor has been doing this, and they get huffy or give a double-barreled answer, such as: "I've had eighteen years' experience in the business and career counseling world,"

(Give them 20 bad points)

What that may mean is: seventeen and a half years as a fertilizer sales-man, and one half year doing career counseling. Persist. "How long have you been with this firm, and how long have you been doing formal career coaching or counseling, as you are here?" You might be interested to know that some executive or career counseling firms hire yesterday's clients as today's new

staff. Such new staff are sometimes given training only after they're "on-the-job." They are practicing . . . on you.

If they try to answer the question of their experience by pointing to their degrees or credentials,

(Give them 3 bad points)

Degrees or credentials tell you they've passed certain tests of their qualifications, but often these tests bear more on their expertise at career assessment, than on their knowledge of creative job-hunting techniques.

If, when you ask about that firm's success rate, they say they have never had a client who failed to find a job, no matter what,

(Give them 500 bad points)

They're lying. I have studied career counseling programs for more than thirty years, have attended many, have studied records at state and federal offices, and have hardly ever seen a program that placed more than 86 percent of their clients, tops, in their best years. And it goes downhill from there. A prominent executive counseling firm was reported by the Attorney General's Office of New York State to have placed only 38 out of 550 clients (a 93 percent failure rate). On the other hand, if they make it clear that they have had a good success rate, but if you fail to work hard at the whole process, then there is no guarantee you are going to find a job, give them three stars.

If a firm shows you letters from ecstatically happy former clients, but when you ask to talk to some of those clients, you get stonewalled,

(Give them 200 bad points)

Man, these guys can be slick! No, no, not honest career coaches; I'm referring to *the crooks* in this field. Here is a job-hunter's letter about his experience with one of those firms:

"I asked to speak to a former client or clients. You would have thought I asked to speak to Elvis. The counselor stammered and stuttered and gave me a million excuses why I couldn't talk to some of these 'satisfied' former clients. None of the excuses sounded legitimate to me. We went back and forth for about thirty minutes. Finally, he excused himself and went to speak to his boss, the owner. The next thing I knew I was called into the owner's office for a more 'personal' sales pitch. We spoke for about forty-five minutes as he tried to convince me to use his service. When I told him I was not ready to sign up, he became angry and asked my counselor why I had been put before 'the committee' if I wasn't ready to commit? The counselor claimed I had

given a verbal commitment at our last meeting. The owner then turned to me and said I seemed to have a problem making a decision and that he did not want to do business with me. I was shocked. They had turned the whole story around to make it look like it was my fault. I felt humiliated. In retrospect, the whole process felt like dealing with a used car salesman. They used pressure tactics and intimidation to try to get what they wanted. As you have probably gathered, more than anything else this experience made me angry."

If you ask the firm what is the cost of their services, and they reply that it is a lump sum that must all be paid "up front" before you start or shortly after you start, all at once or in rapid installments,

(Give them **300 bad points**)

We're talking about firms here, not the average individual counselor or coach. The basic problem is that both "the good guys" and "the crooks" do this. The good guys operate on the theory that if you give them a large sum up front, you will then be really committed to the program. The crooks operate on the theory that if you give them a large sum up front, they don't have to give you anything back, except endless excuses and subterfuge, after a certain date (quickly reached). And the trouble is that, going in, there is absolutely no way for you to distinguish crook from good guy; they only reveal their true nature after they've got all your money. And by that time, you have no legal way to get it back, no matter what they verbally promised.[1]

You may think I am exaggerating: I mean, can there possibly be such mean men and women, who would prey on job-hunters, especially executive job-hunters, when they're down and out? Yes, ma'am, and yes, sir, there sure are. That's why you have to do your own preliminary research so thoroughly.

Trust me on this. There is no way to distinguish the good guys from the crooks. I have tried for years to think of some way around this dilemma, but there just is none. So if you decide to pay up front, be sure it is money you can afford to lose.

---

1. Sometimes the written contract—there is *always* a written contract, when you are dealing with the bad guys, and they will probably ask your partner to sign it, too—will claim to provide for an almost complete refund, at any time, until you reach a cutoff date in the program, which the contract specifies. Unfortunately, fraudulent firms bend over backward to be extra nice, extra available, and extra helpful to you, from the time you first walk in, until that cutoff point is reached. Therefore, when the cutoff point for getting a refund has passed, you let it pass because you are very satisfied with their past services, and believe there will be many more weeks of the same. Only, there aren't. At fraudulent firms, once the cutoff point is passed, the career counselor suddenly becomes virtually impossible for you to get ahold of. Call after call will not be returned. You will say to yourself, "What happened?" Well, what happened, my friend, is that you paid up in full, they have all the money they're ever going to get out of you, and now, they want to move on.

If Money Is a Problem for You: Hourly Coaching

There are career coaches or counselors who charge by the hour. In fact, they are in the majority. With them, there is no written contract. You sign nothing. You pay only for each hour as you use it, according to their set rate. Each time you keep an appointment, you pay them at the end of that hour for their help, according to that rate. Period. Finis. You never owe them any money (unless you made an appointment, and failed to keep it). You can stop seeing them at any time, if you feel you are not getting the help you wish.

What will they charge? You will find, these days, that the best career coaches or counselors (*plus some of the worst*) will charge you whatever a good therapist or marriage counselor charges per hour, in your geographical area. Currently, in major metropolitan areas, that runs around $150 an hour, sometimes more. In suburbia or rural areas, it may be much less—$40 an hour, or so.

That fee is for *individual time* with the career coach or counselor. If you can't afford that fee, ask whether they also run groups. If they do, the fee will be much less. And, in one of those delightful ironies of life, since you get a chance to listen to problems that other job-hunters in your group are having, the group will often give you more help than an individual session with a counselor would have. Not always; but often. It's always ironic when *cheaper* and *more helpful* go hand in hand.

If the career counselor in question does offer groups, there should (again) never be a contract. The charge should be payable at the end of each session, and you should be able to drop out at any time, without further cost, if you decide you are not getting the help you want.

There are some career counselors who run free (or almost free) job-hunting workshops through local churches, synagogues, chambers of commerce, community colleges, adult education programs, and the like, as their community service, or *pro bono* work (as it is technically called). I have had reports of workshops from a number of places in the U.S. and Canada. They exist in other parts of the world as well. If money is a problem for you, in getting help with your job-hunt, ask around your community to see if workshops exist in your community. Your chamber of commerce will know, or your church or synagogue.

You can find an incredibly useful list of all the job clubs in the U.S. compiled by my friend Susan Joyce, on her site: www.job-hunt.org (www.job-hunt.org/job-search-networking/job-search-networking.shtml).

If Your Location Is a Problem for You: Distance Coaching or Telephone Counseling

The assumption, from the beginning, was that career counseling would always take place face to face. Both of you, counselor and job-hunter, together in the same room. Just like career counseling's close relatives: marriage counseling, or even AA.

Of course, a job-hunter might—on occasion—phone his or her counselor the day before an interview, to get some last-minute tips or to answer some questions that a prospective interviewer might ask, *tomorrow*.

What is different, today, is that in some cases, career counseling is being conducted exclusively over the phone from start to finish. Some counselors now report that they haven't laid eyes on over 90 percent of their clients, and wouldn't know them if they bumped into them on a street corner. I call this "distance-coaching" or "telephone-counseling."

With the invention of the Internet, with the invention of Internet *telephoning*, we are witnessing "the death of distance"—that is to say, the death of distance as an obstacle. The world, as Thomas Friedman has famously written, is in effect *flat*.

An increasing number of counselors or executive coaches are doing this *distance-counseling*. For the job-hunter, it's not all that expensive. True, counselors who offer this, charge between $80/hour and "sky-high" (usually, in that case, paid by the company).[2] But you can shop around, and ask questions to find the best price for your budget.

To their fee must be added, of course, the cost of the phone calls. *No problem*—the cost of the telephoning doesn't have to break your budget, especially if your counselor is using a technology known as Public Switched Telephone Network (PSTN) conferencing, or has an Internet phone service—technically called VoIP (Voice-over-Internet-Protocol)—which makes your phone calls free or available for a low fee.

---

2. Two famous "distance coaches" are Joel Garfinkle in Oakland, California, www.dreamjobcoaching.com; and Marshall Goldsmith of www.marshallgoldsmithlibrary.com, international coach to the executive elite, and author (with Mark Reiter) of the currently popular book, *What Got You Here Won't Get You There*.

Indeed, that's available right now. And, a program called *Skype* is especially useful. (Details, for counselor and job-hunter alike, may be found at www.skype.com/download or in the official definitive written guide by Harry Max and Taylor Ray, called—surprise!—*Skype: The Definitive Guide*.[3]) Skype requires telephones, but not necessarily computers. Or computers, but not necessarily telephones. Your options are many.

Now, this increasing availability of "distance-counseling" is good news, and bad news.

Why good news? Well, in the old days you might be a job-hunter in some remote village, with a population of only eighty-five, back in the hills somewhere, or you might be living somewhere in France or in China, miles from any career counselor or coach, and so, be totally out of luck. Now, these days you can be anywhere in the world, but as long as you have the Internet on your desk, you can still find the best distance-counseling there is.

And the bad news?

Well, just because a counselor or coach does distance-counseling or phone-counseling, doesn't mean they are really good at doing it. Some are superb; but some are not so hotsy-totsy.

So, you're still going to have to research any distance-counselor who interests you *very carefully*. It is altogether too easy for a counselor to get sloppy doing distance-counseling—for example, browsing the newspapers while you are telling some long personal story, etc., to which they are giving only the briefest attention. Since you can't see the counselor, you don't know. Because of this, I personally, were I job-hunting or changing careers, would want to sign up only for one session at a time. In case a flaw suddenly appears. *Outtahere!*

To avoid any kind of sloppiness, *you* and the counselor need discipline. Experienced distance-counselors, such as Joel Garfinkle,[4] insist on forms being used, both before and after each phone session. With his permission, I have adapted his forms, and print them here. *And, P.S., they are equally useful for just normal, face-to-face counseling, as well.*

---

3. Published by Que Publishing, Pearson Education.
4. www.dreamjobcoaching.com/about

Client Coaching Forms

1. Before You Start

Prior to beginning the counseling, it helps if your coach or counselor asks you to fill out the following kind of form, for you to give to him or her. They are written by the counselor, addressed to you, the potential counselee. (And if they don't ask for a form like this to be filled out, you might volunteer to give them such a form on your own.)

Questions to Understand You Better

(Copy this onto another sheet of paper, and leave lots of space on the form for your answer, after each question below.)

1. Why have you decided to work with me?
2. How can I have the most impact on your life in the next ninety days (three months)?
3. List three key goals you want to accomplish through our work together.
4. What stops you from achieving what you want in question #2 or #3 above?
5. Project ahead one year: As you look back, and things went well, how did you benefit from our coaching relationship?
6. What are your expectations from our work together? How can we exceed these expectations?
7. What else is helpful for me to know about you?
8. Explain your background (use the same format as the examples below).

Examples:

1. After thirty years as a commercial insurance broker, I hit a wall last May, and decided to change careers . . .
2. After twelve successful years in the high-tech industry, I found myself unfulfilled in finding a satisfying career. Over the years, I read countless books on the topic of finding one's true purpose in career pursuits, but was still missing a sense of purpose and clarity on what I wanted to do . . .

3. After working for twenty years in the investment industry I decided to start my own company . . .

4. Etc.

2. Before Each Session, Preparation Form

Please fill out this form #2 for each coaching session. It should be filled out and e-mailed to me twenty-four hours before the next coaching session to assist me in preparing for that session.

(Copy this onto another sheet of paper, and leave lots of space on the form for your answer, after each question below.)

Commitments that I made to myself on the last coaching session and what I accomplished since we had the coaching session:

The challenges and opportunities I am facing now:

The one action I can take that will most affect my current goals and provide the highest payoff:

My agenda for the coaching session is:

3. After Each Session: Reflection Form

Immediately after each coaching session e-mail me form #3.

(Copy this onto another sheet of paper, and leave lots of space on the form for your answer, after each question below.)

This week's commitment:

My greatest insights during this session were:

What you, my coach, said or asked during the session that impacted me most:

What I'd like you, as my coach, to do differently/more of/less of:

How I feel I am evolving from our work together:

What happens in a counseling session is our responsibility, not just the counselor's or coach's.

The forms, above, are one way of our taking responsibility. Another, is that when you first contact prospective coaches for distance-counseling in particular, you have a right to ask them: (1) "What training have you completed, relevant to distance-counseling, such as telephone skills, and supervised counseling?" (2) "How will our distance-counseling be organized and scheduled?" and (3) "What will the two of us do if and when interruptions occur during a session, at either end?"

You must always remember: distance-counseling, attractive as it will be for many, as necessary as it will be for some, definitely has its limits.

To the caveman, the technology that enables all this to happen in this twenty-first century, would be jaw-droppingly awesome. But, good career counseling or coaching *is not just about technology*. What is really truly awesome, in the end, is simply our power to help each other on this Earth. And how much that power resides, not in techniques or technology, though these things are important—but in each of us just being a good human being. A *loving* human being.

A Sampler

The following Appendix is exactly what its name implies: a Sampler. Were I to list all the career coaches and counselors who are out there, we would end up with an encyclopedia. Some states, in fact, have encyclopedic lists of counselors and businesses, in various books or directories, and your local bookstore or library should have these, in their Job-Hunting Section, under such titles as "How to Get a Job in . . ." or "Job-Hunting in . . ."

I did not choose the places listed in this Sampler; rather, they are listed at their own request, and I offer their information to you simply as suggestions of where you can begin your investigation—when you're trying to find decent help.[5]

Do keep in mind that many truly helpful places and coaches are not listed here. If you discover such a coach or place, which is very good at helping people *with Parachute* and creative job-hunting or career-change, do send us the pertinent information. We will ask them, as we do all the listings here, a few intelligent questions, and if they sound okay, we will add that place as a suggestion in next year's edition.

We do ask a few questions—because our readers want counselors and places that have some expertise *with Parachute*, and can help job-hunters or career-changers finish their job-hunt using this book. So, if they've

---

5. Yearly readers of this book will notice that we do remove people from this Sampler, without warning. First of all, there are accidents: we drop places we didn't mean to, but a typographical error was made, somehow (it happens). *Oops!* Call this to our attention; we'll put you back in next year.

We deliberately remove: places that have moved, and don't bother to send us their new address. *Coaches and counselors: If you are listed here, we expect you to be a professional at communication. When you move, your first priority should be to let us know, immediately. As one exemplary counselor wrote: "You are the first person I am contacting on my updated letterhead . . . hot off the press just today!" So it should always be, if you want to continue to be listed here. A number of places get removed every year, precisely because of their poor communication skills, and their sloppiness in letting us know where they've gone to.*

Other causes for removal: Places that have disconnected their telephone, or otherwise suggest that they have gone out of business. Places that our readers lodge complaints against with us, as being unhelpful or even obnoxious. The complaints may be falsified, but we can't take that chance. Places that change their personnel, and the new person has never even heard of *Parachute*, or "creative job-search techniques." College services that we discover (belatedly) serve only "Their Own." Counseling firms that employ salespeople as the initial "intake" person that a job-hunter meets. If you discover that any of the places listed in this Sampler fall into any of the above categories, you would be doing a great service to our other readers by dropping us a line and telling us so (P.O. Box 370, Walnut Creek, CA 94597).

Appendix B

never even heard of *Parachute*, we don't list them. On the other hand, we can't measure a place's expertise at this distance, no matter how many questions we ask.

So, even if listed here, they need to be thoroughly researched *by you*. You must do your own sharp questioning before you decide to go with anyone. If you don't take time to research two or three places, before choosing a counselor, you will deserve whatever you get (or, more to the point, don't get). So, please, do your research. The purse or wallet you save, will be your own.

The listings that follow are alphabetical within each state, except that counselors listed by their name are in alphabetical order according to their last name.

Some offer group career counseling, some offer testing, some offer access to job-banks, etc.

One final note: Generally speaking, these places counsel anybody. A few, however, may turn out to have restrictions unknown to us ("we counsel only women," etc.). If that's the case, your time isn't wasted. They may be able to help you with a referral. So, don't be afraid to ask them, "Who else in the area can you tell me about, who helps with job-searches, and are there any (among them) that you think are particularly effective?"

Area Codes

If you call a phone number in the Sampler that is any distance away from you, and they tell you "this number cannot be completed as dialed," the most likely explanation is that the area code was changed—maybe some time ago. Throughout the U.S. now, area codes are subdividing constantly, sometimes more than once during a short time span. (We ask counselors listed here to notify us when the area code changes, but some do and some don't.) Anyway, call Information and check.

Of course, if you're calling a local counselor, you probably don't need the area code anyway (unless you live in one of the metropolitan areas in the U.S. that requires ten-digit dialing).

Throughout this Sampler, an asterisk before their name, in green, means they offer both secular and religious counseling, that is, they're not afraid to talk about God if you're looking for some help, in finding your Mission in life.

Appendix C

Sampler List of Coaches

UNITED STATES

Alabama

Chemsak, Maureen J., NCC, LPC, MCC,
Counselor,
Athens State University,
300 N. Beaty St.,
Athens, AL 35611
Phone: 256-233-8285 or 256-722-0449
E-mail: maureen.chemsak@athens.edu

Vantage Associates,
2100-B Southbridge Pkwy., Ste. 240,
Birmingham, AL 35209
Phone: 205-879-0501
Contact: Michael A. Tate

WorkMatters, Inc.,
PO Box 130756,
Birmingham, AL 35213
Phone: 205-879-8494
Contact: Gayle H. Lantz
E-mail: lantz@workmatters.com
www.workmatters.com

Alaska

Career Transitions,
2600 Denali St., Ste. 430,
Anchorage, AK 99503
Phone: 907-274-4500
Fax: 907-274-4510
Contact: Deeta Lonergan, President
E-mail: deeta@alaska.net
www.careertransitions.biz

Arizona

Boninger, Faith, PhD,
10965 E. Mary Katherine Dr.,
Scottsdale, AZ 85259
Phone: 480-551-7097
E-mail: faithboninger@cox.net

*Career Discovery Services, LLC,
3145 E. Chandler Blvd., Ste. 110-212,
Phoenix, AZ 85048
Phone: 480-706-1262
Contact: Sandy Somers, RN, MS, ACC
E-mail: careerdiscovery@msn.com
www.careerdiscoveryservices.com

Davenport, Debra, CEO,
DavenportFolio,
Licensed Career Counselors/Certified
Professional Mentors,
10645 N. Tatum Blvd., Ste. 200-362,
Phoenix, AZ 85028
Phone: 480-348-7875
Toll-free: 866-232-6492
E-mail: info@davenportfolio.com
www.davenportfolio.com

Renaissance Career Solutions,
PO Box 30118,
Phoenix, AZ 85046-0118
Phone: 602-867-4202
Contact: Betty Boza, MA, LCC
E-mail: bboza@cox.net
www.rcareer-solutions.com

California

Bauer, Lauralyn Larsen,
Career Counselor & Coach,
Napa, CA 94558
Phone: 707-363-7775
E-mail: lauralynbauer@hotmail.com

Bay Area Career Center,
Mechanics Institute Library Bldg.,
57 Post St., Ste. 804,
San Francisco, CA 94104
Phone: 415-398-4881
Fax: 415-398-4897
E-mail: info@bayareacareercenter.com
www.bayareacareercenter.com

Berrett & Associates,
533 E. Mariners Cir.,
Fresno, CA 93730
Phone: 559-284-3549
Contact: Dwayne Berrett, MA, RPCC
E-mail: dberrett3@fresno.com
www.berrett-associates.com

California Career Services,
6024 Wilshire Blvd.,
Los Angeles, CA 90036
Phone: 323-933-2900
Fax: 323-933-9929
Contact: Susan W. Miller, MA
E-mail: swmcareer@aol.com
www.californiacareerservices.com

Career Balance,
215 Witham Rd.,
Encinitas, CA 92024
Phone: 760-436-3994
Fax: 760-632-9871
Contact: Virginia Byrd, MEd,
Career and Work-Life Consultant
E-mail: virginia@careerbalance.net
www.careerbalance.net

°Career Choices,
Dublin, CA
Contact: Dana E. Ogden,
MS Ed, CCDV, Career & Educational
Counselor, Workshop Facilitator
E-mail: dana@careerchoices.us
www.careerchoices.us

**Career Counseling and
Assessment Associates,**
9229 W. Sunset Blvd., Ste. 502,
Los Angeles, CA 90069
Phone: 310-274-3423
Contact: Dianne Y. Sundby, PhD,
Director and Psychologist
E-mail: DYSD99@aol.com

**A Career Counseling and
Psychotherapy Practice,**
1330 Lincoln Ave., Ste. 210 A,
San Rafael, CA 94901
Phone: 415-789-9113
Contact: Suzanne Penney Lindenbaum,
MSW, LCSW, MCC
E-mail: lindenccs@aol.com
www.therapistfinder.com/TherapistDetail
.cfm?id=55886

Career Development Life Planning,
3585 Maple St., Ste. 237,
Ventura, CA 93003
Phone: 805-642-9180
Contact: Norma Zuber, MSC; Associates
www.normazubercareers.com

Career Possibilities,
3009 Lantana Ave.,
Fullerton, CA 92835-1945
Phone: 714-990-6014
Contact: Cheryl A. Heil, MEd, JCTC, CPCM
E-mail: keytosuccess1@sbcglobal.net

**Career and Personal
Development Institute,**
582 Market St., Ste. 410,
San Francisco, CA 94104
Phone: 415-982-2636
Contact: Bob Chope
www.cpdicareercounseling.com

**Center for Career Growth
and Development,**
453 Alberto Way, Ste. 257D,
Los Gatos, CA 95032
Phone: 408-354-7150
Contact: Steven E. Beasley
E-mail: stevenbeasley@verizon.net

*Center for Life & Work Planning,
1133 Second St.,
Encinitas, CA 92024
Phone/Fax: 760-943-0747
Contact: Mary C. McIsaac,
Executive Director
E-mail: mmcisaac@aol.com

*Cheney-Rice, Stephen, MS,
2113 Westboro Ave.,
Alhambra, CA 91803-3720
Phone: 626-824-5244
E-mail: sccheneyrice@earthlink.net

Christen, Carol, Consultant,
Career & Job Search Strategy,
Coauthor, *What Color Is Your Parachute?
for Teens*
Atascadero, CA
Phone: 805-462-8795
E-mail: carol@carolchristen.com

Collaborative Solutions,
3130 W. Fox Run Way,
San Diego, CA 92111
Phone: 858-268-9340
Contact: Nancy Helgeson, MA, LMFT

Cypress College,
Career Planning Center,
9200 Valley View St.,
Cypress, CA 90630
Phone: 714-484-7120

Dream Job Coaching,
6918 Thornhill Dr.,
Oakland, CA 94611
Phone: 510-339-3201
E-mail: joel@dreamjobcoaching.com
www.dreamjobcoaching.com,
www.garfinkleexecutivecoaching.com, or
www.14daystoajob.com

Experience Unlimited Job Club
There are many Experience Unlimited
clubs in California, found at the Employ-
ment Development Department (EDD) in
the following locations: Anaheim, Canoga
Park, Contra Costa, Corona, Fremont,
Fresno, Irvine, Lancaster, Manteca,
Oakland, Pasadena, San Francisco, San
Rafael, Santa Cruz/Capitola, Simi Valley,
Sunnyvale, Torrance, and West Covina.
Contact the chapter nearest you through
your local EDD office.

Floyd, Mary Alice, MA,
Career Life Transitions,
3233 Lucinda Ln.,
Santa Barbara, CA 93105
Phone: 805-687-5462
E-mail: maryalicefloyd@cox.net
www.careerlifetrans.com

*Frangquist, Deborah Gavrin, MS,
Chosen Futures,
1801 Bush St., Ste. 121,
San Francisco, CA 94109
Phone: 415-346-6121
Fax: 415-346-6118
E-mail: Deborah@ChosenFutures.com
www.ChosenFutures.com

Fritsen, Jan, MS, LMFT,
Career Counseling and Coaching,
23181 La Cadena Dr., Ste. 103,
Laguna Hills, CA 92653
Phone: 949-497-4869
E-mail: janfritsen@cox.net
www.janfritsen.com

Geary & Associates, Inc.,
1100 Coddingtown Ctr., Ste. A,
PO Box 3774,
Santa Rosa, CA 95402
Phone: 707-525-8085
Fax: 707-528-8088
Contact: Jack Geary, MA;
Edelweiss Geary, MEd, CRC
E-mail: esgeary@sbcglobal.net
www.geary@gearyassociates.com

Hilliard, Larkin, MA,
Counseling Psychology,
1411 Holiday Hill Rd.,
Santa Barbara, CA 93117
Phone: 805-683-5855
E-mail: larkinhilliard@yahoo.com
(English, French, German, and Russian.)

HRS,
4421 Alla Rd., #2,
Marina del Rey, CA 90292
Phone: 310-577-0972
Contact: Nancy Mann, MBA,
Career Coach
E-mail: nanmanhrs@aol.com

Jewish Vocational Service,
6505 Wilshire Blvd., Ste. 200 and Ste. 700,
Los Angeles, CA 90048
Phone: 323-761-8888

Judy Kaplan Baron Associates,
6046 Cornerstone Ct. W., Ste. 208,
San Diego, CA 92121
Phone: 858-558-7400
Contact: Judy Kaplan Baron, Director
E-mail: careergyde@aol.com

Life's Work Center,
109 Bartlett St.,
San Francisco, CA 94110
Phone: 415-821-0930
Contact: Tom Finnegan, Executive Director
E-mail: tom@lifesworkcenter.org

*Miller, Lizbeth, MS, NCC,
3425 S. Bascom Ave., Ste. 250,
Campbell, CA 95008
Phone: 408-486-6763
Fax: 408-369-4990
E-mail: lizmillercareers@yahoo.com
www.lizmillercareers.com

Nemko, Marty, PhD,
Career and Education Strategist,
5936 Chabolyn Terr.,
Oakland, CA 94618
Phone: 510-655-2777
E-mail: mnemko@comcast.net
www.martynemko.com

Passport to Purpose,
333 Somerset Cir.,
Thousand Oaks, CA 91360
Phone: 805-496-5654
Contact: Cathy Severson, MS
E-mail: cathys997@verizon.net
www.passporttopurpose.com
www.retirementlifematters.com

Saraf, Dilip G., Career and
Worklife Strategist,
Career Transitions Unlimited,
39159 Paseo Padre Pkwy., #221,
Fremont, CA 94538
Phone: 510-791-7005
E-mail: dilip@7keys.org
www.7keys.org

*Schoenbeck, Mary Lynne, MA, NCCC,
Career/Retirement Counselor,
Coach, Consultant,
Schoenbeck & Associates,
Los Altos, CA
Phone: 650-964-8370
E-mail: schoenbeck@mindspring.com

Struntz and Associates,
Career Change and Job Search Consulting,
Saint Helena, CA 94574
Phone: 707-963-0843
Contact: Wolfgang Struntz, MA
E-mail: Struntz@netwiz.net

*Visions into Form, Coaching,
223 San Anselmo Ave., Ste. 6,
San Anselmo, CA 94960
Phone: 415-488-4998
Contact: Audrey Seymour, MA, PCC, CPCC
E-mail: inquiry@visionsintoform.com
www.visionsintoform.com

Wilson, Patti,
Career Company,
PO Box 35633,
Los Gatos, CA 95030
Phone: 408-354-1964
E-mail: patti@careercompany.com
www.pattiwilson.com

Zitron Parham Career and Life Counseling,
4724 25th St., Ste. A,
San Francisco, CA 94114
Phone: 415-602-5595
Contact: Nick Parham,
Career & Life Coach
E-mail: npcoach@gmail.com
www.zitronparhamcareerservices.com

Colorado

**Arapahoe Community College
Career Center,**
5900 S. Santa Fe Dr.,
PO Box 9002,
Littleton, CO 80160-9002
Phone: 303-797-5805
E-mail: careers@arapahoe.edu

Arp, Rosemary, MS, GCDF,
Career Counselor,
Boulder, CO
Phone: 303-527-1874
E-mail: rsarp@comcast.net

Gary Ringler & Associates,
1747 Washington St., #203,
Denver, CO 80203
Phone: 303-863-0234
E-mail: garyringler@msn.com

Helmstaedter, Sherry,
5040 S. El Camino,
Englewood, CO 80111-1122
Phone: 303-794-5122

Pivotal Choices, Inc.,
PO Box 1098,
Durango, CO 81302
Phone: 970-385-9597
Contact: Mary Jane Ward, MEd, NCC, NCCC
E-mail: mjw@pivotalchoices.com
www.pivotalchoices.com

Women's Resource Agency,
750 Citadel Dr. E., #3116,
Colorado Springs, CO 80909
Phone: 719-471-3170

Connecticut

Accord Career Services, LLC,
The Exchange, Ste. 305,
270 Farmington Ave.,
Farmington, CT 06032
Phone: 800-922-1480 or 860-674-9654
Contact: Tod Gerardo, MS, Director
E-mail: tod@accordcareerservices.com
www.accordcareerservices.com

Career You Love Counseling Services,
761 Valley Rd.,
Fairfield, CT 06825
Phone: 203-374-7649
Contact: Robert N. Olsen, MA, MCC, LPC
E-mail: counselor@yourpassion.com
www.yourpassion.com

Center for Professional Development,
50 Elizabeth St.,
Hartford, CT 06105
Phone: 860-768-5619
Contact: Eleta Jones, PhD, LPC
E-mail: ejones@hartford.edu
www.thecenterforprofessionaldevelopment
.org

Cohen, James S., PhD,
8 Barbara's Way,
Ellington, CT 06029
Phone: 860-871-7832
E-mail: vocdoc56@yahoo.com

The Offerjost-Westcott Group,
263 Main St.,
Old Saybrook, CT 06475
Phone: 860-388-6094
Contact: Russ Westcott
E-mail: russwest@snet.net

Pannone, Bob, MA,
Career Specialist,
62 Lane St.,
Huntington, CT 06484
Phone: 203-513-2291
E-mail: upstartinc@yahoo.com

Preis, Roger J.,
RPE Career Dynamics,
PO Box 16722,
Stamford, CT 06905
Phone: 203-322-7225
rjpreis@rpecareers.com
www.rpecareers.com

Delaware

Bronson, Kris, PhD,
1409 Foulk Rd., Ste. 204,
Foulkstone Plaza
Wilmington, DE 19803
Phone: 302-477-0708, ext. 4
www.krisbronsonphd.com

Florida

Career Choices Unlimited,
4465 Baymeadows Rd., Ste. 7,
Jacksonville, FL 32217
Phone: 904-443-0059, 904-262-9470
Contact: Marilyn A. Feldstein, MPA,
JCTC, MBTI, PHR,
Career Coach and Professional Speaker
www.careerchoicesunlimited.com

Center for Career Decisions,
3912 S. Ocean Blvd., #1009,
Boca Raton, FL 33487
Phone: 561-276-0321
Contact: Linda Friedman, MA, NCC
www.career-decisions.com

The Centre for Women,
305 S. Hyde Park Ave.,
Tampa, FL 33606
Phone: 813-251-8437
Contact: Alice Thompson,
Employment Services

Chabon-Berger, Toby, MEd, NCC, NCCC,
Career and Professional Development
Coach,
4900 Boxwood Cir.,
Boynton Beach, FL 33436
Phone: 561-596-3656
E-mail: tberger@chabongroup.com
www.tobycareer.com

The Clarity Group,
PO Box 110084,
Bradenton, FL 34211
Phone: 941-388-8108
Contact: George Schofield, PhD
E-mail: george.schofield@clarity-group.com
or george@georgeschofield.com
www.clarity-group.com or
www.georgeschofield.com

Crossroads,
Palm Beach Community College,
4200 Congress Ave.,
Lake Worth, FL 33461-4796
Phone: 561-868-3586
Contact: Bobbi Marsh, Program Manager
www.pbcc.edu/crossroads.xml

**Focus on the Future: Displaced
Homemaker Program,**
Santa Fe College,
3000 NW 83rd St.,
Gainesville, FL 32606
Phone: 352-395-5047
Contact: Nancy Griffin,
Program Coordinator
E-mail: focusonthefuture@sfcollege.edu
www.sfcollege.edu
(Classes are free.)

Harmon, Larry, PhD,
A Career Counseling Center, Inc.,
2000 S. Dixie Hwy., Ste. 103,
Miami, FL 33133
Phone: 305-858-8557

Life Designs, Inc.,
19526 E. Lake Dr.,
Miami, FL 33015
Phone: 305-829-9008
Contact: Dulce Muccio Weisenborn
E-mail: dmw@lifedesigns-inc.com

Rosanne R. Hartwell Women's Center,
Florida Community College at Jacksonville,
South Campus, Building E-100,
11901 Beach Blvd.,
Jacksonville, FL 32246
Phone: 904-256-6982
Contact: Harriet Courtney,
Project Coordinator
E-mail: hcourtney@fccj.edu
Fax: 904-646-2018

TransitionWorks,
Delray Beach, FL
Phone: 301-233-4287
Contact: Nancy K. Schlossberg, EdD,
Principal; Stephanie Kay, MA, LCPC,
Principal
E-mail: skay4@verizon.net
(They also have an office in Rockville, Maryland.)

Georgia

Ashkin, Janis, MEd, MCC, NCC, NCCC,
2365 Winthrope Way Dr.,
Alpharetta, GA 30009
Phone: 678-319-0297
E-mail: jashkin@bellsouth.net

Career Quest/Job Search Workshop,
St. Ann's Catholic Church,
4905 Roswell Rd. NE,
Marietta, GA 30062-6240
Phone: 678-641-0346
Contact: John Marotto

D & B Consulting,
3355 Lenox Rd., Ste. 750,
Atlanta, GA 30326
Phone: 404-504-7079
Contact: Deborah R. Brown, MBA, MSW,
Career Consultant
E-mail: Debbie@DandBconsulting.com
www.dandbconsulting.com

Jewish Family and Career Services,
4549 Chamblee Dunwoody Rd.,
Atlanta, GA 30338
Phone: 770-677-9300

Satterfield, Mark,
720 Rio Grand Dr.,
Alpharetta, GA 30022
Phone: 770-643-8566
E-mail: msatt@mindspring.com

Waldorf, William H., MBA, LPC,
Path Unfolding Career Development,
314 Maxwell Rd., Ste. 400,
Alpharetta, GA 30004
Phone: 770-442-9447, ext. 14
E-mail: wwaldorf@earthlink.net

Idaho

*Career Coaching 4U,
Secular and Christian Career Coaching/
Counseling,
9882 W. View Dr.,
Boise, ID 83704
Phone: 208-323-2462
Contact: Michael W. Reed, MEd, MS
Counseling
E-mail: michael@careercoaching4u.com
www.careercoaching4u.com

Illinois

Alumni Career Center,
University of Illinois Alumni Association,
200 S. Wacker Dr., First Floor,
Chicago, IL 60606
Phone: 312-575-7830
Contact: Claudia M. Delestowicz, Associate
Director; Julie Hays Bartimus, Vice President

Another Horizon Coaching,
P.O. Box 7174,
Buffalo Grove, IL 60089
Phone: 847-808-9982
Contact: Deb Morton, Certified Executive
Career Coach
E-mail: deb@horizonccc.com
www.horizonccc.com

*Career Path,
1240 Iroquois Ave., Ste. 100,
Naperville, IL 60563
Phone: 630-369-3390
Contact: Donna Sandberg, MS, NCC,
LCPC, Owner/Counselor

Career Vision/The Ball Foundation,
800 Roosevelt Rd., E-200,
Glen Ellyn, IL 60137
Phone: 800-469-8378
Contact: Peg Hendershot, Director;
Paula Kosin, MS, LCPC
E-mail: info@careervision.org
www.careervision.org

Davis, Jean, MA,
Counseling Psychology, specializing in
adult career transitions,
1405 Elmwood Ave.,
Evanston, IL 60201
Phone: 847-492-1002
E-mail: jdavis@careertransitions.net
www.careertransitions.net

**Dolan Career & Rehabilitation
Consulting,** Ltd.,
307 Henry St., Ste. 407,
Alton, IL 62002
Phone: 618-474-5328
Fax: 618-462-3359
Contact: J. Stephen Dolan, MA, CRC,
Career & Rehabilitation Consultant
E-mail: dolanrehab@att.net

Grimard Wilson Consulting, Inc.,
333 W. Wacker Dr., Ste. 500,
Chicago, IL 60606
and
1140 W. Lake St., Ste. 302,
Oak Park, IL 60301
Phone: 312-925-5176
Contact: Diane Wilson
E-mail: info@grimardwilson.com
www.grimardwilson.com

**Harper College Community Career
Services,**
1200 W. Algonquin Rd., Rm. A-347,
Palatine, IL 60067
Phone: 847-925-6293
Contact: Kathleen Canfield, Director
E-mail: careers@harpercollege.edu

*Lansky Career Consultants,**
100 N. LaSalle St., Ste. 2207,
Chicago, IL 60602
Phone: 312-444-1500
Contact: Judith Lansky, MA, MBA,
President
E-mail: lanskycareers@yahoo.com

LeBrun, Peter,
Career/Leadership Coach,
Executive Career Management,
4333 N. Hazel St., Ste. 100,
Chicago, IL 60613
Phone: 773-281-7274
E-mail: peterlebrun@aol.com

Lifescopes,
427 Greenwood St., Ste. 3W,
Evanston, IL 60201
Phone: 847-733-1805
Contact: Barbara H. Hill,
Career Management Consultant
E-mail: Lifescopes@comcast.net

Loftus, Jessica, PhD,
Licensed Clinical Psychologist,
National Certified Career Counselor,
62 Orland Square Dr., #007,
Orland Park, IL 60462
Phone: 708-478-0444
www.counselinks.com

*Midwest Ministry Development Service,**
(an Interdenominational Church Career
Development Center),
1840 Westchester Blvd., Ste. 204,
Westchester, IL 60154
Phone: 708-343-6268
www.midwestministry.org

**Moraine Valley Community College,
Job Resource Center,**
9000 College Pkwy.,
Palos Hills, IL 60465
Phone: 708-974-5737
www.morainevalley.edu/jrc

The Summit Group,
PO Box 3794,
Peoria, IL 61612-3794
Phone: 309-657-7156
Fax: 312-896-7411
Contact: John R. Throop, DMin, President

Iowa

Sucher, Billie Ruth, MS, CTMS,
CTSB, JCTC, CCM,
Private Practice Career Transition
Consultant,
7177 Hickman Rd., Ste. 10,
Des Moines, IA 50322
Phone: 515-276-0061
E-mail: billie@billiesucher.com
www.billiesucher.com

University of Iowa, Career Center,
100 Pomerantz Center, Ste. C310,
Iowa City, IA 52242
Phone: 319-335-1023

Zilber, Suzanne, PhD,
Licensed Psychologist,
Catalyst Counseling,
600 5th St., Ste. 302,
Ames, IA 50010-6072
Phone: 515-232-5340
Fax: 515-232-2070
www.catalystcounseling.com

Kansas

Keeping the People, Inc.,
13488 W. 126th Terr.,
Overland Park, KS 66213
Phone: 913-620-4645
Contact: Leigh Branham
E-mail: LB@keepingthepeople.com
www.keepingthepeople.com

Kentucky

Career Span, Inc.,
505 Lemon Drop Ln.,
Lexington, KY 40511
Phone: 859-233-7726 (233-SPAN)
Contact: Carla Ockerman-Hunter, MA,
MCC, NCC
E-mail: careerspan@aol.com
www.careerspanUSA.com

Louisiana

Career Center,
River Center Branch, EBR Parish Library,
120 St. Louis St.,
Baton Rouge, LA 70802
Phone: 225-381-8434
Fax: 225-389-8910
Contact: Anne Nowak, Program Director
E-mail: anowak@careercenterbr.com
www.careercenterbr.com

Maine

D. Gallant Management Associates,
75 Pearl St., Ste. 204,
Portland, ME 04101
Phone: 207-773-4800
Contact: Deborah L. Gallant, SPHR, CBP,
CCP
E-mail: dhma@dgallant.com

*Heart at Work,
25 Middle St.,
Portland, ME 04101
Phone: 207-775-6400
Contact: Barbara Babkirk, LCPC
E-mail: barb@barbarababkirk.com
www.heartatwork.biz

Women's Worth Career Counseling,
9 Village Ln.,
Westbrook, ME 04092
Phone: 207-856-6666
Contact: Jacqueline Murphy,
Career Counselor
E-mail: wethepeople@maine.rr.com

Maryland

**The Career Evaluation and Coaching
Center,**
21 West Rd., Ste. 150,
Baltimore, MD 21204
Phone: 410-825-0042
Fax: 410-825-0310
Contact: Ralph D. Raphael, PhD
E-mail: drraphael@ralphraphael.com
www.ralphraphael.com

College of Notre Dame of Maryland,
4701 N. Charles St.,
Baltimore, MD 21210
Phone: 410-532-5301
Contact: Continuing Education Depart-
ment, Sr. Sharon Slear, ext. 3169

CTS Consulting, Inc.,
3126 Berkshire Rd.,
Baltimore, MD 21214-3404
Phone: 410-444-5857
Contact: Michael Bryant
www.go2ctsonline.com

Friedman, Lynn, PhD,
Clinical Psychologist, Psychoanalyst, and
Work-Life Consultant,
5480 Wisconsin Ave., Ste. 206,
Chevy Chase, MD 20815
Phone: 301-656-9050
E-mail: drlynnfriedman@mindspring.com
Twitter: www.twitter.com/drlynnfriedman
www.drlynnfriedman.com or
www.corporationsonthecouch.com

Headley, Anne S., MA,
6510 41st Ave.,
University Park, MD 20782
Phone: 301-779-1917
E-mail: asheadley@verizon.net
www.anneheadley.com
Blog: www.anneheadley.wordpress.com

Mendelson, Irene N.,
BEMW, Inc.,
Counseling and Training for the
Workplace,
7984-D, Old Georgetown Rd.,
Bethesda, MD 20814-2440
Phone: 301-657-8922

**Positive Passages Life/Career Transition
Counseling and Coaching,**
4702 Falstone Ave.,
Chevy Chase, MD 20815
Phone: 301-580-5162
Contact: Jeanette Kreiser, EdD
E-mail: jskreiser@yahoo.com

Prince George's Community College,
Career Assessment and Planning Center,
301 Largo Rd.,
Largo, MD 20772
Phone: 301-322-0608
Contact: Stephanie Cunningham, Career
Adviser

TransitionWorks,
Rockville, MD
Phone: 301-233-4287
Contact: Nancy K. Schlossberg, EdD,
Principal; Stephanie Kay, MA, LCPC,
Principal
E-mail: skay4@verizon.net
*(They also have an office in Delray Beach,
Florida.)*

**White Ridgely Associates, Success
Management,**
76 Cranbrook Rd., #248,
Hunt Valley, MD 21030
Phone: 410-356-5575
Contact: Daisy Nelson White, PhD
E-mail: Daisy@CareerAid.com
www.CareerAid.com

Massachusetts

Berke & Price Associates,
Newtown Way #6,
Chelmsford, MA 01824
Phone: 978-256-0482
Contact: Judit E. Price, MS, CDFI, IJCTC,
CCM, CPRW,
Career Consultant and Career Coach,
Certified Resume Writer, and
Certified Brand Specialist
E-mail: jprice@careercampaign.com
www.careercampaign.com

The Boston Career Coach,
26 Shanley St.,
Brighton, MA 02135
Phone: 617-254-0791
Contact: Ellen Jackson
www.thebostoncareercoach.blogspot.com

Boston Career Development,
5 Brackett St.,
Needham, MA 02492
Phone: 781-453-9008
Contact: Debbie Lipsett, MA,
Career Coach/Consultant
E-mail: deblipsett@gmail.com
www.BostonCareerDevelopment.com

Career Management Consultants,
108 Grove St., Ste. 19A,
Worcester, MA 01605
Phone: 508-756-9998
Contact: Patricia Stepanski Plouffe,
Founder/Consultant
E-mail: info@careermc.com

Career Planning,
Northern Essex Community College,
Elliott St.,
Haverhill, MA 01830
Phone: 978-556-3722
www.necc.mass.edu

Career Source,
186 Alewife Brook Pkwy., Ste. 310,
Cambridge, MA 02138
Phone: 617-661-7867
www.yourcareersource.com

*Center for Career Development & Ministry,
30 Milton St., Ste. 107,
Dedham, MA 02026
Phone: 781-329-2100
Fax: 781-407-0955
Contact: Stephen Ott, Director
E-mail: info@ccdmin.org
www.ccdmin.org

Changes, Career Counseling and
Job-Hunt Training,
2516 Massachusetts Ave.,
Cambridge, MA 02140
Phone: 617-868-7775
Contact: Carl J. Schneider

Hadlock, Joanne, EdD, NCCC,
Career/Life Transitions,
223 Sandy Pond Rd.,
Lincoln, MA 01773
Phone: 781-259-3752
E-mail: joannehadlock@comcast.net
www.joannehadlock.us

Jewish Vocational Service, Career Moves,
29 Winter St., 5th Floor,
Boston, MA 02108
Phone: 617-399-3131 or 617-339-3101
Contact: Judy Sacks, Director
www.career-moves.org

Jewish Vocational Service,
Career counseling and testing,
Career Moves at the JCC,
333 Nahanton St.,
Newton, MA 02159
Phone: 617-965-7940
Contact: Amy Mazur, career counselor
amazur@jvs-boston.org

*Liebhaber, Gail,
40 Cottage St.,
Lexington, MA 02420
Phone: 781-861-9949
Fax: 781-863-5956
Contact: Gail Liebhaber, MEd
E-mail: gail@yourcareerdirection.com
www.yourcareerdirection.com

Miller, Wynne W., Career & Executive
Coaching,
1443 Beacon St.,
Brookline, MA 02446-4707
Phone: 617-232-4848
Fax: 617-232-4846
E-mail: wynne@win-coaching.com

Stein, Phyllis R.,
Career Counseling and Coaching,
59 Parker St.,
Cambridge, MA 02138
Phone: 617-354-7948
E-mail: p_stein@ziplink.net

Szekely, Bill,
10 Doral Dr.,
N. Chelmsford, MA 01863
Phone: 978-251-3693
Cell: 978-423-3196
www.lifeworkdiscovery.com

Michigan

*Career Consulting Services,
PO Box 135,
Union Lake, MI 48387
Phone: 248-363-6233
Contact: Marybeth Robb, MA Counselor
E-mail: greatresumes@sbcglobal.net

*Careers Through Faith,
3025 Boardwalk St.,
Ann Arbor, MI 48108
Phone: 734-332-8800, ext. 228
Contact: Cathy Synko
E-mail: csynko@CareersThroughFaith.org
www.CareersThroughFaith.org

*Keystone Coaching & Consulting, LLC,
22 Cherry St.,
Holland, MI 49423
Phone: 616-396-1517
Contact: Mark de Roo
E-mail: mderoo@keystonecoach.com
www.keystonecoach.com

Appendix C

*LifeSteward/EaRN Employment & Resource Network,
6670 Kalamazoo SE, Ste. E-114,
Grand Rapids, MI 49508
Phone: 616-698-3125
Contact: Ken Soper, MDiv, MA, Director
E-mail: kensoper@yahoo.com
www.kensoper.com

New Options: Counseling for Women in Transition,
Ann Arbor, MI 48108
Phone: 734-973-8699 or 734-973-0003
Contact: Phyllis Perry, MSW, MFA
E-mail: pepstar27@yahoo.com

Synko Associates, LLC,
3025 Boardwalk St.,
Ann Arbor, MI 48108
Phone: 734-332-8800
Contact: Nick Synko
E-mail: nsynko@SynkoAssociates.com
www.SynkoAssociates.com

Minnesota

Human Dynamics,
3036 Ontario Rd.,
Little Canada, MN 55117
Phone: 651-484-8299
Contact: Greg J. Cylkowski, MA, Founder
E-mail: gregjcy@yahoo.com

*North Central Ministry Development Center,
(an Interdenominational Church Career Development Center),
516 Mission House Ln.,
New Brighton, MN 55112
Phone: 651-636-5120
Contact: Mark Sundby, MDiv, PhD, LP, Executive Director
E-mail: ncmdc@comcast.net
www.ncmdc.org

Prototype Career Service,
626 Armstrong Ave.,
St. Paul, MN 55102
Phone: 800-368-3197
Contact: Amy Lindgren,
Job Search Strategist
E-mail: getajob@prototypecareerservice
.com
www.prototypecareerservice.com

Missouri

Eigles, Lorrie, MSED, LPC,
Authentic Communication,
Life and Career Coach,
432 W. 62nd Terr.,
Kansas City, MO 64113
E-mail: coachlor@swbell.net
www.linkedin.com/in/lorrieeigles

The Job Doctor,
505 S. Ewing,
St. Louis, MO 63103
Phone: 314-863-1166
Contact: M. Rose Jonas, PhD
E-mail: jobdoc@aol.com
www.jobdoctoronline.com

MU Career Center,
Student Success Center,
University of Missouri,
Columbia, MO 65211
Phone: 573-882-6801
Fax: 573-882-5440
Contact: Craig Benson
E-mail: career@missouri.edu

Robert J. Murney Clinic of Forest Institute,
1322 S. Campbell,
Springfield, MO 65807
Phone: 417-865-8943
Contact: Leslie Bailey, Assistant Clinic Director

Women's Center,
University of Missouri-Kansas City,
5100 Rockhill Rd., 105 Haag Hall,
Kansas City, MO 64110
Phone: 816-235-1638
Contact: Brenda Bethman, Director

Montana

Career Transitions,
20900 E. Frontage Rd., B-Mezz,
Belgrade, MT 59714
Phone: 406-388-6701
Contact: Darla Joyner, Executive Director
www.careertransitions.com

IES,
1 New Hampshire Ave., Ste. 125,
Portsmouth, NH 03801
Phone: 603-570-4850 or 800-734-JOBS
(5627)
Contact: James Otis, Career Counselor/
Recruiter/Principal; Anita Labell, Certified
Professional Resume Writer/Career Coach
E-mail: ies@losnh.com
Fax: 603-766-1901

Tucker, Janet, MEd,
Career Counselor,
10 String Bridge,
Exeter, NH 03833
Phone: 603-772-8693
E-mail: jbtucker@comcast.net

*CareerQuest,
2165 Morris Ave., Ste. 15,
Union, NJ 07083
Phone: 908-686-8400
Fax: 908-686-8400 (on request)
Contact: Don Sutaria, MS, IE (Prof.),
Founder, President, and Life-Work Coach
E-mail: don@careerquestcentral.com
www.careerquestcentral.com
Blog: www.careerquestcentral.blogspot.com

Cohen, Jerry, MA, NCC, NCCC,
Licensed Professional Counselor,
PO Box 184,
Hackettstown, NJ 07840
Phone: 908-813-1188
E-mail: cohencareers@comcast.net

Creating Life Options,
26 Wexford Dr.,
Mendham, NJ 07945
Phone: 201-874-3264, 973-543-3458
Contact: Katie McGinty
E-mail: katie@creatinglifeoptions.com
www.creatinglifeoptions.com

Grundfest, Sandra, EdD,
Certified Career Counselor, Licensed
Psychologist,
601 Ewing St., C-1,
Princeton, NJ 08540
Phone: 609-921-8401
and
35 Clyde Rd., Ste. 101,
Somerset, NJ 08873
Phone: 732-873-1212

Job Seekers of Montclair,
St. Luke's Episcopal Church,
73 S. Fullerton Ave.,
Montclair, NJ 07042
Phone: 973-783-3442
(Meets Wednesdays, 7:30-9:15 P.M.)

JobSeekers in Princeton, NJ,
Trinity Church,
33 Mercer St.,
Princeton, NJ 08540
Phone: 609-924-2277
www.trinityprinceton.org
(Meets Tuesdays, 7:30-9:30 P.M.)

Mercer County Community College,
Career Services,
Student Center Room 229D,
1200 Old Trenton Rd.,
West Windsor, NJ 08550
Phone: 609-570-3399
Contact: Gail C. La France, Career Counselor
Fax: 609-570-3880

*W. L. Nikel,
459 Passaic Ave., Ste. 171,
W. Caldwell, NJ 07006
Phone: 973-439-1850
Contact: William L. Nikel, MBA Wharton
E-mail: wnikel@verizon.net

Bernstein, Alan B., LCSW, PC,
122 E 82nd St.,
New York, NY 10028
Phone: 212-288-4881

*CareerQuest,
c/o TRS, Inc., Professional Ste.,
44 E. 32nd St.,
New York, NY 10016
Phone: 908-686-8400
Fax: 908-686-8400 (on request)
Contact: Don Sutaria, MS, IE (Prof.),
Founder, President, and Life-Work Coach
E-mail: don@careerquestcentral.com
www.careerquestcentral.com
Blog: www.careerquestcentral.blogspot
.com

Careers in Transition, LLC,
Professional Career Services and Counseling,
11 Computer Dr. W., #112,
Albany, NY 12205
Phone: 518-366-8451
Contact: Dr. Thomas J. Denham, MCDP,
Founder and Career Counselor
E-mail: careersintransition@yahoo.com
www.careersintransitionllc.com

*Center for Creativity and Work,
19 W 34th St.,
New York, NY 10001
Phone: 212-490-9158, 845-336-8318
Contact: Allie Roth, President
E-mail: allie@allieroth.com
www.allieroth.com

Greene, Kera, MEd,
200 E. 24th St.,
New York, NY 10001
Cell: 917-496-1804
E-mail: kera1010@yahoo.com

*Judith Gerberg Associates,
250 W. 57th St., Ste. 2315,
New York, NY 10107
Phone: 212-315-2322
E-mail: judith@gerberg.com
www.gerberg.com
www.linkedin.com/in/judithgerberg

Optima Careers,
575 Madison Ave., between 56th and
57th Streets,
Tenth Floor,
New York, New York 10019
Phone: 212-876-3488
Contact: Marianne Ruggiero, President
and Founder
E-mail: mcruggiero@optimacareers.com
www.optimacareers.com

Orange County Community College,
Counseling Center,
115 South St.,
Middletown, NY 10940
Phone: 845-341-4070

Personnel Sciences Center,
140 Briarcliff Rd.,
Westbury, NY 11590
Phone: 516-338-5340
Fax: 516-338-5341
Contact: Jeffrey A. Goldberg, PhD,
President, Licensed Psychologist
E-mail: jag_psc@juno.com
(Services also provided in Manhattan.)

The Prager-Bernstein Group,
122 E. 42nd St., Ste. 2815,
New York, NY 10168
Phone: 212-697-0645
Contact: Leslie B. Prager, MA, CMP,
Senior Partner/Career Counselor
Updated E-mail address: Leslie-PBG@
msn.com
www.prager-bernsteingroup.com

**Professional Experience and Career
Planning,**
Long Island University,
CW Post Campus,
Brookville, NY 11548 -9988
Phone: 516-299-2251
Contact: Jeanette Grill, Director

Psychological Services Center,
Career Services Unit,
University at Albany, SUNY,
299 Washington Ave.,
Albany, NY 12206
Phone: 518-442-4900
Contact: George B. Litchford, PhD, Director

North Carolina

Career Focus Workshops,
8301 Brittains Field Rd.,
Oak Ridge, NC 27310
Phone: 336-643-1419
Contact: Glenn Wise, President
E-mail: gwise001@triad.rr.com

Crossroads Career Network,
9621-G Commons East Dr.,
Charlotte, NC 28277
www.CrossroadsCareer.org
(Nonprofit Christian network of member churches equipped to help people find jobs, careers, calling.)

Joyce Richman & Associates, Ltd.,
2911 Shady Lawn Dr.,
Greensboro, NC 27408
Phone: 336-288-1799
E-mail: jerichman@aol.com
www.joycerichman.com
Blog: www.richmanresources.com

Kochendofer, Sally, PhD,
2218 Lilac Lane
Indian Land, SC 29707
Phone: 803-396-0979
E-mail: westiefriend@comporium.net

*The Life/Career Institute,
131 Chimney Rise Dr.,
Cary, NC 27511
Phone: 919-469-5775
Contact: Mike Thomas, PhD
E-mail: mikethomas@nc.rr.com
www.LifeCareerInstitute.com

Life Management Services, LC,
127 Chimney Rise Dr.,
Cary, NC 27511
Phone: 919-481-4707
Contact: Marilyn and Hal Shook

Ohio

Community Services of Stark County, Inc.,
625 Cleveland Ave. NW,
Canton, OH 44702
Phone: 330-305-9696
Contact: Victor W. Valli, Director, Career and Business Services
E-mail: vvalli@csstark.org

Cuyahoga County Public Library,
The Career Center,
5225 Library Ln.,
Maple Heights, OH 44137-1291
Phone: 216-475-2225
E-mail: beaston@cuyahogalibrary.org
www.cuyahogalibrary.org/careerexpert.aspx

*Diversified Career Services, Inc.,
Columbus, OH 43212
Phone: 614-488-3359
Contact: Laura Armstrong,
Career Coach for the 50+ generation
E-mail: armstronglaura4@gmail.com
www.MakeADifferenceAfter50.com

*Flood, Kay Reynolds,
MA Ministry degree,
3600 Parkhill Cir. NW,
Canton, OH 44718
Phone: 330-493-1448

J&K Associates and Success Skills Seminars, Inc.,
607 Otterbein Ave.,
Dayton, OH 45406-4507
Phone: 937-274-3630
Fax: 937-274-4375
Contact: Pat Kenney, PhD, President

New Career,
328 Race St.,
Dover, OH 44622
Phone: 330-364-5557
Contact: Marshall J. Karp, MA, NCC, LPC, Career Counselor
E-mail: marshallkarp@hotmail.com

Woods, Anne,
8225 Markhaven Ct.,
Columbus, OH 43235
Phone: 614-888-7941
E-mail: awoods@columbus.rr.com

Career Development Partners, Inc.,
4137 S. Harvard Ave., Ste. A,
Tulsa, OK 74135
Phone: 918-293-0500
Toll free: 866-466-1162
Fax: 918-293-0503
E-mail: Nancy@cdpartnersinc.com
www.cdpartnersinc.com

Careerful Counseling Services,
12555 SW First St.,
Beaverton, OR 97005
Phone: 503-997-9506
Contact: Andrea King, MS, NCC,
Career Counselor
E-mail: aking@careerful.com
www.careerful.com

*****Exceptional Living Coach,** LLC,
1230 Arthur St.,
Eugene, OR 97402
Phone: 541-484-6785
E-mail: lisa@ExceptionalLivingCoach.com
www.ExceptionalLivingCoach.com
Contact: Lisa R. Anderson, MA, NCC,
GCDF
(English and Spanish.)

Verk Consultants, Inc.,
1190 Olive St.,
PO Box 11277,
Eugene, OR 97440
Phone: 541-687-9170
Contact: Larry H. Malmgren, MS, President
E-mail: larry@verk.net

*****Bartholomew, Uda,**
"Your Very Own Hidden Job Markets!"
Workshops,
PO Box 2112,
Center City Philadelphia, PA 19103
Phone: 215-618-1572
Contact: Uda Bartholomew,
Lead Facilitator
E-mail: VocTransVocLib@comcast.net

Career by Design,
340 N. Main St.,
Telford, PA 18969
Phone: 215-723-8413, ext. 204
Contact: Henry D. Landes, Consultant
E-mail: henry@dvfbc.com
www.dvfbc.com

*****Hannafin, Christine,** PhD,
Personal and Career Counseling,
Bala Farm,
380 Jenissa Dr.,
West Chester, PA 19382
Phone: 610-431-0588
E-mail: chrishannafin@aol.com
www.christinehannafin.com

Haynes, Lathe, PhD,
401 Shady Ave., Ste. C107,
Pittsburgh, PA 15206
Phone: 412-361-6336

JEVS Career Strategies,
1845 Walnut St., 7th Floor,
Philadelphia, PA 19103-4707
Phone: 215-854-1874
Fax: 215-854-1880
E-mail: cs@jevs.org
www.jevs.org

Kessler, Jane E., MA,
Licensed Psychologist,
252 W. Swamp Rd., Ste. 56,
Doylestown, PA 18901
Phone: 215-348-8212, ext. 1
E-mail: jane@kesslerandclark.com
Fax: 215-348-0329

Priority Two,
PO Box 425,
Warrendale, PA 15086
Phone: 724-935-0252
Contact: Don Priestley, Executive Director
www.ptwo.org

Crystal-Barkley Corp.,
(formerly The John C. Crystal Center),
293 E. Bay St.,
Charleston, SC 29401
Phone: 800-333-9003
Fax: 800-560-5333
Contact: Nella G. Barkley, President
E-mail: crystalbarkley@careerlife.com
www.careerlife.com
*(John Crystal, the founder of the Crystal
Center, died in 1988; Nella, his business
partner for many years, now continues
his work in the US, the UK, and the
Netherlands.)*

**White Ridgely Associates, Success
Management,**
26 River Bend Dr.,
Okatie, SC 29909
Phone: 410-356-5575
Contact: Daisy Nelson White, PhD
E-mail: Daisy@CareerAid.com
www.CareerAid.com

*Career Resources, Inc.,
208 Elmington Ave.,
Nashville, TN 37205
Phone: 615-957-0404
Contact: Jane C. Hardy, Career Strategist/
Founder
E-mail: JHardy@CareerResources.net
www.CareerResources.net

Polangin, Robin,
Career Coach
Phone: 888-REAL-008
E-mail: robin@myauthenticcareer.com
www.myauthenticcareer.com

*Slay, Patrick, MA, NCC,
Career Counselor,
3200 West End Ave., Ste. 500,
Nashville, TN 37203
Phone: 615-585-7529
E-mail: patrickslay@yahoo.com

Career Action Associates PC,
8350 Meadow Rd., Ste. 272,
Dallas, TX 75231
Phone: 214-378-8350
Contact: Joyce Shoop, LPC;
Rebecca Hayes, MEd, CRC, LPC
Phone: 817-926-9941
E-mail: rhayescaa@aol.com

Career Art Innovators,
1902 E. Common St., Ste. 400,
New Braunfels, TX 78130
Phone: 830-626-6334
Cell: 830-832-7448
Contact: Shell Herman, MS
E-mail: shell@kidzart.com

Career and Recovery Resources, Inc.,
2525 San Jacinto,
Houston, TX 77002
Phone: 713-754-7000
Contact: Vernal Swisher, Director

Life Transitions, Inc.,
6800 Park Ten Blvd., Ste. 298 W,
San Antonio, TX 78213
Phone: 210-737-2100
www.life-career.com

*New Life Institute,
PO Box 4487,
Austin, TX 78765
Phone: 512-469-9447
Contact: Bob Breihan
E-mail: newlifetexas@sbcglobal.net
www.newlifetexas.org

Quereau, Jeanne, MA, LPC,
9500 Jollyville Rd., #121,
Austin, TX 78759
Phone: 512-342-9552
E-mail: jeanneq19@gmail.com

Lue, Keith,
PO Box 971482,
Orem, UT 84097-1482
Phone: 801-885-1389
E-mail: keithlue@keydiscovery.com

Vermont

Career Networks, Inc.,
1372 Old Stage Rd.,
Williston, VT 05495
Phone: 802-872-1533
Contact: Markey Read
E-mail: markey@careernetworksvt.com
www.careernetworksvt.com

Preis, Roger J.,
RPE Career Dynamics,
PO Box 115,
Shelburne, VT 05487
Phone: 802-985-3775
E-mail: rjpreis@rpecareers.com
www.rpecareers.com

Virginia

Beach Counseling and Career Center,
Offices in Virginia Beach and Norfolk,
Free 10-Minute Phone Consult
Phone: 757-560-0357
Contact: Suzan K. Thompson, PhD, LPC,
Director
E-mail: info@BeachCounselingCenter.com
www.BeachCounselingCenter.com

The BrownMiller Group,
312 Granite Ave.,
Richmond, VA 23226
Phone: 804-288-2157
Contact: Bonnie Miller
E-mail: tbmgroup@aol.com
www.BrownMiller.com

**Fairfax County Office for Women &
Domestic and Sexual Violence Services,**
12000 Government Center Pkwy, Ste. 339
Phone: 703-324-5730
Fax: 703-324-3959
E-mail: ofw@fairfaxcounty.gov
www.fairfaxcounty.gov/ofw

Hollins University,
Career Center,
PO Box 9628,
Roanoke, VA 24020-1628
Phone: 540-362-6364
Contact: Ashley Glenn, Interim Director

Mary Baldwin College,
Rosemarie Sena Center for Career and
Life Planning,
Kable House,
Staunton, VA 24401
Phone: 540-887-7221

McCarthy & Company,
Career Transition Management,
4201 S. 32nd Rd.,
Arlington, VA 22206
Phone: 703-671-4300
Contact: Peter McCarthy, President
E-mail: mccarthy@careertran.com
www.careertran.com

Northern Virginia Community College,
Career Education Department (on each
campus),
Extended Learning Institute,
8000 Forbes Pl.,
Springfield, VA 22151
www.nvcc.edu

Psychological Consultants, Inc.,
6724 Patterson Ave.,
Richmond, VA 23226
Phone: 804-288-4125

The Women's Center,
127 Park St. NE,
Vienna, VA 22180
Phone: 703-281-2657
E-mail: twc@thewomenscenter.org
(Subject line should read, "Attention:
Lauren Kellar)
www.thewomenscenter.org

Washington

Bridgeway Career Development,
227 Bellevue Way NE, PMB 264,
Bellevue, WA 98004
Phone: 1-877-250-2103
Contact: Janet Scarborough Civitelli,
PhD, MCC, Owner
E-mail: js@bridgewaycareer.com
www.bridgewaycareer.com

Career Management Institute,
8404 27th St. W.,
University Pl., WA 98466
Phone: 253-565-8818
Contact: Ruthann Reim McCaffree, MA,
NCC, LMHC, CPC
E-mail: careermi@nwrain.com
www.CareerMI.com

**Centerpoint Institute for Life and
Career Renewal,**
4000 NE 41st St., Bldg. D, Ste. 2,
Seattle, WA 98105-5428
Phone: 206-686-LIFE (5433)
www.centerpointseattle.org

The Individual Development Center, Inc.,
(I.D. Center),
1020 E. John,
Seattle, WA 98102
Phone: 206-329-0600
Contact: Margaret Porter, MEd, President
E-mail: porters@foxinternet.net

MJT Consulting,
302 Park Ave.,
Yakima, WA 98902
Contact: Marilyn J. Tellez, MA
Cell: 509-307-2396
E-mail: doitnow-1@peoplepc.com
www.doitnowcareercoach.info

Washington, DC

Horizons Unlimited, Inc.,
717 D St. NW, Ste. 300,
Washington, DC 20004
and
17501 McDade Ct.,
Rockville, MD 20855
Phone: 301-258-9338
Contact: Marilyn Goldman,
LPC, NCCC, MCC
E-mail: horizons@career-counseling.com
www.career-counseling.com

The Women's Center,
1025 Vermont Ave. NW, Ste. 310,
Washington, DC 20005
Phone: 202-293-4580
www.thewomenscenter.org

West Virginia

Ticich, Frank E., MS, CRC, CVE, Career
Consulting,
153 Tartan Dr.,
Follansbee, WV 26037
Phone: 304-748-1772
E-mail: frankticich@comcast.net

Wisconsin

*•***Career Momentum, Inc.,**
Career Focus, Assessment, Job Search
Coaching, Resume Writing,
49 Kessel Court, Ste. 214,
Madison, WI 53711
Phone: 608-274-2430, 888-776-0246
Contact: Clara Hurd Nydam,
MDiv, MCC, SPHR
E-mail: Clara.Nydam@CareerMomentum.com
www.CareerMomentum.com

Guarneri Associates,
Career Coaching, Personal Branding, and
Professional Resumes,
6670 Crystal Lake Rd.,
Three Lakes, WI 54562
Phone: 715-546-4449 or 866-881-4055
Contact: Susan Guarneri, NCCC, DCC,
CERW, CPBS
E-mail: Susan@AssessmentGoddess.com

Wyoming

University of Wyoming,
The Center for Advising and Career
Services,
1000 E. University Ave., Dept. 3195,
Laramie, WY 82071-3195
Phone: 307-766-2398
www.uwyo.edu/cacs

CANADA

British Columbia

CBD Network, Inc.,
201-2033 Gordon Dr.,
Kelowna, BC V1Y 3J2
Phone: 250-717-1821

Curtis, Susan, MEd, RCC, CEAP,
4513 W. 13th Ave.,
Vancouver, BC V6R 2V5
Phone: 604-228-9618
E-mail: susancurtis@telus.net

Appendix C

*Find Work You Love Inc.,
2277 W. 2nd Ave., Ste. 704,
Vancouver, BC V6K 1H8
Phone Local: 604-737-3955
Phone Toll Free: 1-888-737-3922
Fax: 604-737-3958
Contact: Marlene Haley, MEd, RCC
(President, Registered Clinical Counsellor)
www.findworkyoulove.com

Ontario

*Careers by Design,
Coaching and Counseling,
80 Harrison Garden Blvd.,
Toronto, ON, M2N 7E3
Phone: 416-519-8408
Contact: (Ms.) Shirin Khamisa, BA Hons., BEd,
ICF-Certified Coach and Career Counselor
E-mail: shirin@careersbydesign.ca
www.careersbydesign.ca

*CareersPlus Inc.,
55 Village Pl., Ste. 203,
Mississaugua, ON L4Z 1V9
Phone: 905-272-8258
Contact: Douglas H. Schmidt,
BA, MEd, EdD
www.careersplusinc.com

Career Strategy Counselling,
2 Briar Hill Pl.,
London, ON N5Y 1P7
Phone: 519-455-4609
Contact: Ruth Clarke, BA
E-mail: rclarke4609@rogers.com
www.careerstrategycounselling.com

donnerwheeler,
1 Belvedere Ct., Ste. 1207,
Brampton, ON L6V 4M6
Phone: 905-450-1086
Contact: Mary M. Wheeler, RN, MEd, PCC
E-mail: info@donnerwheeler.com
www.donnerwheeler.com

Human Achievement Associates,
22 Cottonwood Crescent,
London, ON N6G 2Y8
Phone: 519-657-3000
Contact: Mr. Kerry A. Hill
E-mail: haa.no.1@rogers.com

Puttock, Judith, BBA, CHRP,
Career Management Consultant,
The Puttock Group,
913 Southwind Ct.,
Newmarket, ON
Phone: 905-717-1738
E-mail: j.puttock@rogers.com
www.puttockgroup.com

YMCA Career Planning & Development,
42 Charles St. E.,
Toronto, ON M4Y 1T4
Phone: 416-928-3362, ext. 4222
E-mail: PersonalAssessmentandDevelopment@ymcagta.org

Quebec

Agence Ometz,
5151 Côte Ste-Catherine,
Montreal, QC H3W 1M6
Phone: 514-342-0000
Fax: 514-342-2371
Contact: Howard Berger, Co-Executive
Director,
Employment, Family, and Immigration
Services
*(Uses both French and English versions of
Parachute. Utilise des versions Françaises
et Anglaises de Parachute.)*

La Passerelle Career Transition Centre,
1255 Phillips Square, Ste. 903,
Montreal, QC H3B 3G1
Contact: Lorraine Loubier
Phone: 514-866-5982
E-mail: info@lapasserelle.ca
www.lapasserelle.ca

Roy, Marie-Carmelle,
Career Development Consultant,
Phone: 514-992-5219
E-mail: mcroy20@sympatico.ca
*(Marie-Carmelle was on my staff at the
Two-Week Workshop for seven years.)*

OVERSEAS

Australia

Grace du Prie, Career Development &
Training,
P.O. Box 736,
Ipswich, Qld. 4305
Phone: 07 3812 3807
Cell: 0438 760 735
E-mail: graceduprie@optusnet.com.au

The Growth Connection,
56 Berry St., Ste. 402, 4th Floor,
North Sydney, NSW 2060
Phone: 61 2 9954 3322
Contact: Imogen Wareing, Director

Life by Design,
PO Box 50,
Newport Beach, NSW 2106
Phone: 61 2 9979 4949
Contact: Ian Hutchinson, Lifestyle Strategist
E-mail: info@lifebydesign.com.au
www.lifebydesign.com.au

Milligan, Narelle,
Career Consultant (regional NSW)
Cell: 0411 236 124
E-mail: nmilligan2000@yahoo.com.au

Taccori, John, EdD,
Career Counsellor,
Blue Mountains, NSW 2777
Phone: 04 0093 8574
www.careersdoctor.net

France

Chavigny, Catherine,
11bis, rue Huyghens
75014 Paris
Phone: 0033 6 30 51 40 56
E-mail: catherinechavigny@voila.fr

Germany

Buddensieg, Marc,
Spechtweg 6,
30938 Burgwedel
Phone: 49 0 163 624 2639
Fax: 49 0 12120 277 627
E-mail: buddensieg@gmx.de
www.lwp-institut.de

Hoff, Rüdiger,
Zum Karpfenteich 11,
25826 St. Peter-Ording
Phone: 49 0 163 63 94 680
E-mail: ruediger.hoff@gmx.de
www.life-work-planning.de

Leitner, Madeleine, Dipl. Psych.,
Ohmstrasse 8,
80802 Munchen
Phone: 089 33079444
Fax: 089 33079445
E-mail: ML@Karriere-Management.de
www.Karriere-Management.de

Webb, John Carl,
Meinenkampstr 83a,
48165 Munster-Hiltrup
Phone: 49 0 2501 92 16 96
E-mail: john@muenster.de
www.lifeworkplanning.de
*(Universities offering Life/Work Planning
courses based on Parachute are located in
Berlin, Bochum, Bremen, Freiburg,
Hannover, Konstanz, and Münster.)*

Ireland

Brian McIvor & Associates,
Newgrange Mall, Unit 4B,
Slane, County Meath
Phone: 353 41 988 4035
E-mail: brianmcivor@gmail.com
www.brianmcivor.com
*(Brian was on the staff at my international
Two-Week Workshop for five years.)*

Israel

Mendel, Lori,
PO Box 148,
Caesarea, Israel 38900
Phone: 972 3 524 1068
Cell: 972 54 814 4442
E-mail: bizcom@bezeqint.net

Transitions & Resources, Ltd.,
6 Tzipornit, Apt. 3,
Modiin, Israel 71808
Phone: 08 926 6102
Cell: 050 5739496;
U.S. phone line in Israel until 4 p.m. EST:
516-216-4457
Fax: 08-926-6103
Contact: Judy Feierstein, CEO
E-mail: info@maavarim.biz
www.maavarim.biz

The Netherlands

Pluym Career Consultants,
Career Executive Coaching Services,
Boshoekerweg 16,
NL/8167 LS EPE/OENE
Contact: Johan Veeninga, Senior Consultant
E-mail: johan.veeninga@gmail.com or
info@careerconsultants.nl

New Zealand

The Career Company,
191 Peachgrove Rd., PO Box 24 195,
Hamilton 3253
Contact: Megan Smith
Phone: 64 7 853 9177
E-mail: info@thecareercompany.co.nz
www.thecareercompany.co.nz

Career Lifestyle,
175 Queen St., Level 5,
Auckland Central 1143
Contact: Paula Stenberg
E-mail: pfstenberg@gmail.com
www.careerlifestyle.blogspot.com
www.cvstyle.co.nz
www.cvstyle.blogspot.com
www.paulastenberg.blogspot.com

*CV.CO.NZ (NZ) Limited,**
373 Masters Rd.,
Auckland 2682
Free: 0800 282 669
Phone: 09 235 8484
Contact: Tom O'Neil
E-mail: tom@cv.co.nz
www.cv.co.nz

Poland

JC Coaching,
Tarniny 5a,05-500 Nowa Iwiczna
Cell: 48 600 327 163
Contact: Justyna Ciecwierz, ACCC,
Career Coaching, Work/Life Planning
E-mail: justyna.ciecwierz@jc-coaching.pl
www.jc-coaching.pl

Singapore

Transformation Technologies Pte Ltd.,
122 Thomson Green,
574986 Singapore
Phone: 65 98197858
Contact: Anthony Tan, Director
E-mail: anthonyt@singnet.com.sg

South Africa

Andrew Bramley Career Consultants,
12 Ridge Way/PO Box 1311,
Proteaville, Durbanville 7550
Phone: 27 0 21 9755573
Fax: 27 0 88 0 21 9755573
Contact: Andrew Bramley
E-mail: info@andrewbramley.co.za
www.andrewbramley.co.za

South Korea

Byung Ju Cho, PhD,
Professor of Business and Career,
Ajou University,
Suwon
Phone: 82 31 219 2709
Fax: 82 2 594 6236
Cell: 82 10 9084 6236
E-mail: chobju@ajou.ac.kr,
chobju@kornet.net
(Byung Ju Cho is the translator of the
Korean version of Parachute.)

Spain

Analisi-Nic,
Via Augusta, 120,
Principal 1,
08006 Barcelona
Phone: 34 932119503
Fax: 34 932172128
Contact: José Arnó
E-mail: analisi@arrakis.es

Switzerland

Baumgartner, Peter,
Hummelwaldstrasse 18a,
8645 Jona,
Phone: 41 0 55 534 1447
lebensunternehmer@bluewin.ch

KLB LifeDesigning,
Alpenblickstrasse 33,
CH-8645 Jona-Kempraten
Phone: 41 0 55 211 09 77
Fax: 41 0 55 211 09 79
Contact: Peter Kessler, LifeDesigning Coach
E-mail: p.kessler@bluewin.ch
www.LifeDesigning.ch

LifeProject,
Career Coaching, Work/Life Planning,
Consulting,
Kaepfnerweg 20,
CH-8810, Horgen/Zurich
Phone: 41 0 44 715 15 63
Cell: 41 0 78 626 11 58
Contact: Dr. Peter A. Vollenweider
E-mail: peter.vollenweider@gmail.com

Porot & Partenaire,
Rue de la Terrassière, 8,
1207 Genève-Suisse
Phone: 41 0 22 700 82 10
Fax: 41 0 22 700 82 14
Contact: Daniel Porot, Founder
E-mail: porot@compuserve.com
www.porot.com, www.careergames.com,
www.cabinet-porot.ch,
www.porot.com/pictocv,
www.outplacement3d.com
(Daniel was co-leader with me each sum-
mer for twenty years, at my international
Two-Week Workshops—though now I only
do five-day workshops.)

Sauser, Hans-U.,
Beratung und Ausbildung,
Im Bungert 2,
CH-5430 Wettingen
Phone: 056 426 64 09
E-mail: husauser@gmx.ch

United Kingdom

Hub Working Centre,
5 Wormwood St.,
London EC2M 1RW
Contact: Duncan Bolam, Dip. CG,
Director and Founder
E-mail: duncanbolam@careerdovetail.co.uk
www.careerdovetail.co.uk

Hawkins, Dr. Peter,
Mt. Pleasant,
Liverpool, L3 5TF
Phone: 0044 0 151 709-1760
Fax: 0044 0 151 709-1576
E-mail: p.Hawkins@gieu.co.uk

John Lees Associates,
37 Tatton St.,
Knutsford, Cheshire WA16 6AE
Phone: 01565 631625
Contact: John Lees
E-mail: johnlees@dsl.pipex.com
www.johnleescareers.com

LEAP Development and Coaching,
East Midlands/Eastern Counties/
Hertfordshire/London
Contact: Alix Nadelman
Phone: 44 7977 930 223 or
44 1438 716 559
E-mail: alix@leapcoach.com
www.leapcoach.com
Blog: www.leapcoach.blogspot.com

Passport Coaching and Consulting,
74 Blenheim Crescent,
South Croydon CR2 6BP
Phone: 0208 405 1670 or
07968 027 344
Contact: Janie Wilson
E-mail: janie@passport.co.uk
www.passport.co.uk

Sherridan Hughes,
Career Management Expert,
110 Pretoria Rd.,
London SW16 6RN
Phone: 020 8769 5737
www.sherridanhughes.com

PHONE AND INTERNET DISTANCE COUNSELING

*__Christian Career Center,__
PO Box 362,
Howell, MI 48844
Phone: 517-552-0328
Contact: Kevin Brennfleck, MA, NCCC;
Kay Marie Brennfleck, MA, NCCC
E-mail: Staff@ChristianCareerCenter.com
www.ChristianCareerCenter.com

__Collaborative Solutions,__
3130 W. Fox Run Way,
San Diego, CA 92111
Phone: 858-268-9340
Contact: Nancy Helgeson, MA, LMFT

__Human Resources Simplified,__
Florida
Phone: 941-926-8888
Contact: Jean Juchnowicz, SPHR, CBM,
Owner
E-mail: 4HRS@comcast.net
www.HumanResourcesSimplified.com

__McKinney, Donald,__ EdD, Career Counselor,
131 River Rd.,
DeQueen, AR 71832
Phone: 879-642-5628
E-mail: eaglenestdmm@yahoo.com

__Piazzale, Steve,__ PhD,
Career/Life Coach,
Mountain View, CA
Phone: 650-904-4366
E-mail: Steve@BayAreaCareerCoach.com
www.BayAreaCareerCoach.com

Index

Update 2010

To: PARACHUTE
   P.O. Box 370
   Walnut Creek, CA 94597

I think that the information in the 2010 edition needs to be changed, in your next revision, regarding (or, the following resource should be added):

_____

_____

_____

_____

_____

I cannot find the following resource, listed on page _____:

_____

_____

_____

_____

_____

Name _____

Address _____

_____

Please make a copy.
Submit this so as to reach us by February 1, 2010. **Thank you.**

OTHER RESOURCES

Additional materials by Richard N. Bolles to help you with your job-hunt

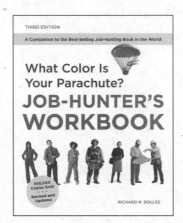

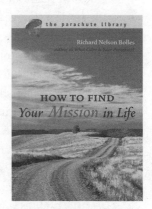

The Job-Hunter's Survival Guide
This little guide shows how to find hope and rewarding work—fast.
$9.99 paper (Can $12.99)
ISBN 978-1-58008-026-2

What Color Is Your Parachute?
Job-Hunter's Workbook
This handy workbook leads the job-seeker through the process of determining exactly what sort of job or career they are most suited for, easily streamlining this potentially stressful and confusing task.
$9.99 paper (Can $12.99)
ISBN 978-1-58008-009-5

The Three Boxes of Life,
And How to Get Out of Them
An introduction to life/work planning.
$18.95 paper (Can $23.00)
ISBN 978-0-913668-58-0

How to Find Your Mission in Life
Originally created as an appendix to *What Color Is Your Parachute?*, this book was written to answer one of the questions most often asked by job-hunters.
$7.95 paper (Can $10.95)
ISBN 978-1-58008-705-6

What Color Is Your Parachute?
for Teens
(WITH CAROL CHRISTEN AND JEAN M. BLOMQUIST)
Using *Parachute*'s central philosophy and strategies, this new addition to the *Parachute* library teaches high school and college students to zero in on their favorite skills and then to apply that knowledge to finding their perfect college major or job.
$15.99 paper (Can $19.99)
ISBN 978-1-58008-141-2

OTHER RESOURCES

Additional materials by Richard N. Bolles to help you with your job-hunt

What Color Is Your Parachute? for Retirement
(WITH JOHN E. NELSON)
Using *Parachute*'s central philosophy and strategies, this new addition to the *Parachute* library teaches those approaching 50, or beyond, how to prepare for the Fourth Movement of their lives.
$16.99 paper (Can $21.99)
ISBN 978-1-58008-205-1

Job-Hunting Online,
Fifth Edition, revised and expanded
(WITH MARK BOLLES)
This handy guide has quickly established itself as the ideal resource for anyone who's taking the logical step of job-hunting on the Internet.
$12.95 paper (Can $15.99)
ISBN 978-1-58008-899-2

Job-Hunting for the So-Called Handicapped, Second Edition
(WITH DALE BROWN)
A unique perspective on job-hunting and career changing, addressing the experiences of the disabled in performing these tasks.
$14.95 paper (Can $18.95)
ISBN 978-1-58008-195-5

The Career Counselor's Handbook, 2nd edition
(WITH HOWARD FIGLER)
A complete guide for practicing or aspiring career counselors.
$19.95 paper (Can $24.95)
ISBN 978-1-58008-870-1

NOTES

continued from back cover

"What are the ten biggest mistakes made during interviews?" SEE PAGE 70.

"How is the way employers hunt for people different from the way people hunt for employers?" SEE PAGE 8.

"How do I figure out what my best skills are?" SEE PAGE 41, 177+.

"If I decide I need some career counseling, how do I avoid getting 'taken'?" SEE APPENDIX B (STARTING ON PAGE 264).

"I had a job dealing with manufacturing. Now it's gone. How do I find jobs in related fields?" SEE PAGE 15.

"I'd like to emphasize my traits in my next job interview, but I don't have 'a trait vocabulary.' Got any lists?" SEE PAGE 20.

"I have a handicap. How can I get around it, in interviews?" SEE PAGE 37.

"I am painfully shy. I dread interviewing. What can I do?" SEE PAGE 42.

"I want to use a resume. What should I include?" SEE CHAPTER 5 (STARTING ON PAGE 49).

"How long should I expect my job-hunt to last?" SEE PAGE 7.

"Since I'm out of work, I'd like to use this opportunity to find more purpose and sense of mission in my next job. How do I do that?" SEE PAGES 17, 245+.

"I'm just starting my job-hunt. I know 'networking' is important. I haven't got a network. How do I build one from scratch?" SEE PAGE 64.

"There are no jobs out there, so I'm thinking of starting my own business. Where do I begin?" SEE CHAPTER 9 (STARTING ON PAGE 124).

PARACHUTE has all the answers you're looking for and more. It's the guide that millions of job-hunters have turned to for more than three decades.